Irene and Peter Ludwig

Insights into the Collectors' International Activities

Irene and Peter Ludwig

Insights into the Collectors' International Activities

Regina Wyrwoll in Conversation
with Contemporary Witnesses

Verlag der Buchhandlung
Walther und Franz König, Köln

Table of Contents

Foreword

More than almost any other collectors in the second half of the twentieth century, Irene and Peter Ludwig dedicated their lives to art. As Peter Ludwig put it in 1993: "Art has to do with life."

Their passion for collecting for the public is the reason—whether directly or indirectly—that the Ludwigs are known today. Twelve museums around the world carry the Ludwig name. The best known of these museums is most likely Cologne's Museum Ludwig, with a further six located throughout Germany, from Aachen to Bamberg, from Koblenz to Oberhausen and Saarlouis. Internationally, there are Ludwig museums in Basel, Beijing, Budapest, St. Petersburg, and Vienna. In addition, the foundation has relationships with sixteen further institutions, which hold donations or permanent loans given by Irene and Peter Ludwig, thereby forming a part of the Ludwig family.

The dynamism and tirelessness of the Ludwigs' work within Germany were matched by the vigour and indefatigability of their dealings in international cultural politics. That is the subject of this publication: How were Irene and Peter Ludwig active in Austria, Hungary, and the former USSR (and later Russia)? What about in Cuba and China? Which of their initiatives proved to be successful and which did not get off the ground? These were the questions that interested Regina Wyrwoll when she interviewed the contemporary witnesses who worked with the Ludwigs in their undertakings.

One of the foundation's objectives is to come to terms with and understand its own history. The Peter and Irene Ludwig Foundation has existed since 1997 and, since Irene Ludwig's death in 2010, has been responsible for administering the couple's legacy. Our core task is to collect art for the broader public and promote exhibitions and projects in the institutions throughout the world that are associated with us.

At the same time, it is important to keep in mind that the Ludwig Collection is synonymous with diversity and cosmopolitanism. Diversity, because the Ludwigs' interests included both ancient and contemporary art, eighteenth-century porcelain and pre-Columbian art, Pablo Picasso and sculpture from the Middle

Ages. Cosmopolitanism, because, long before globalisation, the Ludwigs were interested in art from parts of the world that fell outside the focus of the Western art cognoscenti of the time. For example, the former East Germany, the former USSR, China, Cuba … Irene and Peter Ludwig's profound conviction was that art is an existential expression of human life in its entirety and, at the same time, an essential component of each individual life, independent of one's political context.

Now, the deeds and legacy of the Ludwigs have once more been brought to life through these interviews. Our special thanks must go to Regina Wyrwoll, who, over many years and with great personal commitment, has gathered together this invaluable treasure for the foundation. As a longtime cultural journalist who closely followed the activities of the Ludwigs, later becoming the secretary-general of the Kunststiftung NRW (NRW Art Foundation), she possessed the necessary experience with the chosen format of the interviews. As a member of the Board of Trustees of the Peter and Irene Ludwig Foundation, she has access to our archives, which allowed her to comprehensively prepare for and conduct the interviews with these contemporary witnesses.

I would also like to thank Brigitte Franzen who, as sole Chief Executive Officer (CEO) of the foundation at the time, helped initiate the interview project together with the Board of Trustees, as well as Carla Cugini, the current CEO, who, together with Regina Wyrwoll and Benjamin Dodenhoff, brought this publication to fruition. My thanks go to all those involved in this project—especially the contemporary witnesses who drew on their personal recollections for these interviews, some of which were conducted across multiple sittings, and shared them with Ms. Wyrwoll.

ISABEL PFEIFFER-POENSGEN
Chairperson of the Board of Trustees
Peter and Irene Ludwig Foundation

Introduction

This publication brings together interviews conducted by Regina Wyrwoll with fourteen individuals who personally experienced the international activities of Irene and Peter Ludwig from a variety of perspectives. They take us on a journey to differing countries and regions, a journey through various perspectives and insights, through diverse experiences, anecdotes, and memories. Together, they bring the work of Irene and Peter Ludwig to life, helping to lend it clarity.

Of the couple, Peter Ludwig was much more in the public eye during his lifetime than his wife, Irene. He was undoubtedly the driving force behind the founding of the numerous domestic and international museums that bear their name. On the one hand, he was an entrepreneur, the managing director of Leonard Monheim AG from 1952 and, from 1986, the owner of Ludwig Schokolade GmbH. On the other hand, he held a doctorate in art history and was a passionate collector. His actions reflected the spirit of the couple's mutual belief in both collecting art for the public and exhibiting it in all its diversity in disparate regions of the world.

After his death in 1996, Irene Ludwig took on the responsibility of tending to the far-flung network of museums, donations, and permanent loans that she and her husband had built up over a forty year period. In 1997, she established the Peter and Irene Ludwig Foundation, designed to carry on collecting and promoting art in perpetuity, and continued, in her own personal style, to pursue their vision of collecting from around the world and providing support. As an art historian, she was a generous, self-assured, and, especially, an understanding and knowledgeable patron.

How did we handle the transcribed and authorised interviews that Regina Wyrwoll provided to us? Our archive—whose development is still in its early stages—is substantial, allowing us to verify a great deal of factual information, in particular the dates of travel, contract signings, and exhibition openings, as well as both the content and extent of art purchases. If there were discrepancies between what was said and the sources within our archives, we consulted the relevant individuals. With their approval, we corrected or reformulated the corresponding passages. When we were unable to independently verify the information provided by an interviewee, we left it as the individual had expressed it.

Together with Regina Wyrwoll and the editorial team, we sought to carefully transform the interviews into a written form that is easy to read while still maintaining the interviewees' individual ways of speaking.

We considered it important to accompany each chapter with a brief, factual introduction. This is intended to provide initial insight into the spheres of action of both the Ludwigs and the other people involved in each case, as well as the scope of artworks collected in the country in question. The timeline in the appendix brings together the most important events that are mentioned in the interviews or are otherwise contextually significant. While covering far from all of the Ludwigs' activities, it hopefully gives an idea of just how many initiatives the Ludwigs took on and tenaciously pursued in parallel.

The interviews collected here are not a history of the Ludwig Collection, but rather selected stories about the collectors' international activities. Further stories on other subjects about the collection will have to be told elsewhere. Hopefully, these interviews will provide the stimulus for further research, while also making clear what the Peter and Irene Ludwig Foundation, as sole inheritor of these extraordinary collectors, stands for: collecting for the public, supporting public institutions and rigorous research—and the unconditional love of art.

CARLA CUGINI
Chief Executive Officer
Peter and Irene Ludwig Foundation

BENJAMIN DODENHOFF
Research and Projects
Peter and Irene Ludwig Foundation

FROM AACHEN TO THE WORLD

Irene and Peter Ludwig conducted all their art collecting from Aachen. It was the location of both their home and the headquarters of Leonard Monheim AG (known as the Ludwig Schokolade GmbH from 1986) and was the starting point for their extensive travels. In order to realise their international ambitions, they built up a network of agents and representatives with whom they could directly exchange information and confer. One of them was **Wolfgang Becker**. Through his work in Aachen, the art historian was closely connected to the Ludwigs. In 1970, he became the founding director of Aachen's Neue Galerie (New Gallery). This was the first institution to permanently exhibit part of the Ludwigs' collection, with American Pop Art prominently represented. After its renaming in 1973, it would also carry their name, becoming the Neue Galerie – Sammlung Ludwig (New Gallery – Ludwig Collection). Becker shared the Ludwigs' enterprising spirit, passion for travel, and, in particular, their openness and curiosity when it came to continually seeking out new art from different regions of the world. Their collaboration can be described as synergistic: the Ludwigs amassed an ever-growing collection of contemporary art through both the domestic and international art markets, which allowed Becker to present a programme of world-class exhibitions. It was through Wolfgang Becker that the Ludwigs made many important contacts, such as Radu Dobre-Sima, who stirred their interest in Romanian art. Becker made a constant stream of suggestions to them for both exhibitions and acquisitions, often during their joint travels. One of his tasks as museum director was to integrate the newly acquired international works in the Ludwig Collection into a coherent exhibition programme. When the Ludwig Forum für Internationale Kunst (Ludwig Forum for International Art) opened in 1991, succeeding the

Neue Galerie – Sammlung Ludwig and with Becker remaining as director, its name made clear that its fundamental concept was to be the international nature of the collection and the exhibition programme. It was here that the majority of new acquisitions in the collection—for example, those from Cuba, China, or Romania—were shown for the first time. Some groups of works went on to form touring exhibitions that travelled all over the world, while others remained in Aachen permanently, or were later donated or loaned out to the institutions that formed the globally expanding network of Ludwig museums.

In 1985, when Peter and Irene Ludwig met the gallery owner **Thomas Krings-Ernst**, their collection had already gained its international focus. In the art lover and connoisseur Krings-Ernst, they found a business partner on the same wavelength as them, going on to acquire numerous artworks from his Cologne gallery. Serving as a middleman, Krings-Ernst accompanied them on many trips and conducted numerous negotiations and preliminary discussions on their behalf. In this role, he was regularly in Moscow during the intensive phase of negotiations for a Russian Ludwig museum in the early 1990s, working to push the sometimes faltering discussions forward. As a gallerist, Krings-Ernst repeatedly provided the Ludwigs inspiration for new areas of collecting, such as contemporary art from Cuba and China. Krings-Ernst was not only linked to Peter Ludwig through the twin roles of entrepreneur and art lover, but also through their shared vision of art's capacity to build cultural and political bridges. These always went in both directions: just as the Ludwigs brought art of the world to Germany, they saw to it that parts of their international, contemporary Ludwig Collection, in the form of donations and permanent loans, could be seen in Austria, Switzerland, Hungary, Russia, and China—where they continue to be on view today.

A conversation with **Wolfgang Becker** about his working relationship with Peter Ludwig and his work to enact cultural politics through founding international museums

The interview took place over two sessions in Becker's apartment in Aachen, on February 14 and June 19, 2017. The second part of the interview, which primarily discusses the founding of institutions in Aachen, will be published separately at a later date.

DR. WOLFGANG BECKER (b. 1936, Hanover) was one of Peter and Irene Ludwig's longest and closest associates. Following his secondary education and a commercial traineeship, he studied art history, archaeology, and history in Bonn and Paris. In 1965, he received his doctorate from the University of Cologne. From 1967 to 1969, he worked as publicity manager for the arts in Cologne, where he met the collectors Peter and Irene Ludwig. In 1970, he became the head of the Neue Galerie – Sammlung Ludwig (New Gallery – Ludwig Collection) in the Alten Kurhaus in Aachen, a project he cofounded. There, he was tasked with showcasing the Ludwigs' new acquisitions, expanding their holdings, and presenting them to the public through exhibitions and events. In 1991, the collection moved to the Schirmfabrik, the former Emil Brauer umbrella factory, where Becker continued his multidisciplinary programme under a new name, the Ludwig Forum für Internationale Kunst (Ludwig Forum for International Art). He retired in 2001 and has since been active as an independent curator and author.

Ludwig enthralled me because his full charm and generosity were on display—he was young and dynamic.

REGINA WYRWOLL Mr. Becker, I would like to begin by asking you the classic first question, the one that I've asked every interviewee for this publication: When did you first meet Peter and Irene Ludwig?

WOLFGANG BECKER It was in 1967, when they first became active in Cologne. At the time I was a publicity manager for Cologne's tourism office, and my partner at the time, Evelyn Weiss, was a trainee at the Wallraf-Richartz-Museum.

RW Do you remember your first impression of Peter Ludwig?

WB We were close from our first meeting. Ludwig enthralled me because his full charm and generosity were on display—he was young and dynamic.

RW And what was the relationship between the couple like? It's often said that Irene Ludwig was something of a restraining force when it came to his acquisitions of contemporary art. Was she more interested in acquiring works like medieval art, ceramics, Meissen porcelain, or antiques?

WB As far as I knew her, she had a broad love of visual arts as one component of cultural history. Her husband's extreme engagement with the world of contemporary art was something she occasionally tried to curb.

RW How did their wonderful home come to be, where all their art collecting come together in a wholly unique manner?

WB Peter and Irene Ludwig's house wasn't devoted to modern art. They built their villa in the fifties, and their plan from the beginning was to rescue as many pieces of art as possible from the postwar rubble of the Rhineland. Hundreds of tiles, the small cloister on the first floor, and numerous other reused pieces were incorporated into the fabric of the house. It must have been quite an exhausting task for the architects. But I don't recall anything in my experience that suggested that Irene Ludwig wanted to give much space to modern art. I don't remember ever talking to her in detail about specific works of art.

RW That's an interesting opinion, one that differs from what other interviewees have said. Artworks from every possible era and from all over the world could be found in the Ludwigs' house, from Matisse to Pop Art—with an Arno Breker in the garden.

WB The Breker could go! That's a whole other story. Peter Ludwig and I often argued about it.

RW What was Peter Ludwig's perspective on art, in your opinion? Did you discuss individual works of art with him? The gallery owners Rudolf Zwirner and Rolf Ricke both say that they only ever discussed prices with him, not the works themselves.

WB Of course I did! Naturally we discussed art. Ludwig took pleasure in personally taking people through his collection and talking at length about the artworks! His views on art changed over the years. He saw gallery owners as salespeople with whom you did business. I experienced that once in Paris with Ileana Sonnabend. I saw her when Ludwig had already gone outside. She was sitting there with tears running down her face and she said: "Dreadful, that man is dreadful! He pressures me so much." He had haggled with her, he liked to do that.

In 1978, a new era began which was very exciting, very interesting, but also fraught with problems. It began with the first purchases of East German art …

RW How did your working relationship with him develop after you became the director of the Neue Galerie in Aachen, at Ludwig's recommendation in 1970? Three years later, it would receive the suffix "– Sammlung Ludwig."

WB My job at the Neue Galerie was to observe which international art movements Peter Ludwig followed. He travelled and often bought works in New York. For instance, for three or four years he was chiefly interested in photorealism, ignoring other styles. Those other styles and movements were what I took an interest in. They defined the initial years of my exhibition programme. In 1978, a new era began which was very exciting, very interesting, but also fraught with problems. It began with the first purchases of East German art, along with the exhibition *Kunst Heute in der Deutschen Demokratischen Republik* (*Art Today in the German Democratic Republic*), which ran from January 13 to March 18, 1979, in the Neue Galerie – Sammlung Ludwig in Aachen.

The most important artists from the GDR came to Aachen to take part in a panel discussion: Willi Sitte, Werner Tübke, Bernhard Heisig, and Wolfgang Mattheuer. In a hallway of the Neue Galerie hung three images by A.R. Penck, who would be expatriated from East Germany a year later. We took them down so that we could display works by the others. Penck protested and there was an exchange of letters in which he vehemently bad-mouthed Sitte. The integration of Eastern European art, its opening up and acceptance in the West, was often accompanied by such fighting and challenges.

RW It was a real culture war, one that continues to this day.

WB It's over, today there's no East Germany and no USSR. And at the Leipzig academy—the Academy of Fine Arts in Leipzig as it is now known—there are many students from the West.

RW What was it that spurred Peter Ludwig to collect East German art?

At that time, the beginning of the 1980s, it was clear to everyone that Ludwig was trying to expand the role of art collector into a position of power within cultural politics.

WB Let me set the stage. You remember the scandal that arose when Ludwig sold the medieval manuscripts to the J. Paul Getty Museum in Los Angeles?

RW That was in 1983.

WB The background was that Ludwig was very active in cultural politics at the time and had suggested a national Ludwig foundation into which he wanted to house his entire art collection. Three partners were to come together: the federal government, the state of North Rhine-Westphalia, and the City of Cologne. The City of Cologne negotiated with the federal and state governments with the aim of their taking over the costs of the Ludwig museum. Ludwig's bitter adversary was Werner Schmalenbach, director of the Kunstsammlung Nordrhein-Westfalen (North Rhine-Westphalia Art Collection) in Düsseldorf. Schmalenbach made fervent use of the media to agitate against Ludwig, despite the fact that Ludwig had, for many years, been a member of the acquisitions committee of the museum Schmalenbach directed. At that time, the beginning of the 1980s, it was clear to everyone that Ludwig was trying to expand the role of art collector into a position of power within cultural politics.

RW Ludwig had, in 1981, already founded the national Österreichische Ludwig-Stiftung für Kunst und Wissenschaft (Austrian Ludwig Foundation for Art and Science) in Vienna. Two years later he would begin talks in Budapest that would result in the Ludwig Múzeum.

From the materials I found in the federal archives, it's clear that there was fear in the political sphere that the collection would become scattered and not be kept in Cologne.

WB At the time, he had also housed the Wolfgang Hahn Collection in Vienna.

RW So it was his choice to take the Hahn Collection to Vienna? Did he not want competition within "his" museum?

WB Wolfgang Hahn was a great friend of his, as was Hahn's wife. Hahn was ill and was frequently in Aachen for treatment at the hospital there. I think Ludwig wanted both to create some guaranteed capital for Mrs. Hahn and find a good home for the Hahn Collection. As the latter wasn't possible in Cologne, which would have been the most sensible solution, he instigated Vienna to acquire the collection. And it has a good home there.

The Österreichische Ludwig-Stiftung für Kunst und Wissenschaft was, on the other hand, initiated by the then president of the Künstlerhaus in Vienna.

RW Hans Mayr.

WB Mayr was a character. I loved him, he was a real firebrand and very active in Cologne. By the way, he most likely had a lover there, too. I arranged talks between him and Peter Ludwig and, in 1977, we organised the exhibition *Kunst um 1970. Art around 1970* at the Künstlerhaus in Vienna. The Künstlerhaus had no funds and Ludwig stepped in as a generous sponsor. As a result, both he and I were made honorary members of the Künstlerhaus, Gesellschaft bildender Künstlerinnen und Künstler Österreichs (Künstlerhaus, Austrian Society of Visual Artists).

Mayr expressed interest in having a permanent Ludwig collection in Vienna. The Palais Liechtenstein was empty at the time. Ludwig worked hard for a museum to be established there for his collection and for the Hahn Collection.

RW The contract with the Austrian state came about as a result of the determination of Minister Hertha Firnberg. In my eyes, it was the cleverest of all of Ludwig's contracts because it mandated that both parties pay money into a foundation over many years, allowing the institution to become independent in the future owing to the amassed funds. That's how the Museum Moderner Kunst Stiftung Ludwig Wien (Modern Art Museum Ludwig Foundation Vienna), otherwise known as mumok, came to be. The chairperson of the Board of Trustees, Hermann Fillitz, who I have also interviewed, told me that, unfortunately, not enough money was accumulated.

WB Fillitz knew Ludwig and was just as involved in the negotiations as Mayr.

RW He told me that Mayr spoke in such a working-class Viennese dialect that Ludwig snubbed him twice. It was the only on a third occasion in Aachen that Ludwig met with him.

WB It was Irene Ludwig who was above all appalled by him, because he didn't fit her image of a person of good manners. Mayr was a hearty, loud Viennese type, a photographer by trade. Some of his photos, which were purchased by Peter Ludwig, still hang in the former offices of the Firma Ludwig Schokolade in Süsterfeldstraße in Aachen, which are currently rented by the Peter and

Irene Ludwig Foundation. In Vienna, Ludwig was a collector and donor. His activities in East Germany, in contrast, pertained more to cultural politics and business. He was always the *Pralinenmeister* (master of pralines), as the artist Hans Haacke aptly characterised him in his 1981 fourteen-piece work with the same name. It was also about trying to get a foot in the door in the GDR in relation to chocolate production, an attempt that later proved successful.

[In the countries of the Communist Bloc,] the Western free market system ran up against the Soviet planned economy. During visits to studios, the artists were helpless when Peter Ludwig asked, "What does a work like this cost?"

RW Did Ludwig only buy through the Staatliches Kunsthandelshaus (State Art Trading House) of the GDR, which later became VEH Bildende Kunst und Antiquitäten (VEH Visual Arts and Antiquities), or did he also purchase from other institutions?

WB In the Communist Bloc countries, he could only buy through their respective state art trading houses. It was the same in Moscow.

RW In Moscow, at least, Ludwig acquired some very interesting works of art, works which did not strictly conform with the state ideology. How was that done?

WB During the Brezhnev era, one could easily see the progress of the political thaw since one's previous visit. The range of works and styles available through the art dealership of the Union of Visual Artists of the USSR was constantly expanding, including some that had been completely disregarded at first. As a result, we went back to the studio of Ilya Kabakov on a second visit, followed by a third. People from the union led us to a loft, where Mrs. Kabakov met us. Kabakov and others were now officially recognised. Dissidents were often tolerated, but denounced. In the Union of Visual Artists of the USSR, the painters and sculptors were at the top of the hierarchy, with illustrators at the bottom. Kabakov was an illustrator, he created children's books.

RW But didn't Ludwig also buy works by, for instance, the underground artist Grisha Bruskin, among others—whose prices, in the spectacular Sotheby's auction in Moscow in 1988, were inflated from nothing to as much as 400,000 dollars?

WB Yes. He was able to buy works by these artists earlier, on the recommendation of Vladimir Semyonov, the Soviet ambassador to Bonn from 1978 to 1986. It was the same in the GDR. I don't believe that he was able to buy works by any of the East German artists we know except through the official channels. He could only buy works by A.R. Penck, for instance, from the gallery owner Michael Werner in Cologne.

RW Peter Pachnicke was the general director of the Staatliches Kunsthandelshaus of the GDR from 1974 to 1976. From 1993, he was the deputy director of the Ludwig-Institut für Kunst der DDR (Ludwig Institute for the Art of the GDR) in what is now the Ludwig Galerie Schloss Oberhausen (Ludwig Gallery in the Oberhausen Palace), where he curated numerous interesting exhibitions. Did he have dealings with Ludwig in his earlier role?

WB I don't know if Pachnicke was in contact with Ludwig back then. I first met him in Oberhausen.

RW What happened next with art from the East?

WB After the GDR exhibition in Aachen in 1979, which was controversial but attracted a lot of visitors, Semyonov invited me to Bonn and expressed his interest in seeing some Russian artists represented in the Ludwig Collection and shown in solo exhibitions in the Neue Galerie – Sammlung Ludwig. He showed me some pieces from his private collection, which hung in the Russian embassy, particularly works by the very "Russian" landscape artist Nikolai Andronov and his wife Natalia Yegorshina, and the husband and wife Nina and Dmitry Žilinski. I was very interested in these works and made clear that we knew relatively little about Russian art, but that Ludwig had already demonstrated his interest in it through his considerable collection of art of the Russian Revolution. Semyonov knew about this, and that's how his first personal contact with Ludwig came about. In April 1980, they travelled together to Moscow, together with Karl Ruhrberg, the director of the Museum Ludwig in Cologne from 1978 to 1984, who had fiercely opposed the idea. We were there as official guests and Semyonov showed us not only what we understood Russian art to be—Socialist Realism—but also a collection that was distinctly not Soviet but still in line with a Russian tradition. Ludwig began to enquire about prices very carefully. That's where the Western free market system ran up against the Soviet planned economy. During visits to studios, the artists were helpless when Peter Ludwig asked, "What does a work like this cost?" I can remember that the painter Eduard Steinberg really shocked Ludwig once, when he answered, "You can't afford it." Ludwig left and then he asked, "What did he mean by that?" In the interim, Steinberg asked about Ludwig, "Is he really a millionaire?" Then Ludwig made Steinberg an offer—a very low one because he didn't know what prices a Russian artist might ask for. Steinberg was offended and said, "I'll give it to you." Ludwig reddened and left the room. As always on these trips, Wolfgang Schreiner—Ludwig's general representative for all of his Communist Bloc activities and the general manager of the chocolate factory in Berlin—was present. He bought graphic works there himself and later founded a small private museum with them in Bad Steben, the Grafikmuseum Stiftung Schreiner (Graphic Art Museum Schreiner Foundation). Schreiner came to an agreement with Steinberg on a price that both sides were happy with. This was a time when you could still negotiate with artists.

RW During the period when he was buying art from the East, Peter Ludwig changed the galleries he worked with, because neither Rudolf Zwirner, Rolf Ricke, nor Ileana Sonnabend wanted to move in the same direction as him. The Cologne gallery owner Thomas Krings-Ernst, who worked together with you in getting the Fundación Ludwig de Cuba started, then came onto the scene. Somebody told me that one of the ways Krings-Ernst had gained Ludwig's esteem was through arranging for him to be made a commander of the French Legion of Honour in 1988. How did this new partnership come about?

WB Krings-Ernst's mother came from Aachen and was friends with Peter Ludwig. There were rumours that Peter Ludwig felt obliged to honour the deathbed request of Krings-Ernst's mother to take care of her son. Ludwig felt a kind of paternal duty toward him. Krings-Ernst had followed Ludwig since the 1960s— for instance to New York. When he opened his gallery in Cologne, Ludwig had him conduct negotiations with some of his contacts, such as those in Moscow. Krings-Ernst is a very laid-back, outgoing individual, and handled matters in Moscow that were important to Ludwig. He became accustomed to accompanying us whenever we travelled to Socialist countries. The relationship with Cuba, for instance, began with Jürgen Harten. At a congress of the International Council of Museums (ICOM) in Havana, he discovered the Cuban art scene thanks to Antonio Eligio Fernández, also known as Tonel, an intelligent artist and mediator. He subsequently organised the exhibition *Kuba o.k.* at the Kunsthalle Düsseldorf in 1990. Krings-Ernst saw the exhibition and enthusiastically told Ludwig about it. Ludwig commissioned him to arrange the acquisition of a large part of the exhibition collection. So Krings-Ernst brought us—Ludwig and myself—to Havana in 1991, where we negotiated with Helmo Hernández, who represented the Ministry of Culture and was our most important contact. The establishment of the Fundación Ludwig de Cuba in 1994 was undertaken as a form of public aid because a Ludwig museum in Havana, which was the original idea discussed, proved to be infeasible.

RW I interviewed Helmo Hernández and he told me the whole story. On top of all the problems that you overcame was the issue that Ludwig insisted on receiving two honorary doctorates, although Havana would only give one per person, on principle. But Helmo also managed to sort that out. When Peter and Irene Ludwig were visiting Cuba in 1993, Fidel Castro unexpectedly came for lunch at the government guesthouse where the Ludwigs were staying. Helmo had to wait outside.

At that point in time, Ludwig the cultural politician was interested in influential politicians or dictators, and he found them in history.

WB Yes, that's right, I was there too. When Ludwig returned from the audience with Castro, he said that Castro has asked him if he was the son of Emil Ludwig—Emil Ludwig, the German author who had written monographs about important men from history, such as Stalin or Simon Bolívar. His books had been translated into Spanish too. Castro had apparently read some of them.

RW What did Ludwig think of this meeting?

WB At that point in time, Ludwig the cultural politician was interested in influential politicians and dictators, and he found them in history: Stalin, Hitler—and Fidel Castro.

RW Excuse me?

WB He was interested in what motivated these figures, how many people they affected, and how they created history, regardless of the resulting losses. Ludwig explained to me that he knew I highly disapproved of the story with Arno Breker. He said that I shouldn't forget, however, that he didn't go to Breker to have his portrait painted, or to admire his sculptures. Rather, it was because Breker had been an eyewitness who could tell him about Adolf Hitler and the foolish artists who went down on their knees before him and followed him. In the book I wrote for Ludwig's 70th birthday, *Ein deutscher Sammler – ein Deutsches Auto. Peter Ludwig und der Volkswagen* (*A German Collector – A German Car: Peter Ludwig and the Volkswagen*) I discuss Hans Haacke and his installation *Bodenlos* (*Bottomless*) in the German pavilion at the Venice Biennale in 1993, in which he renamed the pavilion Germania and tore up its floor. I compare the two Ludwig busts by Arno Breker from 1986 with the one by the Russian state sculptor, Lev Kerbel, who portrayed Ludwig very similarly.

About Castro, he once said to me something along the lines of how the man had achieved so many great things. On the streets you could see that all the people in Cuba were skinny, which was much better for their health than being fat. That was really crossing the line. I also told him, "I take offence at Arno Breker's *Alexander* (1990), and when I see it standing in the garden, it pains me."

RW Irene Ludwig didn't comment on her husband's fascination for such figures?

WB No. Peter Ludwig is without question one of the most daring collectors in Germany's history. Others, such as Karl Ströher, weren't motivated to be public figures and expose themselves to denunciation. Ludwig's own essays, interviews, and biographies evince his desire to play a part in global political debates.

RW The public outcry at the beginning of the 1980s—during his negotiations with the federal government, North Rhine-Westphalia, and the City of Cologne regarding a national Ludwig foundation—really got to him. Did he sometimes express his concerns to you?

WB No. He just said, as a great, powerful man like him is prone to say, "It's water off a duck's back." But you could see that it affected him. At the same time, he was convinced that it would benefit his reputation.

Peter Ludwig didn't shy away from the majority of conflicts, but there were some which he stayed out of, such as the discussions surrounding the poor condition of some of the city's storage facilities. I had to handle that. The city eventually understood that we had moved out of those facilities and into better ones because the problems associated with storage and conservation were becoming ever more daunting, the collection's holdings were growing too quickly, Ludwig was buying new works every other day, so to speak!

Today, I still agree with Ludwig: If we are interested in the art of other countries, then we also have to study the systems within which that art is created and we must respect those systems.

RW Large batches of them too …

WB … There were also many things which he was forced to take or buy. Negotiations with the Union of Visual Artists of the USSR and its steering committee in Moscow always included the expected additional purchase of at least one work by the union's president. This was also the case in all the other Communist Bloc countries where one had to negotiate with such a union—Romania, the former Czechoslovakia, Bulgaria …

RW Was that also the case in East Germany?

WB Yes, that's why a number of paintings by Willi Sitte were purchased together, including the large-format works *Im Leichtmetallwerk* (*In the Light Metal Plant*) from 1977 and *Nach der Schicht im Salzbergwerk* (*After the Shift in the Salt Mine*) from 1982. Sitte was the president.

RW The whole situation is beyond comprehension for us now. How did you feel about it, as the recipient of this "flood" of images?

WB At times it amused me. When Peter Ludwig said, "That's the way it has to be," I could only reply, "OK, I understand, that's the way it has to be," because that was the only way that dissident artists like Kabakov or Bruskin could be included in the collection. There was no other way.

Today, I still agree with Ludwig: If we are interested in the art of other countries, then we also have to study the systems within which that art is created and we must respect those systems. We must assume that if the images reach us, it means the systems will collapse, because they can no longer retain their images. If they give them over to us, those who created them will also escape the system. Indeed, quite a number of the artists whose works we bought back then have since emigrated.

[Peter Ludwig] was determined to pursue his vision of world art and, above all, to collect as much art of Communist Bloc countries as possible, chapter by chapter.

RW How did the Ludwig Museum at the Russian Museum come about? The museum was initially supposed to be in Moscow, wasn't it? During that period you were negotiating with the Pushkin Museum and the Tretyakov Gallery, right?

WB The Pushkin Museum is the international museum and the Tretyakov is the national one. Irina Antonova was director of the Pushkin Museum, which holds a multitude of treasures of German art that were seized after the war. We all met Antonova when the curator Pontus Hultén put on the exhibition *Paris-Moscou 1900–1930* in the Centre Pompidou and the Pushkin Museum in 1979. The French iteration of exhibition was more extensive than the

Russian one, because the one in Moscow was heavily censored. I can remember that a picture that showed the Russian revolutionary Leon Trotsky was not allowed to be shown in Moscow. Hultén protested about this in his opening speech, which caused considerable unrest. Antonova defended the censorship with an argument based on national honour. We were unable to find a way into the Pushkin Museum.

RW Isn't it true that during this period you were aided by Andreas Meyer-Landrut, the West German ambassador to Moscow, from 1980 to 1983, and again from 1987 to 1990?

WB He was kind enough to mediate for us, but really it was Semyonov that opened all the doors in Moscow. That was great. I remember another visit to Moscow in 1981, when we were taken to a gloomy church in Polyanka Street, which had been set up as a salesroom for the Union of Visual Artists of the USSR. We were astounded by how many works were now on display by artists who had previously been vilified as dissidents.

RW How, then, did the Ludwig Museum at the Russian Museum in the Marble Palace in St. Petersburg come about?

WB Joseph Kiblitsky was certainly involved. Kiblitsky spoke German well and was—like Mayr in Vienna—communicative and cooperative. He was always present and facilitated communication with the director of the Russian Museum, Yevgenia Petrova, who doesn't speak German.

RW Were you and Ludwig aware at the time that, as a Nonconformist artist, Kiblitsky had left the Soviet Union for Germany in 1982? He painted realistically and had exhibitions in the west for a period. He later had himself named "artistic director of the Russian Museum and the Ludwig Museum in the Marble Palace." Had that already occurred by 1995?

WB No. Kiblitsky was the one who introduced us to those in charge at the Russian Museum, and I assumed he was one of the museum directors. Everyone was complaining about economic constraints and talking about selling off their collection. We would be able to remedy some of their hardships if we were to found a Ludwig museum there, which would be primarily financed by Peter Ludwig.

Later, on their own initiative, they generously exhibited artists like Jörg Immendorff and Aachen-resident Eric Peters in the galleries of the Ludwig Museum—in return for high rent.

RW Who did the money go to?

WB I think it went to the Russian Museum, to the Marble Palace.

RW What kind of role did Peter Ludwig play in the rent arrangements?

WB None. As with other museums, Ludwig offered a selection of works from his collection, half of them donated and the other half on loan. The Marble Palace would bear his name. A quarter of the holdings should always be on display, while the museum could make use of the free rooms. This agreement, as far as I have been able to ascertain, has not been strictly adhered to in either St. Petersburg or Beijing.

RW So, the Ludwig Museum in St. Petersburg was founded. We have already spoken about the role of the two ambassadors, the German Meyer-Landrut and the Russian Semyonov. Do you remember how things went in 1995 with the Ludwig Museum in Beijing? Did Krings-Ernst play an important role?

WB I don't know much about that at all because I was very busy with the activities of the recently-created Ludwig Forum für Internationale Kunst, which opened in 1991 in new rooms in the Schirmfabrik. However, I think it was Chinese antiquities and the Ludwigs' collaboration with the director of the Museum für Ostasiatische Kunst (Museum for East Asian Art) in Cologne, Adele Schlombs, that led to the first contacts. Prior to the negotiations with Beijing, Ludwig had already made loans and donations to the museum in Cologne of antiquities he had acquired on the international market. To this day, the museum still houses magnificent works from the Ludwig Collection. Irene Ludwig once remarked, after her husband's death, that the amount he had spent on ancient Chinese art had surprised her. Schlombs may have helped establish contact with Yang Lizhou, the then deputy director of the National Art Museum of China (NAMOC) in Beijing, which was also responsible for modern art. I wasn't involved in the preparations and was invited to the opening by the Goethe Institute in Beijing in order to explain the works in the collection and their history to those Chinese individuals who were interested. I had an attentive public with little knowledge about Western techniques and imagery—not only the museum staff, but also a number of visitors. We spent hours going through the exhibition. In front of Jörg Immendorff's linocuts, for instance, I had to first explain what a linocut is. It is difficult to imagine that a people with such a long cultural history only first encountered oil painting on canvas and other Western techniques in 1912.

RW Why in 1912?

WB Sun Yat-sen founded the first Chinese republic then and opened its culture to the West. There are barely any older Chinese oil paintings on canvas.

RW Were there also negotiations for the founding of a Ludwig museum in Prague?

WB I believe there were only vague plans for Prague. Ludwig acquired a work by Milan Knížák, the director of the Academy of Fine Arts in Prague. After extensive research in Prague, assisted by the Czech Iva Haendly from Aachen, I organised the exhibition of recent Czechoslovakian art *Zweiter Ausgang: Tschechische und slowakische Künstler* (*Second Exit: Czech and Slovak Artists*) at the Ludwig Forum in 1993. Ludwig bought some works from this exhibition and bought some others in Prague. But I don't know anything about any talks regarding a Ludwig museum. Prague was busy converting the Trade Fair Palace to be used as a museum. They would have been delighted if Ludwig had offered some works on loan, but I don't know of any talks about a museum in Prague. In Bucharest there were concrete discussions about the founding of a museum. The talks began before the breakup of the Communist Bloc in 1989.

RW Who was involved there? How did those discussions transpire? There must have been an exhibition in Bucharest, too?

WB No. One of the middlemen was the Romanian architect Radu Dobre-Sima, who has lived in Aachen for decades. He invited me to Bucharest in 1988, took me to museums and studios, and introduced me to some people. The artist and art critic Călin Dan was beginning to establish a centre in Bucharest, where he would later become its director, in the mould of the Soros Center for Contemporary Art in Budapest. He was the second contact.

RW Was that in 1992, after the fall of the Iron Curtain? George Soros didn't travel there before that.

WB When I was there before the Iron Curtain fell, there were already discussions about how Soros wanted to become involved in Romania. The radical nature of the Communist Bloc's end surprised everyone. Productive talks led to a representative of the Ministry of Culture showing Peter Ludwig rooms in the People's House that could be used for a Ludwig museum, but a new cultural infrastructure began to develop before that could occur. A functionary from the Ministry of Culture put together a comprehensive exhibition of Romanian art for Ludwig in the vestibules of the Teatrul Național Ion Luca Caragiale, the National Theatre in Bucharest, from which he purchased a small collection. A couple of years later, in 1997, I organised a substantial exhibition at the Ludwig Forum that included works from that collection, entitled *Bukarest nach '89. Kunst in Rumänien heute* (*Bucharest After '89: Art in Romania Today*).

RW Was there also something like a state art trading house in Romania?

WB Of course. As there was in all of the Socialist countries.

RW Nicolae Ceaușescu brutally repressed Romania. People were not even allowed to own a typewriter without it being officially registered so that the state could control any writing of subversive letters or texts. Weren't you aware of that?

WB Nevertheless, there were many artists there, whether they were supported, tolerated, or banned. For example, Paula Ribariu, who Dobre-Sima took me to meet, had worked for decades in secrecy. Ludwig purchased the large work *Altar* (1987/1988) from her. I had earlier encountered the problem with so-called "copying machines" in the offices of the Union of Visual Artists in the USSR in Moscow. The secretary hadn't been able to make a copy of the list of purchases, because she had no machine on which to do so. If she had had one, she could have been suspected of reproducing her boyfriend's poems and distributing them in the form of samizdat, literary publications that didn't conform with the state ideology. Dobre-Sima established three businesses in Bucharest after the Communist Bloc collapsed—a business selling copying machines and printers, an import-export firm for art and office supplies, and a building firm—and was very successful. Bank loans were just as difficult to come by as copiers or art supplies. I was asked about them from time to time.

RW Ceaușescu built the People's House back then. After the earthquake in 1977, which destroyed so many houses, he had the city centre essentially levelled in order to build this monumental new inner city. You must have seen that.

WB Of course. We were shown around the state rooms. After 2004, I visited the National Museum of Contemporary Art (MNAC), a haunting place that struggles to attract an audience.

RW Due to construction of the People's House, the dictatorship was, for many years, the largest purchaser of traditional carpets, curtains, and furniture. It had all these produced in Romanian monasteries, convents, and factories according to their own designs. It makes for a bizarre aesthetic experience. Do you know that the corridors on the ground floor of the People's House are so large that a tank can be driven through them?

WB The monumental scale doesn't engender astonishment but bewilderment. We also visited Ceaușescu's country residence outside Bucharest. I visited the monasteries and convents with Dobre-Sima—they are similar to the painted monasteries in Moldavia—and spoke to many friendly monks and nuns.

RW Which buildings were you offered for the Ludwig Collection?

WB A central location in the People's House, where several series of rooms stood empty. I don't think, however, that Ludwig thought about it for too long, because he had heard of Soros's ambitious interests. He wasn't happy about the competition.

RW So the negotiations dragged on for several years?

WB I don't know anything about that.

RW So you weren't always involved?

WB No. But I also don't know anything about Ludwig's later visits. I do remember a visit to the National University of Arts in Bucharest when we were accompanied by Dobre-Sima and another Romanian from Aachen, a musician, who had arranged for Ludwig to be given an honorary doctorate in 1995. And I remember a trip in an official military helicopter to Târgu Jiu, the small town that Constantin Brâncuși made famous with his memorial sculpture ensemble, which includes the *Colonne sans fin* (*The Endless Column*) (1937).

RW And weren't you shocked by what you saw?

WB I was only shocked on my first visit in 1988, when the city and everyone who lived in it were almost suffocating beneath a cloak of silence and whispers. I was more appalled than I had been in Moscow. After Ceaușescu's overthrow, everything was different. I discovered the city. There was this beautiful, airy villa, where a private collection of art from the early twentieth century was on show—a collection that no longer exists. Unfortunately I can't remember the name. I remember the artists I visited, and who I continue to follow, Orthodox believers like Victoria and Marian Zidaru or the "shaman" Paula Ribariu. I have some of her works in my apartment. I knew Horia Damian, whose large installation, *Galaxy (Voie Lactée)* (1974), shone in the ballroom of the Neue Galerie in 1974. In 2009, the MNAC dedicated a large memorial exhibition to him at the People's House, which bore his name as its title.

RW Did you experience any political difficulties on your visits?

WB During the Ceaușescu era, everything was very hidden. We visited the artists in secret, and my guide, Dobre-Sima, was very careful on the phone when he was arranging the visits. We visited his favourite, Ribariu, clandestinely—in 2013 we published an extensive catalogue about her work with the Klartext Verlag publishing house in Essen. I had experienced something similar once in Moscow, when our interpreter had secretively led us to the apartment of a forbidden artist, one we were not allowed to see officially, where we could view his works. Together with her husband, a writer, Ribariu and some of her friends had "hibernated" through the entire Ceaușescu era. In her youth, she had followed in the artistic footsteps of Salvador Dalí and further developed his surrealism into large-scale installations that include many references to Orthodox Christian imagery and to Romanian history, such as the Thracians. She belongs to a generation that walks the streets very warily, as if they are being followed.

RW You said a few minutes ago, that Peter Ludwig had given up on the idea of founding a museum in Bucharest because of competition from Soros.

WB I think he felt a bit superfluous. As I mentioned, there was Călin Dan who was preparing the centre for Soros and who wanted to expand that institute. He may have been worried that we would get in his way.

RW Let's talk about Ludwig's activities in Bulgaria. How did that play out?

WB Hans Mayr arranged all that, in his position as head of the Künstlerhaus in Vienna. He maintained close relations with the union of Bulgarian visual artists and set up an official visit. The leaders of the union invited us to Sofia and to a number of other cities. I remember Plovdiv, where a number of artists lived. They painted modern historical pictures dominated by tragic pathos. Ribariu had explained to me the Romanian history of the Thracians, who fought the Romans. Here we encountered the Dacians, who were their enemies—a people who were repressed by everyone from the Romans to the Soviets. When I leaf through the two catalogues from the Neue Galerie – Sammlung Ludwig, *Aspekte sowjetischer Kunst der Gegenwart* (*Aspects of Contemporary Soviet Art*) from 1982 and *Aspekte bulgarischer Kunst heute. Sammlung Ludwig Aachen* (*Aspects of Bulgarian Art Today: Ludwig*

Collection Aachen) from 1984, the pervasive sadness in the works catches my eye. Ludwig was hesitant about adding a collection of Bulgarian art to the larger body of twentieth century Socialist art.

RW And why did he decide to do so in the end?

WB He was determined to pursue his vision of world art and, above all, to collect as much art of Communist Bloc countries as possible, chapter by chapter. This was especially true of the period when the Communist Bloc collapsed, when it was opening up, when a particular style would never exist again, when everything would be blurred into an international context. The provinces of Europe could still be distinguished from one another then. The circle was closed with the establishment of the foundation in Cuba. It really fascinated him to say: Look, there is the entire Socialist Bloc coming to an end.

[Peter Ludwig] lived twice as fast as everyone else—in cars, in planes, in hotels—and almost always on the move; a frightful, all too futuristic life. ... I would have wished for him to have been able enjoy the fame he won through his hard work for many years to come.

RW Can you explain why the founding of Ludwig museums became an unending activity? The last of them was in Beijing, and Peter Ludwig died unexpectedly before it opened.

WB I think Ludwig sensed that his days were numbered. He suffered from high blood pressure and was quick to anger. So he negotiated quickly in Beijing and surprisingly donated everything—he was in a hurry.

RW But he was only seventy-one years old.

WB He lived twice as fast as everyone else—in cars, in planes, in hotels—and almost always on the move; a frightful, all too futuristic life. We both were in Aachen University Hospital in 1996, in neighbouring rooms. The renowned surgeon Volker Schumpelik operated on both of us. I wanted to congratulate Peter on his birthday, but Irene stopped me. I would have wished for him to have been able enjoy the fame he won through his hard work for many years to come.

RW Thank you very much, Mr. Becker, for taking so much time to talk to us.

A conversation with **Thomas Krings-Ernst** about his close collaboration with Peter Ludwig from 1986 to 1996 and his involvement in Ludwig's founding of new museums around the world

The interview took place in his gallery in Cologne across three meetings, on October 15, 21, and 28, 2020.

DR. THOMAS KRINGS-ERNST (b. 1947, Aachen) studied business administration at the University of Cologne. He worked for a variety of international firms, founded a number of start-ups, completed his MBA from 1978 to 1979 at the European business school INSEAD in Fontainebleau, and built an international network. In 1991, he wrote his doctoral thesis on "Kunstproduktion und Kunstförderung einst und jetzt. Unter besonderer Berücksichtigung ökonomischer Aspekte" ("Art Production and Art Promotion, Past and Present, with Special Consideration of Economic Aspects") at Johannes Kepler University in Linz. In 1982, Krings-Ernst purchased a former factory in Cologne-Bayenthal as the location for his newly-founded Galerie Kunsträume Köln, later renamed Krings-Ernst Gallery, where figures from the international art scene have lived, worked, and exhibited. Many of these artists' works became part of the Ludwig Collection. In 1986, as a close confidant and ally of Peter Ludwig in matters of world art, he began to negotiate with cultural institutions and government representatives regarding the founding of Ludwig museums in Germany and abroad. With his involvement, the museums in Budapest (1989), Koblenz (1992), St. Petersburg (1995), and Beijing (1996), as well as the Fundación Ludwig de Cuba in Havana (1994) were founded.

REGINA WYRWOLL Thank you very much for your willingness to talk about your experiences and work with Peter and Irene Ludwig.

THOMAS KRINGS-ERNST It's my pleasure. To begin with a quote from Joseph Beuys: "Von der Sprache aus … Jo-Jo … Nö-nö …" ("Starting with language … Yes-yes … No-no …") And one from Thomas Krings-Ernst: "Da-da … bla-bla … Alles in Allem." ("Da-da … Blah-blah … All together.")

RW Let's begin with the most important question: What was your relationship to Peter Ludwig?

TKE Let me put it like this: life is essentially about drives—drives of material and form, of greed, envy, and hate. Curiosity is a form of greed. That's what connected me to Peter Ludwig, starting in 1968 when I saw the legendary exhibition *Zeitbild – Provokation – Kunst* (*Image of the Times – Provocation – Art*), which included Pop Art works from his collection at the Suermondt Museum in Aachen (today the Suermondt-Ludwig-Museum). Nietzsche once said, "The happy are curious." In my opinion, art is the best raw material for curiosity! For curiosity and for passion!

I first experienced Ludwig's collection in 1968 as a student, at the Suermondt Museum's Pop Art exhibition. In response to it, the public in Aachen said, "What he is showing here is just nonsense, he is wasting his wife's money." I, however, was electrified.

RW There is a story that as your mother lay on her deathbed, she recommended you, her son, to Peter Ludwig.

TKE No! That's not true! "My mother, on her deathbed, recommended me to Peter Ludwig" is false! Jealousy! My mother died in 1982 as the result of a stroke, and it wasn't until 1985 that I got to know Peter Ludwig as a collector and partner. I was his cicerone. My mother had absolutely nothing to do with the fact that Peter Ludwig and I began working together in 1986.

RW How were you first put into touch with him?

TKE I knew him and his family from Aachen because I grew up there. I'll explain it all for you: my father, Arthur Ernst, was a textile industrialist. In the late 1920s he met my mother, Dalozia, who was also called Szöszy, a Hungarian from a hussar family. We lived in Aachen. In 1956, my parents divorced, and then my mother married Heinz-Otto Krings. H.O. Krings also belonged to a textile dynasty, was the president of the German and European golf federations for fifteen years, and spoke six languages—including Öcher Platt, the regional dialect. The family had many branches, typical for Aachen.

So why am I telling you this? It was, if you like, an Aachen oligarchy. The Monheims, the Cadenbachs (Irmgard Cadenbach was Irene Ludwig's half-sister, she was born a Monheim), the Kringses, the Ernsts—they all moved in the same circles. For me, as a young man, it was an atmosphere that was as impressive as it was oppressive. Politicians were always coming and going at our house. My father, Arthur, and his brother, Alexander, were co-founders of a textiles trade show in Moscow in the 1960s. We had a lot of Russian guests, including Vladimir Semyonov, a high-ranking Soviet diplomat and committed art collector.

RW Let's return to your mother, Szöszy, for a moment.

TKE My mother was an elegant woman and a passionate builder of bridges between people. She found Peter Ludwig and his collection fascinating. As I mentioned, I first experienced Ludwig's collection in 1968 as a student, at the Suermondt Museum's Pop Art exhibition. In response to it, the public in Aachen said, "What he is showing here is just nonsense, he is wasting his wife's money." I, however, was electrified. I began to collect works on paper—by Andy Warhol, Richard Hamilton, Jasper Johns, Roy Lichtenstein, David Hockney, and James Rosenquist, not to mention Michael Buthe, Sigmar Polke, C. O. Paeffgen, and Joseph Beuys.

In 1969, during my business administration studies, I moved to New York. My interest in the city was sparked by, among other things, Professor Hans Büschgen's practice-oriented banking seminar, particularly as the question of universal versus special-purpose banks was being hotly debated then. At the same time, I was curious about art—there were always two hearts beating in my chest. I quickly immersed myself in the New York art scene. I went to Warhol's Factory, the New Lafayette Theatre, Woodstock … it was a wild time.

RW What took you to New York at that time?

TKE On the recommendation of my stepfather, Heinz-Otto Krings, I got an internship at the investment firm Hayden, Stone & Co. (later Loeb, Rhoades & Co.). What I learned during this internship flowed into my thesis on options trading on the New York Stock Exchange. I took my car with me, a VW Beetle. When I arrived in 1969, the opening of Roy Lichtenstein's first retrospective was happening at the Solomon R. Guggenheim Museum. There I ran into the American collector Peter Brant, who I knew from St. Moritz. Peter was the "influencer" in New York—and still is, for that matter. He began collecting very early on, produced films by Warhol, and was in close contact with the gallery owner Leo Castelli—Peter had fantastic connections. And he told me, "Drop in some time." He had a huge apartment, at least four hundred square metres, on United Nations Plaza. I explained to him: "I know Peter Ludwig well. He's my uncle." This wasn't true of course, but it worked. "Ah, you know Ludwig! I've got some works here that I'd like to sell him." So I wrote to Peter Ludwig: "Dear Mr. Ludwig! I'm here in New York …," and so on. Ludwig answered: "Unfortunately I can't come. I'm very interested, but I have a dealer who I trust, Rudolf Zwirner. I'll arrange a meeting. He'll be in contact." Zwirner got in touch and we met with Brant. The two of them made a deal. That was my first "business" encounter with Ludwig. Later, I left my Beetle with Brant's girlfriend, Sandy, and travelled around America. I didn't have anything else to do with Ludwig at this point.

RW What happened next? What did you do after that?

TKE At the beginning of the 1970s I lived in France: initially in Saint-Paul-de-Vence, where I improved my knowledge of French at the Faculté des Lettres in Nice, then in Paris, where I worked for the banking group Crédit Industriel et Commercial for four years. I felt very much at home in France. The best or most special thing about French savoir vivre is not just that they know about good food and elegant clothing, but that the French are open to every kind of beauty and are able to see it, to enjoy it, and—most importantly—to appreciate it. No great distinction is made between the beauty of nature and that of art. That's very much after my own heart. Nature and culture have always belonged together for me. Yuval Noah Harari wrote, "Homo sapiens are animals, and everything that has happened in history [that is, in CULTURE!] has obeyed the laws of physics, chemistry and biology [that is, NATURE!]"[1] In other words, culture is unthinkable without nature. If you can't see the beauty in a horse, then you won't see it in an artwork either! You should keep your eyes open, be curious about the world, and not be visually illiterate—that's how I see it, that's what I was taught at home growing up. That's probably what drew me to France time and again. I would have been happy to stay there forever.

In 1979, during my time at the private business school INSEAD in Fontainebleau, I met Jean-Claude Decaux, founder of the JCDecaux group, which specialises in street furniture and outdoor advertising. The design and architecture of their furniture and advertising media were created in the 1970s. I was impressed by the overall idea of the company: the aesthetic component—designed by architects; the social—part of the concept is that the company takes care of the upkeep and maintenance of their products, in turn creating jobs; the economic—the trilateral contracts between the company, local government, and transport operators were important for the development of PPP, public-private partnerships. Their street furniture was a new medium for visual communication in public urban spaces! It inspired me to bring the concept to Germany, so I founded the GUVE—Gesellschaft für Urbane Verkehrseinrichtungen (Society for Urban Transport Facilities) in Cologne.

To sum it all up: the Kaiserstadt (imperial city), my parent's house, the Kringses and the Ernsts, the competition-oriented world of American finance, the dignified and tasteful life in France, the furnishing of streets, and always, parallel to all this, art and culture—which would later prove pivotal, even defining, for my work with Ludwig.

Before Pontus Hultén opened the Centre Pompidou in Paris in 1977, he contacted Ludwig: "We have nothing here! Could you loan us some Pop Art?" The works from the Ludwig Collection remained on loan in Paris for several years.

RW When did you set up your gallery?

TKE In 1982, a disused factory from the turn of the century caught my eye—I saw it and bought it. What was the motivation? At the end of the 1970s, the Marais area of Paris was redeveloped and the Centre Pompidou (Beaubourg) was built. In the early 1980s, my travels often took me to New York where, in SoHo, former industrial buildings were being converted into studios and lofts. Slogan: old buildings reborn, revitalisation of the city! Similar to Decaux, I was preoccupied by the idea of restructuring urban space. So I transformed the old drive-belt factory into a gallery. In 1985, after I had sold my share of GUVE to Decaux, I opened the Kunsträume Köln with 1,200 square metres of floorspace. It is now known as the Krings-Ernst Gallery.

RW In August 1985, an extensive newspaper article, "A Venturesome Gallery in Cologne," appeared in the International Herald Tribune, discussing you and the Kunsträume Köln.

TKE Yes, it was written by the American journalist David Galloway. During those years, Cologne was one of the artistic centres of the world. Galloway was the chief curator for Farah Diba, the Iranian empress, and was tasked by her with setting up the Tehran Museum of Contemporary Art.

RW How did you come to Peter Ludwig's attention?

TKE In 1985, after I had opened the Kunsträume Köln, he came to the gallery with Wolfgang Hahn. At the time, Hahn was the head of restoration at the Wallraf-Richartz-Museum and the Museum Ludwig and the key figure when it came to discovering and collecting contemporary art. A very important person for me at that time. When they visited the gallery, I was exhibiting the five artists Daniel Poensgen, Bertram Jesdinsky, Thomas Kesseler, Antonius Höckelmann, and Benjamin Katz. I said, "Oh, Mr. Ludwig!" Hahn interrupted me and quietly told me: "That's Professor Ludwig! Call him Professor Ludwig!" Professor Peter Ludwig went through the gallery and looked at everything very closely. He was quite enthusiastic and said, "I'll buy a work from every floor." Then Hahn said to me: "Listen to me, Mr. Krings-Ernst, Ludwig has ceased working with the gallerist Zwirner. This is your big chance!"

RW And you took the opportunity? What happened next?

TKE At first, Ludwig visited my exhibitions over the next nine months. Then he had a project for which he required a partner: founding a museum in Koblenz. I guess he thought to himself: “Let’s see. Let’s ask Krings-Ernst first.” That’s how I interpreted it. In any case, one day Ludwig said to me: “Listen, all of your colleagues say that there has been no art in France since the École de Paris. However, I want to establish a museum for contemporary French art in the Deutschherrenhaus in my home city, Koblenz. I want to create an institution that represents a dialogue between Germany and France in that unique, historical location. I need your help! You lived in France for a long time.”

RW A big opportunity for you.

TKE Yes! I enjoy speaking French and speak it fluently. During my time in Paris, I familiarised myself with the art scene there, visiting galleries, exhibitions, and artist’s studios. I considered the idea of cultural exchange, of cooperative cultural coexistence, to be extremely important and relevant. I could make use of my knowledge and contacts, especially my contacts among museum directors and curators, like Bernard Ceysson and Jean-Hubert Martin. I still work together with Ceysson today, an art historian, cultural mediator, and in his day, director of the Centre Pompidou and founder of the Museé d’Art Moderne et Contemporain (Museum of Modern and Contemporary Art) in Saint-Etienne. Martin curated the important exhibition *Les Magiciens de la Terre* (*Magicians of the Earth*) in 1989 at the Centre Pompidou in Paris, at which non-European art was presented for the first time on equal terms with that from the West.

I would also like to mention Marie Luise Syring at this point, the former curator of the Kunsthalle Düsseldorf, who has written a great deal about French art. She curated the exhibition *Geschichte als Widerstand – Aspekte zeitgenössischer Kunst in Frankreich* (*History as Resistance – Aspects of Contemporary Art in France*) there in 1985. That exhibition was enlightening for me. I knew some of the artists. There followed, in 1986, a series of exhibitions of French art in my gallery. In February 1987, the gallery exhibited various styles of French painting. Around then, the idea of a cooperative arrangement with the Institut Francais in Cologne arose. I was able to win over the director at the time, Christian Dumon, for the exhibition project, for which he converted the cinema at the institute into an exhibition space. The exhibition *Le Nouveau Pari(s) – Neue Malerei in Frankreich* (*New Challenges/New Paris – New Art in France*)—including works by Georges Autard, Robert Combas, François Boisrond, Hélène Delprat, Hervé di Rosa, Pierre Nivollet, and others—was held concurrently in the gallery and the Institut Francais, and in parallel to Art Cologne. Ludwig acquired a number of works from it. These, together with some works by French artists that had been acquired earlier, formed the basis of the collection for the Ludwig Museum in the Deutschherrenhaus in Koblenz, which opened in 1992. This exhibition marked the beginning of the close collaboration between Ludwig and myself. Many works of French contemporary art that Ludwig purchased in the second half of the 1980s and the early 1990s—works by Daniel Buren, Martial Raysse, the artist couple Judith Bartolani and Claude Caillol, and Claude Viallat—were acquired through me.

RW You also arranged for Peter Ludwig to receive a French Order of Merit!

TKE Not just one, many. For him, official honours meant public appreciation. Initially, I focussed on getting him a French order of merit, as I knew the French minister of culture, Jack Lang. However, it wasn't so easy due to the history of the Monheim chocolate company under the Third Reich, during which time the company used forced labour. Nevertheless, the French government couldn't easily refuse, because Ludwig had already shown enormous generosity: before Pontus Hultén opened the Centre Pompidou in Paris in 1977, he contacted Ludwig: "We have nothing here! Could you loan us some Pop Art?" The works from the Ludwig Collection remained on loan in Paris for several years. In 1988, Peter Ludwig was made a commander of the Legion of Honour. He was as excited as a child at Christmas: "That's fantastic! Fantastic! We have the commandership ..." In 1992, the Ludwig Museum in Koblenz opened with a focus on French art. Ludwig was determined that his wife should also receive a French order of merit. Finally, in 1995, she was made a Knight of the Legion of Honour.

RW While we're on the subject: What other awards given to Peter Ludwig did you help organise?

TKE In 1988, there was an Ordre des Arts et des Lettres given to Peter and Irene Ludwig; in 1991 an honorary doctorate from the Havana Instituto Superior de Arte (University of Arts of Cuba); in 1993 an honorary doctorate from the University of Havana given to Irene Ludwig; and there was a Russian Order of Merit which couldn't be awarded in the end as, at the time, there were no legal guidelines on the awarding of orders between Russia and Germany. In 1995, Peter Ludwig also received an honorary doctorate from the University of Havana.

We both had a vision and a mission: to capture the zeitgeist and historical momentum by building bridges between countries, both through art donations and the creation of museums.

RW You worked together with Peter Ludwig from 1986 to 1996. A number of Ludwig museums were founded during those years. In 1991, the Ludwig Múzeum in Budapest opened; in the same year, the Ludwig Collection moved from the Neue Galerie (New Gallery) in the Alten Kurhaus to the redesigned Schirmfabrik (umbrella factory), which became the Ludwig Forum für Internationale Kunst (Ludwig Forum for International Art) in Aachen. One year later, the Ludwig Museum in Koblenz opened, followed in 1994 by the founding of the Fundación Ludwig de Cuba in Havana, and, in 1995, the opening of the Ludwig Museum at the Russian Museum in St. Petersburg. In 1996, only a few months after Peter Ludwig passed away, the Ludwig Museum for International Art in the National Art Museum of China (NAMOC) in Beijing opened to the public, with the celebrations attended by the presidents of both Germany and China. That was an extremely important period of Peter Ludwig's life.

TKE Before our collaboration began, I had considered giving up my gallery in Cologne. I wanted to be more than just a typical art dealer! Then our work got going and became increasingly exciting. We both had a vision and a mission: to capture the zeitgeist and historical momentum by building bridges between countries, both through art donations and the creation of museums.

These were splendid years. Everything happened at once. I was involved in almost all of Peter Ludwig's endeavours in cultural politics. Apart from the ones you just mentioned, there was the establishment of the Ludwig Foundation in Hungary, of which I sat on the board of trustees. In 1990, negotiations for the founding of a museum in Havana began, eventually culminating in the founding of the Fundación Ludwig de Cuba in 1994, which you just mentioned, and which continues to promote and curate art in and from Cuba. In 1991, there were also negotiations regarding the expansion of the Österreichische Ludwig-Stiftung für Kunst und Wissenschaft (Austrian Ludwig Foundation for Art and Science) in Vienna. Later in 1992, a contract regarding cooperation between the Istanbul Foundation for Culture and Arts and the Ludwig Stiftung für Kunst und Internationale Verständigung (Ludwig Foundation for Art and International Understanding) was drafted, although, in the end, nothing came of it. Additionally, planning for a Ludwig museum in China began in 1993 and, in the same year, negotiations with the National Gallery in Prague took place, which reached an advanced stage but were ultimately abandoned.

RW Do you know why?

TKE We weren't satisfied with what was being offered from the Czechoslovakian side; we also wanted to concentrate on the projects that were already underway at the time.

RW Did you write all the offers and contract drafts?

TKE No, there were lawyers for that. For the negotiations in Moscow and St. Petersburg, I hired Helmuth Liesegang as legal counsel. Besides that, Peter and Irene Ludwig put together a list of possible donations. Afterwards, Ludwig and I compiled a final selection, which I then called upon during negotiations. I was constantly travelling and keeping him informed about new trends. The exhibitions, which I now organised in particular consideration of our partnership, were about the current art scene as a whole, the tremendous shifts in discourse. Of course, there were artists I was particularly interested in, such as Dmitri Prigov, Ai Weiwei, David Goldblatt, and Bertram Jesdinsky—all of them outstanding artists and individuals. But most of all, I wanted to know, and also show, what—apart from the Western canon—was happening globally, which movements were changing the zeitgeist in a sustainable way. Ludwig would then purchase whole batches of works.

RW Ludwig was known for his haggling. What was he like when it came to paying?

TKE We negotiated about the prices, and he would always pay two or three months later or when he had funds available. I was always relaxed about it. I had my own money. I usually settled the costs for my travel with his secretary, Elke Beyer, or I paid them myself. Don't forget, Ludwig was a businessman and felt a sense of responsibility to his company. At the end of the day, his business was the financial basis for his art collecting. Naturally, we inspected chocolate factories in Moscow and Beijing, but that wasn't his first priority, and I was only responsible for negotiations that concerned art.

RW Did you ever argue with Peter Ludwig, or were you always in agreement?

TKE We each had our own opinions. We always discussed things! That was the motor that drove our partnership!

RW And Mrs. Ludwig?

TKE Always friendly, always polite, but she always kept some distance.

RW Were you Ludwig's only adviser?

TKE No, but I believe that I was his closest adviser for a long period. There were a number of people who were frequently involved: Evelyn Weiss, for example, who was the deputy director of the Museum Ludwig in Cologne from 1983 to 2003. She played an important role in everything to do with the GDR, East Europe, and Russia. Then there was Marc Scheps, who was the successor to Siegfried Gohr and director of the Museum Ludwig from 1991 to 1997. Scheps was very cosmopolitan and I was delighted when he was named director. He got on very well with Ludwig, in contrast to his predecessor. And, of course, there was Wolfgang Becker, director of the Neue Galerie in Aachen.

RW Were you also involved with Ludwig's activities in East Germany, Romania, and Bulgaria?

As was generally the case with Ludwig, his involvement with Russia was two-pronged: on the one hand there was the official founding of the museum and his donation, on the other was his intellectual engagement with the local art scene.

TKE No.

RW Let's talk about your activities in Russia. How did it all start?

TKE Peter Ludwig had been collecting works of the Russian avant-garde since as early as the mid-1970s, although not in Russia, but primarily through Antonina Gmurzynska's gallery in Cologne. The Soviet ambassador at the time, Vladimir Semyonov, who was himself a collector, had also encouraged Ludwig to engage with Soviet art. It has to be said that Ludwig had been looking around the Communist Bloc for a long time and had acquired a lot of works. The Soviet Union was very important to him. He travelled to Moscow and Leningrad, as well as other cities and regions, and bought official USSR art through the so-called export salon, the official contact point for exporting cultural works. He attracted a lot of criticism in the West as a result.

In regard to Russia, I came on the scene in 1987. I had come into contact with Russian or Soviet art in the 1970s when I saw it at Dina Vierny's gallery in Paris and the Galerie Gmurzynska in Cologne. The exhibition *Progressive russische Kunst. Der Aufbruch bis 1930 + Lev Nusberg und die Moskauer Gruppe ‚Bewegung'* (*Progressive Russian Art: From the Awakening to 1930 + Lev Nusberg and the Moscow Group "Movement"*) at the Galerie Gmurzynska in 1973, where I saw Ilya Kabakov's drawings for the first time, made a huge impression on me. An interest in the alternative scene of the 1980s was aroused in me through a number of ways: through the German-Russian philosopher and cultural theorist Boris Groys, the Swiss art historian Claudia Jolles, and the Swiss diplomats Alfred Hohl and Paul Jolles. In the West at that time, it was terra incognita. At the opening of my exhibition of French contemporary art in 1987, I told Peter Ludwig, "Professor, I am going to Russia soon, to Moscow." I was financially independent and had, through my father among others, good contacts in Moscow. I knew for certain that this would interest Ludwig.

RW Was that the beginning of the chapter with Soviet Russia? Did you have a contract from Ludwig?

TKE No, no contract, but Ludwig sent letters to the negotiating parties before my departure notifying them that I was empowered to negotiate on his behalf. In the months after my exhibition of French art in 1987, as contact between us became more regular—he visited the gallery once a week and we spoke on the phone every Sunday—I had the feeling that Ludwig saw me as a comrade-in-arms and trusted my negotiating abilities, especially when it came to international relations. Ludwig definitely needed someone like-minded. It was still a difficult time for him. He had solved his company's problems through the sale of his medieval manuscripts in 1983, but he was preoccupied with the idea of world art, the big picture, moving away from the viewpoint of the West and toward a globalised art.

The former president of Germany, Theodor Heuss, said in his 1951 speech "Kräfte und Grenzen einer Kulturpolitik" ("Forces and Limits in Cultural Policy"), "You cannot create culture with politics, but perhaps you can create politics through culture."[2] At that time it was, for us, all about the political power of culture. The power with which one can really move things! Nobody wanted to follow Ludwig on that path, not even Siegfried Gohr, who was the director of the Museum Ludwig in Cologne from 1984 to 1991. It was different in Aachen, though. Becker, the director of the Neue Galerie, understood it, but that was "only" Aachen.

RW Who was Krings-Ernst to Ludwig?

TKE I believe I was a kind of cicerone, a catalyst for Ludwig. The catalyst is like vitamins for the pear [a German idiomatic term for brain], oxygen for the soul, what we all need, what Ludwig needed too. Just like Egon Bahr, the foreign policy adviser to Willy Brandt, who pursued his own ideas and didn't necessarily stick to what had been agreed with Brandt beforehand—that's how it was with me too! At the risk of sounding presumptuous: I brought my own ideas and vision to the negotiations—whether on the political side, with the ministers of culture Nikolai Gubenko, Yevgeni Sidorov, or Mikhail Shvydkoy; or on the museum side, with Irina Antonova from the Pushkin Museum in Moscow or Yevgenia Petrova from the Russian Museum in St. Petersburg. I always had to convince Ludwig about them first.

RW Could you tell us what you mean by that?

TKE As was generally the case with Ludwig, his involvement with Russia was two-pronged: on the one hand there was the official founding of the museum and his donation, on the other was his intellectual engagement with the local art scene. Prior to my involvement, beginning in 1982, Ludwig had been negotiating with Antonova, at first for an exhibition of his collection at the Pushkin Museum, and then about the possibility of a Ludwig museum combined with the promise of an extensive endowment. An extension to the Pushkin Museum was planned, because Ludwig's collection would have caused it to burst at the seams, so to speak. But we're talking about the mid-1980s—the political landscape had started to change. Gorbachev had been in power since 1985 and had heralded glasnost and perestroika. That had transformed society a great deal: on the one hand, old and ailing state structures collapsed and many government positions changed hands; on the other, agreements were no longer so secure or were simply not kept at all. When I mentioned my trip to Ludwig, he spontaneously said, "I'm coming with you, Mr. Krings-Ernst!" And then he arranged the appointments together with a Russian translator who he knew from previous trips.

You always had to show everything down to your fingernails when you travelled to the Soviet Union. It took six months before everything was prepared and had been discussed with the Russians. Besides the political situation, we could only communicate at that time, apart from letters, with fax, and that didn't always function well. We finally flew there in the spring of 1988. There were three of us, as Evelyn Weiss came too, one of the few supporters of Ludwig's world art activities. For me, it was an enormously exciting situation. The KGB was everywhere. Ludwig had always made his purchases through the official export salon and worked together with the artist's union of the USSR. He primarily bought what could be called, if you like, Soviet academic art. The head of the official export body was Marina Bakuleva, an elegant woman with a large dacha, to which she invited us. We ate dinner together with Vladimir Semyonov and drank quite a bit, which is the norm there, with thousands of toasts and grand speeches.

RW Did you gain access to the nonofficial art scene at all?

TKE I had been in contact with Boris Groys in Cologne, who was a central figure in Moscow Conceptualism. He told me a lot about the scene in Moscow. But independently of him, I discovered Furmannyi Lane, where many artists lived and worked in its squats—the younger generation, the second Russian avant-garde, so to speak. I went from cellar to cellar throughout the night as they showed me their works. Officially, an exhibition was put on for Ludwig in a former church in Polyanka Street. It was made up of works like those Ludwig had selected and acquired on previous trips, including from Dmitry Žilinsky and his wife, Nina, among others. I had given Pavel Khorošilov, who worked in the Ministry of Culture at the time, a list of nonofficial artists. Khorošilov, who oversaw all of the official export body's operations, took me aside: "Mr. Krings-Ernst, we can't see these people, they aren't artists." Then I said to Peter Ludwig: "Yes, that's fine, Professor. I'll go anyway, take a look at the studio, and negotiate directly on site." Khorošilov buckled a bit then: "Wait a minute. Maybe I can organise something in the next few days." The following evening he let us know, "We can visit all of the artists and studios you have listed, Mr. Krings-Ernst." They were younger artists: Yuri Albert, Olga Černyševa, Andrei Filippov, the brothers Vladimir and Sergei Mironenko, Vadim Zakharov, Larisa Rezun-Zvezdočetova, Constantin Zvezdochotov, and others. Many of the works were acquired and brought to Germany through the export salon, including works by Ilya Kabakov, Erik Bulatov, Grisha Bruskin, and Eduard Steinberg. The export salon wanted to have the purchase done in deutsche marks, as the rouble was worth nothing. They needed foreign currency.

RW Did Ludwig discuss the possibility of a Ludwig museum during that trip?

TKE He had begun that years earlier with Irina Antonova, but with little success. In April 1988, a few months after our trip, Peter and Irene Ludwig sent an official letter to the general secretary of the Communist Party, Mikhail Gorbachev, in which they suggested founding a museum of international contemporary art in Moscow. Ludwig tasked me with leading the negotiations. I travelled repeatedly to Moscow and spoke to a variety of people—the situation was quite chaotic. The Russian diplomatic corps in Bonn was helpful, they supported our activities. In 1989, we were able to deliver an initial draft contract to the Russian minister of culture, Gubenko. Three more drafts followed in the period up until 1992, which went to the interim minister, Alexander Schkurko, and his successor, Yevgeni Sidorov. On the condition that the planned museum carried his name and was housed in its own building, Ludwig was prepared to provide around 150 works from his collection, initially on loan and later to be donated.

RW Did the German government know about Ludwig's activities?

TKE Every step we took was discussed with the Foreign Ministry and the office of the chancellor. Every single step! The government was informed. The cultural bridge building between the two nations ran in parallel to domestic and foreign policy developments, to reunification, and to the fall of the Iron Curtain. Ludwig's offer was: we donate! It needs to be stated here, that the Ludwigs, with my support, were the first to found museums outside the standard cultural terrain. These days, many museums open branches both domestically and overseas—including the Guggenheim, the Pompidou, and the Louvre. However, they take a different approach: they lend, they show their own collections, they "expand."

Peter Ludwig was a missionary seeker of power. Through his dealmaking, he wanted to alter the existing situation, to drive cultural policy, and he freely admitted as much. That's why his idealistic gesture of donating was so important to him. Because only unconditional giving elicits a positive reaction from one's opposition. The donations to Russia, as was the case in other countries too, included not only works by Western artists, but also works from Russia's own underground—works by Dmitry Prigov, Igor Makarevič, Viktor Pivovarov, and so on. Their works hadn't previously been exhibited or collected by any official institutions. By donating them to the new museum, we brought them into a broader artistic context. We made them a part of the discourse among international museums.

RW Did you visit other artists on those trips?

TKE Of course! Bruskin, Prigov, Makarevič, and Elena Elagina, just to name a few. I generally stayed with the TV correspondent Gerd Ruge. Brigitte Willisch, who everyone called Gitti, was also a great help; she was a good friend and worked at the WDR studios in Moscow. I invited some of the artists to Germany. They came to my gallery and stayed in an artist's apartment on the first floor. For example, Prigov—in my eyes the most important and interesting figure of Moscow Conceptualism and beyond—was a regular visitor to Cologne. Those invitations paved the way to the West for those artists. In Russia, they received only a fraction of the profits from sales of their work, or sometimes nothing at all. That's why I invited them.

RW Let's return to museum planning. In March 1992, Irina Antonova wrote a letter to Peter Ludwig stating that the question of who the new museum should report to, the Ministry of Culture or the president, was unresolved. On top of that, the financing had been put on hold and it was unclear if and when it would be reinstated.

TKE It all developed very slowly. Ludwig and I were included in the delegation of a state visit by Chancellor Helmut Kohl. As part of this visit in October 1988, a declaration of intent between the Ludwig Stiftung für Kunst und Internationale Verständigung and the Pushkin Museum regarding the creation of a Ludwig museum in the Pushkin Museum was signed. In the official final communiqué of the state visit, it was stated that both sides had "received Ludwig's initiative with interest." However, the situation became increasingly complicated, in part because the question of looted art and its return had arisen and was a subject of discussion at the highest levels.

RW Do you believe that this—at the time—quite heated debate played a role?

TKE Both Irina Antonova, who had deposited art taken from Nazi Germany after the war in the cellars beneath the Pushkin Museum, and Peter Ludwig took part in the debate in the form of public statements. I was of the opinion that restitution should not be insisted upon, that a new collaboration was of much greater importance. What was decisive for our negotiations, however, was the fact that the Soviet Union fell and there was no longer a unified political stance, not even when it came to questions of cultural policy.

RW How did you arrive at the decision to open the Ludwig Museum in St. Petersburg?

TKE I can only matter-of-factly list a few events for you. In 1993, the first preparatory discussions about a guest exhibition of works from the Russian Museum took place in Bonn at the Bundeskunsthalle (Federal Kunsthalle). The Russian side was represented by the deputy director of the museum, Yevgenia Petrova. She came to Cologne and visited the exhibition *Russische Avantgarde im 20. Jahrhundert. Von Malevich bis Kabakov. Die Sammlung Ludwig* (*Russian Avant-garde in the Twentieth Century: From Malevich to Kabakov. The Ludwig Collection*). She was impressed and invited the Ludwigs and the then director of the Cologne museum, Scheps, to St. Petersburg. In April 1994, we travelled there together and held official talks with her. There is a statement of understanding from May 1994, in the form of the minutes of a meeting, signed by Ludwig, Scheps, and Petrova. It states that Petrova offered Peter Ludwig the ability to set up a department of international and Russian contemporary art in the Russian Museum. The department would bear Ludwig's name and would be given a permanent home in the historic Marble Palace. It is important to know that the German-born Empress Catherine the Great had this palace built for her lover, Prince Grigory Orlov.

RW A worthy home! What happened next?

TKE As Ludwig's talks with the Pushkin Museum since 1982 had resulted in little more than promises, the offer from St. Petersburg was naturally attractive, especially as the building was not only available, but also prestigious. Furthermore, everyone supported the plan, including the city government headed by Mayor Sobchak. We sent a draft contract to St. Petersburg in May 1994. At the same time, Ludwig informed Ms. Antonova in Moscow of the plans and made clear that he wanted to continue negotiations with her. On September 2, 1994, a contract between the Ludwigs and the Russian Museum was signed. Shortly afterwards, on March 10, 1995, the Ludwig Museum at the Russian Museum was opened.

RW At the beginning of our conversation, you mentioned the strange situation between Moscow and St. Petersburg and of the radical break on the part of Antonova.

TKE It was highly stressful for me personally, but I advised Ludwig to go with St. Petersburg, for obvious reasons. The then deputy minister of culture, Shvydkoy, had said to me, "It's easier with St. Petersburg, it will be quicker." I remembered that and relayed it to Ludwig. Ludwig reacted appropriately: "Then you will lose your credibility with Ms. Antonova. Let's make her a new proposal." I still can't say whether or not this decision was a mistake. I was the emissary, tasked with continuing the negotiations in Moscow. She welcomed me, holding under her arm architectural plans for the conversion of the Dolgorukov Palace, the former Marx-Engels Museum, into a Ludwig museum. She already knew about everything. She turned to me and said, "I trusted you, your generation, but I never trusted Ludwig." Then she turned and walked away. I never saw her again. Anyway …

Peter Ludwig saw an opportunity to become active in cultural policy and to fulfil his mission of enlightenment. He took on Cuba as a new challenge.

RW Now we come to Cuba. What was your role in establishing the Fundación Ludwig de Cuba?

TKE In April 1990, Jürgen Harten curated the exhibition *Kuba o.k.* at the Kunsthalle Düsseldorf, a survey of recent Cuban art. A few artists from the art scene in Cuba had travelled to the exhibition. I saw the exhibition and met the artist Tonel, who had cocurated the exhibition with Harten. I was inspired by the works, and I called Ludwig: "I have a fantastic project! I'll buy the entire exhibition!" The theme of the exhibition interested him a great deal because Cuba was at a turning point in terms of culture, economics, politics, indeed all aspects of civic life—much like the Soviet Union at the end of the 1980s, which was breaking apart. Peter Ludwig saw an opportunity to become active in cultural policy and to fulfil his mission of enlightenment. He took on Cuba as a new challenge.

The works for the exhibition in Düsseldorf were brought to the Federal Republic via the still-existing East Germany. As was stated in the contracts, they had to be returned to Cuba via the Communist Bloc. In August 1990, I was in Havana. I had connections in Cuba through my friend and mentor Jean-Pierre Saltiel—to Armando Blanco, the head of the Central Bank, among others. I met Helmo Hernández, who was the Cuban minister of culture and responsible for the import and export of art and, as such, also for *Kuba o.k.* He accompanied me everywhere. We visited a number of studios, including Tonel's, and I met museum staff and representatives of state institutions, like Llilian Llanes, the director of the Centro Wifredo Lam and director of the Havana Biennial. I can remember how, during a dinner in Havana, she danced with a former sugar baron who had returned to Cuba as a tourist. There was a unique atmosphere in Cuba at that time.

A day before my return to Germany, I was finally able to sign the sales agreement for the works of recent Cuban art. It included almost the entirety of the *Kuba o.k.* exhibition. Twenty-eight crates came via Amsterdam to Cologne. In January 1991, the Ludwig Stiftung für Kunst und Internationale Verständigung purchased the majority of the consignment.

RW On November 26, 1991, Peter Ludwig received a letter from the Cuban ambassador in Germany with an official invitation to Havana from the Ministry of Culture. Did you travel with him?

TKE Yes, as did Wolfgang Becker. In December 1991, we were official guests of the Ministry of Culture and stayed in a government guesthouse. The occasion was the awarding of an honorary doctorate to Peter Ludwig from the Instituto Superior de Arte, the famed ISA, the art university that occupied the grounds of a former golf club. I had arranged for this award to be given during my first visit. Peter Ludwig gave a historic speech, which elicited highly emotional reactions. We were shown around everywhere—the museums, the restoration workshops, the writer's and artist's union—and we visited the fourth Havana Biennial. We negotiated for the acquisition of further Cuban works and discussed the possibility of founding a museum of modern art in Havana. An agreement was made to invite two Cuban artists to Aachen on scholarships. An exhibition of contemporary Cuban art in Aachen was also planned.

RW Did the exhibition in the Ludwig Forum in Aachen come to fruition?

TKE Yes, it was titled *Von dort aus: Kuba* (*From There: Cuba*), and it opened on March 11, 1992. The deputy minister of culture, Omar González, travelled from Cuba for the occasion, together with Hernández. We continued our discussions on founding a museum. If I remember correctly, Becker and Irene Ludwig both took part. Peter Ludwig offered to provide around eighty to one hundred works from Europe and North America, as well as a sum of 100,000 deutsche marks for building renovations. It was agreed that an exhibition of these loans from the Ludwig Collection would be planned and that further works from the upcoming biennial would be acquired. I then held a large Cuban exhibition in my gallery in January 1993, entitled *Made in Cuba*.

RW When were you next in Cuba?

TKE Together with Peter and Irene Ludwig and a large delegation, we arrived in Havana on November 6, 1993. Hernández had succeeded, after some difficulties, in securing an honour for Irene Ludwig. She received an honorary doctorate from the University of Havana.

RW Did you also meet Fidel Castro during that trip?

TKE Peter and Irene Ludwig were invited to an audience with Castro. Wolfgang Becker and I accompanied them. When we arrived at Castro's residence, he came out to meet us and greeted Peter Ludwig with the words, "My dear Mr. Ludwig, I have read all your books, all of your philosophical tracts!" Fidel acted as if he had mistaken Professor Ludwig for the philosopher Ludwig Wittgenstein. I guess that was his way of lightening the mood, of turning on the charm. During their talks, Becker and I remained in an antechamber.

RW Was there any progress with plans for the museum? After the collapse of the Soviet Union, Cuba found itself in enormous financial difficulties, as payments to the country had almost completely ceased.

TKE Yes, it was difficult. Ludwig had given those responsible in Cuba another list of fifty-nine possible loans and had also chosen further acquisitions. Everyone was interested in cooperation with

Cuba—not only our Cuban connections, but, especially, Peter Ludwig himself, as it would allow him to leave a footprint behind in yet another part of the world. But it was clear that the commercial and conservation conditions there, despite all the respect and appreciation for art, were not up to par for founding a museum. In the Cuban museums, there was no climate control in spite of the tropical heat; the professional handling of artworks—proper storage and transport—was also very important for us. The idea of setting up a foundation subsequently arose. I don't know who came up with it, but I suspect it may have been Helmo Hernández.

RW In a memorandum dated November 1993, signed by Ludwig and González, it says, "The German and Cuban sides strive to establish a Cuban Ludwig foundation according to Cuban law, which should pursue the aim of promoting young Cuban artists."

TKE That's how it was! A scholarship programme had already begun. Becker had been tasked with assisting the selection process. In 1992, Antonio Eligio Fernández (Tonel) and Luis Gomez Armenteros were the first two Cuban recipients. A year later, Monika von Wedel and Klaus Osterwald were sent from Germany for a sojourn in Cuba. And so it continued.

RW Did you go to Cuba again after that?

TKE No.

RW During those turbulent years, Peter Ludwig's relationship with China developed. Together with his wife, he had collected Chinese antiquities and porcelain for many years, most of which can now be found in the Museum für Ostasiatische Kunst (Museum for East Asian Art) in Cologne. At the end of the 1970s, when it became possible to travel to China, Irene Ludwig travelled there as part of a tour group. There was a lot of interest in China.

TKE Yes, but none of us had any idea about contemporary Chinese art until 1993, when the exhibition *China Avantgarde!* was held at the Haus der Kulturen der Welt (House of the World's Cultures) (HKW) in Berlin. One of the curators was the German artist Andreas Schmid, who had lived in China, could speak the language, and is an acknowledged expert on China. The exhibition presented a new generation bursting with energy. The exhibition then travelled from Berlin to the Kunsthal Rotterdam, the Museum of Modern Art in Oxford, and the Danish Kunsthallen Brandts Klaedefabrik in Odense. Later, I showed part of the exhibition in my gallery.

RW What was the Ludwigs' reaction?

TKE Rather reserved. There was a lot of catching up to do in terms of understanding these artworks. As such, I invited Schmid to give a presentation about contemporary Chinese art for Peter Ludwig in my gallery.

In 1994, Schmid and I travelled for several weeks to visit the most important locations for contemporary art in China. I got to know many of the artists personally, the most important for me being Ai Weiwei, who had just returned from New York because his father was on his deathbed. It must be said, of course, that the social systems in China and the West were extremely different. Ai Weiwei also opened the door to politics for me. He put me in touch with the deputy director of the Chinese Museum of Art in Beijing (later the National Art Museum of China or NAMOC), Yang Lizhou, as well as the director of the Shanghai Art Museum, Li Xiangyang. Although lacking a mandate, I held initial talks with the two of them regarding a possible donation. When I returned to Germany and reported my unauthorised negotiations, Ludwig was enthusiastic. At the beginning of November, he wrote a letter to the two men and expressed his immense interest in the donation. In this context, I had the honour of receiving Mei Zhaorong, the Chinese ambassador to Germany, at my home.

RW When did you hold your first exhibition of contemporary Chinese art?

TKE I had acquired the majority of the *China Avantgarde!* exhibition. When the exhibition tour was finished, I showed it in Cologne, in January 1995. It was a great success. I showed works by Ai Weiwei, Ding Yi, Fang Lijun, Huang Yong Ping, Hu Zhiying, Ji Wenyu, Li Bangyao, Liu Wei, Wang Guangyi, Wang Keping, and Xu Tan.

RW How did you get around in China? Did you learn the language?

TKE No, we had a marvellous translator, Chen Ping. He worked in the cultural department of the Chinese embassy in Bonn, had studied German language and literature, and spoke excellent German. The role of the translator can't be valued highly enough! Chen Ping—called Siegfried by his German friends—was a dedicated mediator and greatly helped us throughout the negotiations. Thanks to him, the two sides were able to communicate in spite of the differences in mentality. Yang, the former deputy director of NAMOC, knew about the international museums Ludwig had founded and asked him to make a donation to the Beijing museum. In March 1996, Scheps, the Ludwigs, and I travelled to China once more to initial the endowment contract. As early as 1993, Ai Weiwei had undertaken critical research about the state of the Chinese Museum of Art in Beijing, with the aim of turning it back into a cultural institution with an educational purpose. We were able to realise this project.

At almost the same time, we made offers to Shanghai and Nanjing. We then suggested forming a foundation, for which both sides would pay 100,000 deutsche marks per year into an endowment fund, based on the model of the Österreichische Ludwig-Stiftung für Kunst und Wissenschaft. The Chinese couldn't understand or accept that model, because in their system at the time such endowment funds didn't exist. It's different today. That meant, however, that a Ludwig museum could not have an independent structure, but would have to function as a department of the National Museum, which is what it became and continues to be.

Under these conditions, the negotiations for a donation progressed at an astonishing pace. There would be eighty-nine works of art from eighty-two different artists from the US, Europe, and Russia, including four works by Pablo Picasso. This was a unique offer! At the time, there was no American or European art that could be seen in China, with the exception of a Käthe Kollwitz print that had been a gift from Erich Honecker. Our progress in these negotiations was, without question, thanks to Chen's talent as a mediator. We agreed on the name Ludwig Museum for International Art in the National Art Museum of China.

RW Did Ludwig sign the donation contract?

TKE No, he only initialled it at that time. In July 1996, he died completely unexpectedly. That called into question the entire project. Irene Ludwig was in mourning and didn't want to travel to China again.

RW The opening of the Ludwig Museum was to take place in October 1996 during a state visit to China by President Roman Herzog.

TKE We all did our best to convince Mrs. Ludwig to keep this date. To everyone's great relief, she relented. In October 1996, I travelled to China with Elke Beyer, Ludwig's secretary, and Barbara Thiemann, the curator of the Museum Ludwig in Cologne, to clarify the final contractual points and to install the artworks in the museum. On November 18, 1996, the opening of the Ludwig Museum for International Art in the National Art Museum of China was celebrated with the attendance of presidents Roman Herzog and Jiang Zemin. Ai Weiwei, who had helped us a great deal, was not invited, despite my emphatic appeals. Irene Ludwig signed the donation contract. My collaboration with the Ludwig Stiftung für Kunst und Internationale Verständigung came to an end with that trip.

RW Do you have any concluding thoughts about your work with Peter Ludwig?

TKE "Art is one of the manifestations of the intellectual and spiritual life of humanity. … Consequently, our art must be topical in any given moment. You only have to know where the art is to be found."[3] A quote from Leo Tolstoy, 1896!

Together, Peter Ludwig and I occupied ourselves with this "manifestation of intellectual and spiritual life" for ten years. Our vision/mission was to recognise, preserve, and manifest it in the area of world art, globalised art. In that period of ideological and geopolitical upheaval, we focussed on art that captured the essence of the era. We didn't seek individual trophies, and we didn't see this art as a local phenomenon. We understood it as part of a global cultural context and attempted to do justice to the complexity of that context.

What did we set in motion? Our approach pursued cooperative cultural coexistence as opposed to cultural egotism! And, of course, Ludwig's founding of museums and his donations were a part of our mission. Indeed, that was the core of our activities! It was always about education through and about images. It was always about the global cultural legacy and about the social functions of museums. All of these questions had to be addressed! The issues that we brought to the public's attention back in the 1980s still drive me today. They're more topical now than ever. The idea of world art, of globalised art, is closely linked with the educational mission of museums today: How should the history of human culture be told? Which point of view should be adopted in order to present it appropriately? Furthermore, the concept of visible or open storage has developed in recent years, similar to the idea behind the Ludwig Forum: a place where art may be directly encountered, where the perception and appreciation of art may be enriched through cross-pollination with music, dance, or theatre. I always say: interest yourself in …, occupy yourself with …, in order to gain insights from … That's the approach that united Ludwig and I, that drove the two of us.

For me, the name Peter Ludwig stands first and foremost for an undisguised commitment to culture and the willingness to overcome limitations, regardless of their nature—whether ideological, political, economic, or having to do with art theory. A quality which, fortunately, he manifested in the form of numerous museums and foundations. That is his most valuable legacy, one which I see as a basis that can and should be built upon. That is my conclusion!

RW Mr. Krings-Ernst, thank you for taking the time to talk to us!

Thomas Krings-Ernst would like to take the opportunity to thank his long-time employees Claus Bach, Ekaterina Eloshvili, and Julia Teplitzky for their support in the research for this interview.

1. **Yuval Noah Harari, *Sapiens: A Graphic History: The Birth of Humankind (Vol. 1)* (Harper Perennial: New York, 2020), 11.**

2. **Theodor Heuss, "Kräfte und Grenzen einer Kulturpolitik," in *Theodor Heuss: Die großen Reden. Der Staatsmann* (Wunderlich: Tübingen, 1965), 137 (translated by Darren Mann).**

3. **Ludwig Rubiner (ed.): *Leo Tolstoy. Tagebuch 1895–1899*, trans. Frida Ichak-Rubiner, (Max Rascher Publishing: Zürich, 1918), 21 (translated by Darren Mann).**

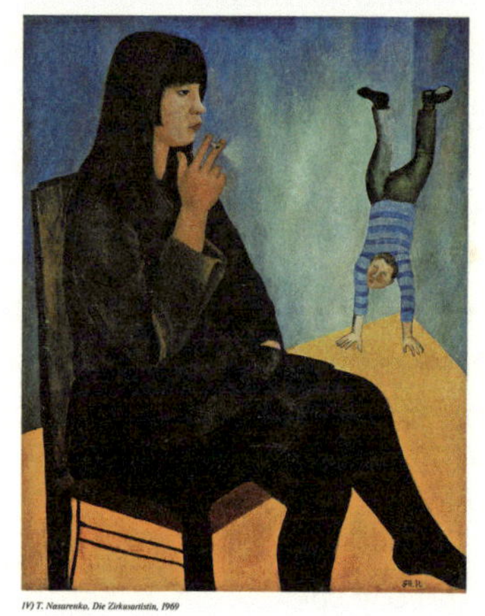

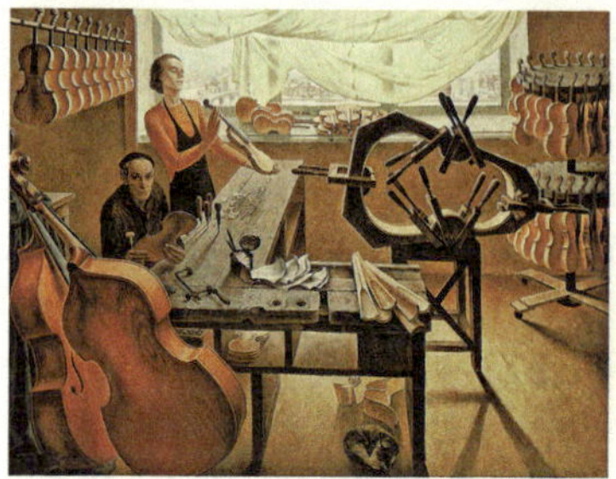

Double-page spread from the exhibition catalogue *Aspekte sowjetischer Kunst* der Gegenwart (*Aspects of Contemporary Soviet Art*), 1982. Left: Tatyana Nazarenko, *The Circus Performer*, 1969. Right: Galina Neledva, *Workshop*, 1975.

Der sowjetische Gesandte in Bonn, Wladislaw Tirechow, bei der Eröffnung der Ausstellung. Rechts das Ehepaar Ludwig. Foto: Hansen

Sowjetische Kunst-Schau „ein kulturpolitisches Ereignis"

Ausstellung in der Neuen Galerie eröffnet – Dank an Köln

AACHEN. – „Wir dürfen sicher sein, daß die Ausstellung zu einem wichtigen kulturpolitischen Ereignis wird. Sie ist ein weiterer Schritt zum gegenseitigen Verständnis und zur Entwicklung gutnachbarlicher Beziehungen zwischen Deutschland und der UdSSR", dies sagte der russische Gesandte Wladislaw Tirechow zur Eröffnung der Ausstellung „Sowjetische Kunst der Gegenwart" in der Neuen Galerie Aachen.

Tirechow war in Vertretung des sowjetischen Botschafters in der Bundesrepublik, Semjonow, erschienen. Bei der Ausstellungs-Eröffnung waren ebenfalls eine Abordnung des sowjetischen Künstlerverbandes, ein Professor aus Leipzig sowie der deutsche Botschafter in Moskau zugegen.

Die Teilnehmer der Feier umstanden die weißen Gipsfiguren des Künstlers Baranow, die an das Leben des Dichters Puschkin erinnern. Die Gruppe von Standbildern fügt sich eigenartig gut in den hellen Rokoko-Saal mit seinen üppigen Stuck-Bildwerken an den Wänden.

Gesandter Tirechow würdigte die „geduldige und kreative Arbeit" des Aachener Kunstsammlers Peter Ludwig, der bei mehreren Reisen in die UdSSR die Stücke der Ausstellung erworben hatte.

Aachens Bürgermeister Clemens Gläßer, der den verhinderten Oberbürgermeister Kurt Malangré vertrat, erklärte: „Wir danken dem Ehepaar Ludwig, daß es sich für einen wenig betrachteten Teil der Weltkunst so engagiert." In der Bundesrepublik fehlten die Kenntnisse über das Schaffen der heutigen sowjetischen Künstler. Hier biete die Ausstellung – „ein bedeutendes und lohnenswertes Unternehmen" – Abhilfe.

Als beispielhaft lobte Bürgermeister Gläßer die Zusammenarbeit zwischen den Städten Köln und Aachen (in Köln wird der andere Teil der Erwerbungen Ludwigs gezeigt). „Aachen profitiert von Köln. Für dieses Entgegenkommen danke ich dem Nachbarn herzlich", sagte Clemens Gläßer.

Der Leiter der Neuen Galerie, Dr. Becker, sagte, die Stücke der Ausstellung erzählten „Geschichten aus einem anderen Land". Die hier gezeigten Bilder würden mehr Aufschlüsse über die Menschen in diesem riesigen Land geben, als man dies aus Zeitungen erfahren könnte.

Kunstsammler Peter Ludwig betonte, sein Ziel sei es gewesen, sowjetische Kunst zur Diskussion zu stellen. „Was Sie dann davon halten, mag jeder selbst entscheiden." Die Frage, ob es überhaupt Kunst im sowjetischen Machtbereich geben könne, müsse mit einem klaren Ja beantwortet werden.

Peter Ludwig ist bei seinen Reisen in der Sowjetunion „die große Deutschfreundlichkeit" aufgefallen, „die weit und breit herrscht". Diese bezeichnete er als „Kapital für die Zukunft". W. Erdweg

Newspaper article about the opening of the exhibition *Aspekte sowjetischer Kunst der Gegenwart* at the Neue Galerie (New Gallery), Aachen, and the Kölnisches Stadtmuseum (Cologne City Museum). *"Soviet Art Exhibition, a Cultural-Political Event," Aachener Nachrichten, 5.7.1982*

Seite K/Bo EXPRESS 2. VIII. 82 EXPR

Kunst-Königs Kosmonauten im Westen hart gelandet

Super-Sammlung langweilt die Kritiker

Endlich im Westen: Schoko-König Ludwigs 500 Stück Russen-Kunst. Fast 4 Jahre verhandelte der Sammler mit Moskau, kaufte Werke, die eigentlich sowjetischen Museen vorbehalten waren. Allein das ist eine Sensation. Jetzt werden die Bilder, Grafiken und Plastiken im Kölner Stadtmuseum und in der Neuen Galerie Aachen gezeigt, die umfassendste Sammlung außerhalb der UdSSR. Doch die entsetzten Kritiker fast einstimmig: „Langweilig!"

Schöne Bilder von höchster handwerklicher Qualität aus einem bislang unbekannten Land. Doch ein Westkunst-Fan vermißt avantgardistischen Schwung, stattdessen Zitate bekannter Kunstrichtungen: Expressionismus und Impressionismus, etwas Chagall oder Goya.

Kölns Museumschef Hugo Borger: „Man muß diese Kunst aus ihrem Umfeld heraus verstehen: Abgeschnitten von der übrigen Kunstwelt lebt russische Kunst von der Weiterentwicklung der Tradition." Dieses Umfeld aber fehlt in der Ausstellung, dem Westler bleiben so inhaltliche Spitzen verborgen.

Er sieht biedere Landschaften, verspielte Akte, strahlende Kosmonauten, überraschend viel religiöse Motive, gekonnte, aber biedere Buchillustrationen, viel Innerlichkeit.

Nur wenige Dissidenten, die meisten erst in letzter Minute der Sammlung beigefügt. Allerdings auch verblüffend wenig Lenin oder Sozialistischen Realismus. Offizielle Kunst: Vom Staat angekauft, aber nicht in den Museen ausgestellt.

Ludwig zu seiner Sammlung: „Ich habe die besten Amerikaner gekauft, jetzt wollte ich die besten Russen. Ich bekam, was ich wollte."

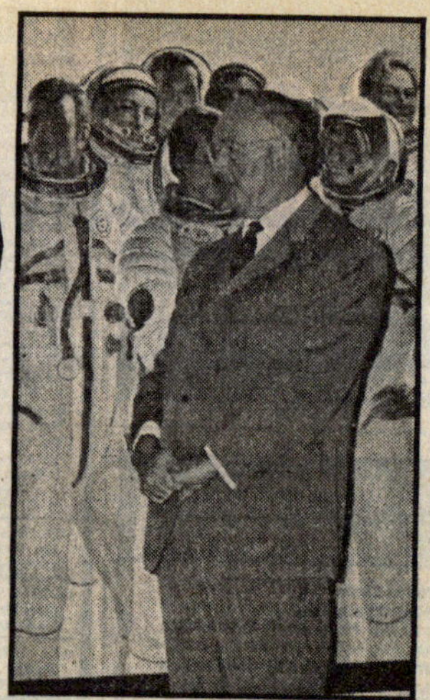

Peter Ludwig: Vor russischer Kosmonauten-Mannschaft im Stil alter Ikonen

Newspaper article about the opening of the exhibition *Aspekte sowjetischer Kunst der Gegenwart* at the Neue Galerie, Aachen, and the Kölnisches Stadtmuseum. *"The King of Art's Cosmonauts Landed Hard in the West," Express, 2.8.1982*

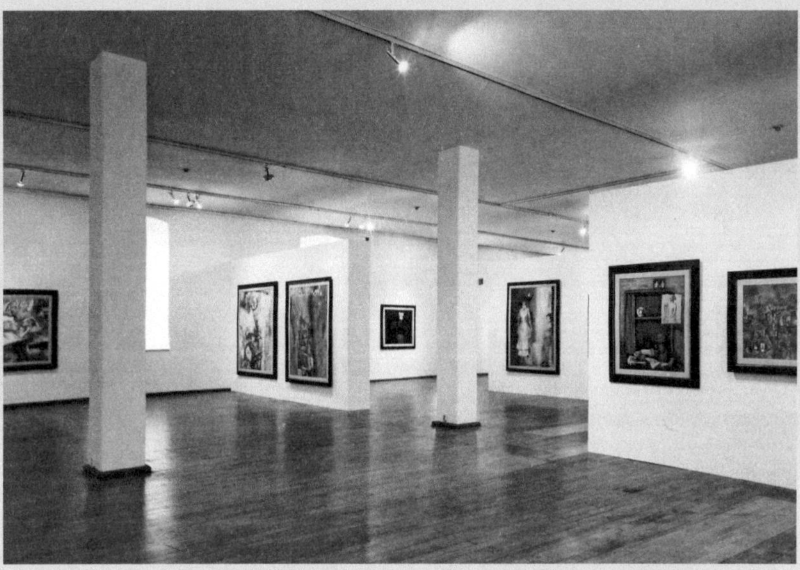

View of the exhibition *Aspekte sowjetischer Kunst der Gegenwart* in the Kölnisches Stadtmuseum (Zeughaus), 1982.
Photo: unknown

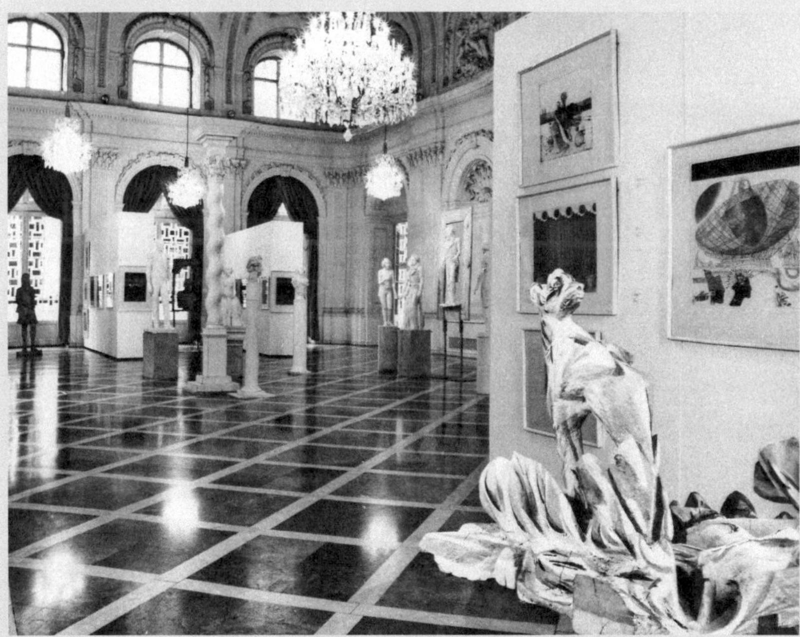

View of the exhibition *Aspekte sowjetischer Kunst der Gegenwart* in the Neue Galerie, Aachen, 1982.
Photo: unknown

Exhibition catalogue, *Die 5. Biennale von Havanna – Kunst, Gesellschaft, Reflexion: Eine Auswahl* (*The 5th Havana Biennial – Art, Society, Reflection: A Selection*), Aachen, 1994.

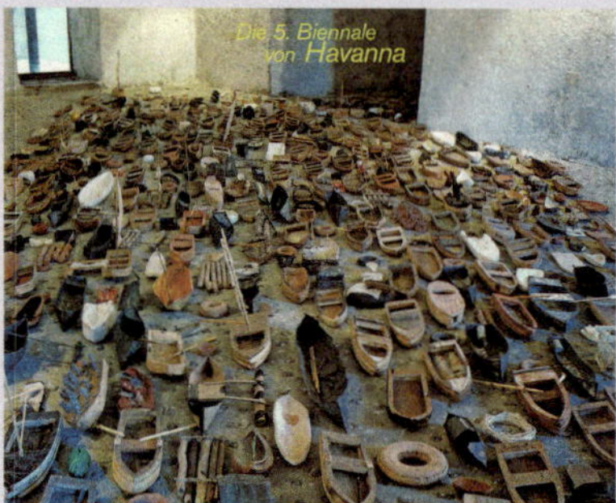

Feuilleton FAZ 7.V.92

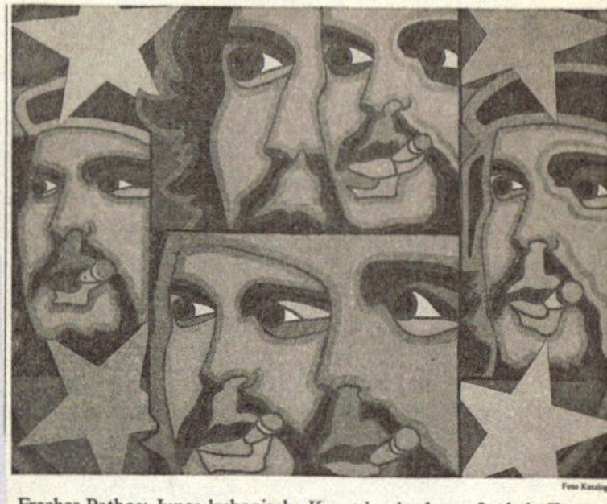

Freches Pathos: Junge kubanische Kunst im Aachener Ludwig-Forum

Newspaper article about the fifth Havana Biennial at the Ludwig Forum in Aachen. *"Havana Biennial in Europe for the First Time," Der Bund, 20.10.1994*

FEUILLETON

KUNST Biennale von Havanna im Ludwig Forum Aachen

Biennale von Havanna erstmals in Europa

Newspaper article about the opening of the exhibition *Von dort aus: Kuba* (*From There: Cuba*) at the Ludwig Forum in Aachen. *"Cheeky Pathos: Young Cuban Art at the Ludwig Forum in Aachen," FAZ, 7.5.1992*

Newspaper article regarding the opening of the fifth Havana Biennial at the Ludwig Forum in Aachen. *"Sparks Flew at Opening," Aachener Nachrichten, 17.9.1994*

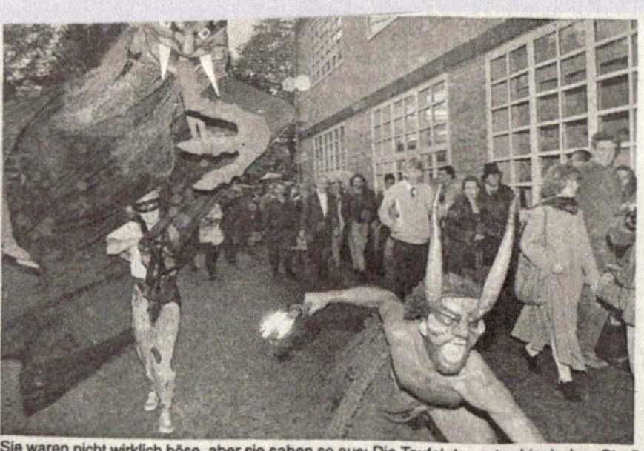

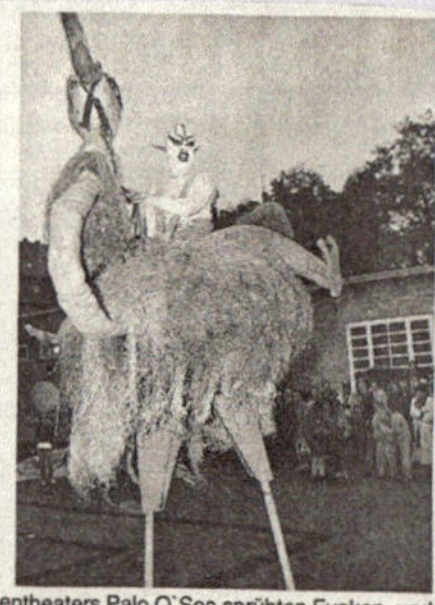

Sie waren nicht wirklich böse, aber sie sahen so aus: Die Teufel des columbianischen Straßentheaters Palo Q'Sea sprühten Funken, und riesige Phantasiekreaturen auf Stelzen mischten die Menge im Hof des Ludwig Forums ordentlich durch. Immer wieder wichen die Zuschauer vor krachenden Knallern und glühenden Fackeln zurück, um danach sofort wieder in die erste Reihe zu drängen. Fotos: Krömer

Zur Eröffnung sprühten die Funken

Mitreißendes Theaterspektakel zum Auftakt der „5. Biennale von Havanna"

Von Silke Niewenhuis

Aachen. Es war kalt, hat gequalmt, gebrannt und geregnet. Und laut war es außerdem. Die Besucher des Ludwig Forums waren begeistert, ließen sich willig durchregnen, in Rauchwolken hüllen und von halbnackten Teufeln an den Haaren zerren. Die Eröffnung der 5. Biennale von Havanna war ein voller Erfolg.

Die Truppe Palo Q'Sea fand den richtigen Rhythmus, um die Besucher unter der Überdachung hervorzulocken und lieferte ein farbenprächtiges Straßentheater in der Tradition karnevalistischer Umzüge der Karibik. Da flogen den Leuten im Hof des Ludwig Forums Knaller um die Ohren, und Funken sprühten aus allen Richtungen.

Am ganzen Körper rot bemalte Teufel rannten mit Fackeln in die Menge, schrien und warfen sich vor erschrocken zurückweichenden Gästen auf den Boden. Das Kunstsammlerehepaar Ludwig verfing sich in schwarzem Tüll, den groteske Phantasievögel auf meterhohen Stelzen hinter sich herschleppten.

Kurz: Es war ein Spektakel der Extraklasse das die Columbianer den Aachenern lieferten. Und die Leute tanzten so versessen mit, daß die schrille Veranstaltung länger dauerte als geplant. „Dafür habe ich nicht mehr bezahlt", sagte der Pressesprecher und Programmleiter des Ludwig Forums, Rick Takvorian, voller Begeisterung.

Nach der feurigen Eröffnung sprachen dann Oberbürgermeister Jürgen Linden und der Direktor des Ludwig Forums, Wolfgang Becker, sowie die Direktorin der Biennale von Havanna, Lilian Llanes, zu den zahlreichen Gästen, die sich noch die Knallerfetzen von der Kleidung klopften. „Kunst," so Linden, „darf nicht die Beschäftigung einer Elite sein und schon gar nicht die der Mitteleuropäer." Es sei mit der Ausstellung gelungen, den teilweise sehr eurozentristische Blickfeld in der Kunstszene zu erweitern, sagte Becker. Und Rick Takvorian prophezeite, daß Themen der „dritten Welt" auch in der Kunst zukünftig eine größere Rolle spielen würden. Vor diesem Hintergrund ist es erstaunlich, daß sich kaum eine andere westeuropäische Stadt um diese Ausstellung bemüht hatte.

„In Aachen hat sich die Befürchtung, Westeuropäer könnten an der Kunst der 'dritten Welt' kein Interesse zeigen, jedenfalls nicht bestätigt", freute sich die Direktorin der Biennale in Havanna, Lilian Llanes. Sie bedankte sich für das Interesse und lobte die guten Beziehungen, die zwischen Aachen und Havanna entstanden seien.

Die Ausstellung ist noch bis zum 11. Dezember in Aachen zu sehen und wird in keiner anderen deutschen Stadt gezeigt werden. Umrahmt und begleitet wird sie von zahlreichen Tanz-, Film- und anderen Vorführungen (weiterer Bericht siehe Kultur).

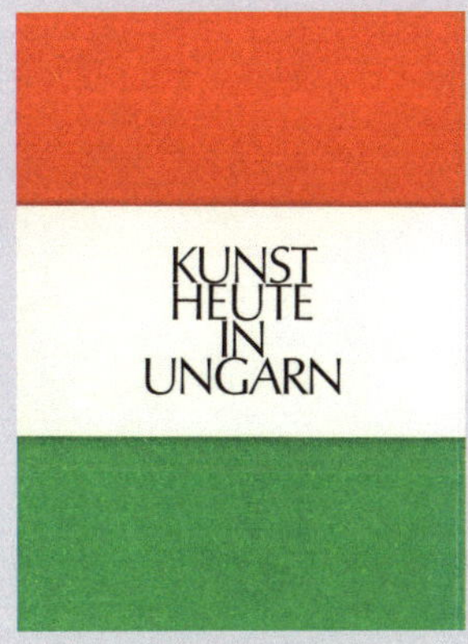

Exhibition catalogue, *Kunst heute in Ungarn* (*Art Today in Hungary*), Aachen, 1989.

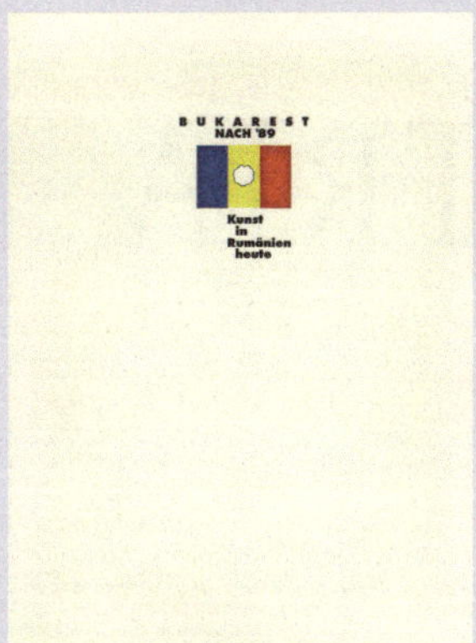

Exhibition catalogue, *Bukarest nach '89. Kunst in Rumänien heute* (*Bucharest After '89: Art in Romania Today*), Aachen, 1998.

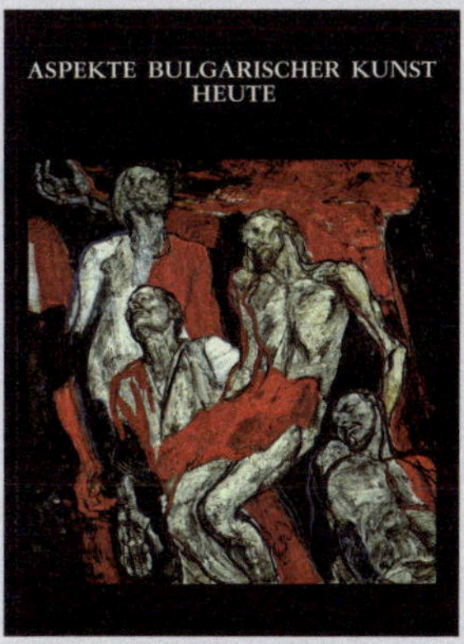

Exhibition catalogue, *Aspekte Bulgarischer Kunst heute* (*Aspects of Bulgarian Art Today*), Aachen, 1984.

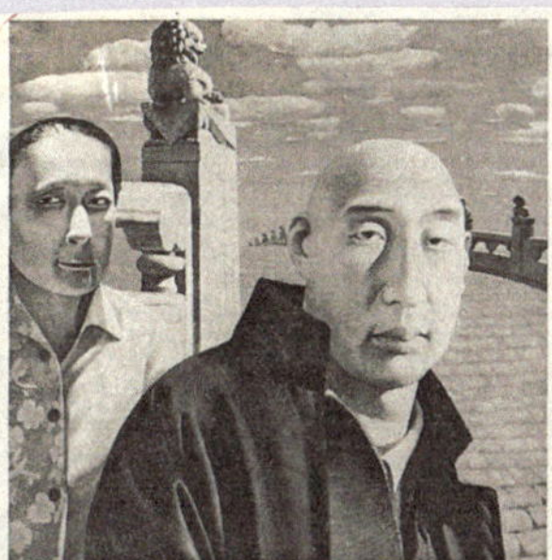

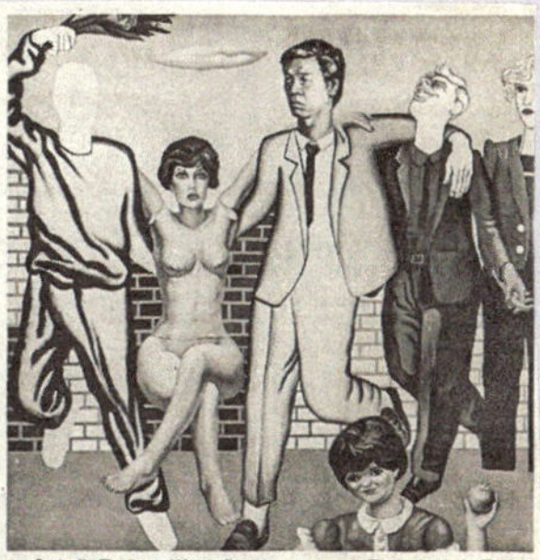

Zweimal Kunst aus China: „Gruppe Eins, Nr.2" von Fang Lijun und „Der große helle Tag" von Wang Jingsong. Fotos: Ludwig-Forum

Doppelter Mao und eine nackte Venus

Peter Ludwigs Neuerwerbungen aus China - Breites Veranstaltungsprogramm in Aachen

Von Gernot Geduldig

Aachen. Das Ludwig-Forum sieht auf den gerade erschienenen Plakaten leicht verändert aus: Rot gefärbt und mit Pagodendach wirbt es für das große Projekt, das unter dem Motto „Begegnungen mit China" in diesem Hause stattfindet. Der Schwerpunkt ist zweifellos die Kunst aus Taiwan, die ab Anfang Mai gezeigt wird, den Auftakt macht bereits ab heute eine Auswahl von Peter Ludwigs Neuerwerbungen aus dem riesigen Reich der Mitte. Der Sammler war schon mehrmals in die Volksrepublik gereist, gestern erst kam er aus Peking zurück, wo bald ein Ludwig-Museum für moderne Kunst eröffnet werden soll. Der Mäzen will für dieses Haus ungefähr hundert Beispiele westlicher Kunst zur Verfügung stellen.

Rund zwei Dutzend Werke aus China sind jetzt, auf zwei Räume verteilt, im Forum ausgestellt; dazu gibt es einen als Katalog gedachten großformatigen, informativen Prospekt (8 Mark) aber, eher ungewöhnlich, keine Vernissage. Zweifellos steht diese Präsentation etwas im Schatten der großen China-Schau im Bonn, wo rund hundertsiebzig Werke gezeigt werden, allerdings auch dort mit der Unterstützung Ludwigs.

Ein sozialistisches Reich im Umbruch, die kommunistischen Dogmen wanken, Konsumlust und Marktwirtschaft unterlaufen die überkommenen gesellschaftlichen Strukturen. In den Bildern der zeitgenössischen Künstler ist der Einfluß des Westens unübersehbar: Man orientiert sich gerne an kunterbunter amerikanischer Pop-Art, aber auch an der surrealistischen Malerei eines René Magritte. Der Künstler Wang Jingson zum Beispiel arrangiert vor einer Mauer eine Gruppe von Schaufensterpuppen, darunter eine nackte Frau, am Himmel schwebt eine rosa Wolke, die als Lippenpaar, aber auch als Vulva deutbar ist.

Aktbilder verpönt

Aktbilder sind in China immer noch ein Tabu-Thema, und wenn Ji Wendyu in einem Gemälde neben ein traditionelles chinesisches Liebespaar Boticellis nackte Venus plaziert, ist dies sehr gewagt.

Dennoch: Etliche der hier vertretenen Künstler lehren an Staatsakademien und genießen überraschend weitgehende Freiheiten. Was sie in ihren Ateliers produzieren, ist allerdings nicht für die Einheimischen gedacht, sondern für den westlichen Markt.

Während einige Maler mehr oder minder locker mit dem modernen Bilderfundus umgehen und ihn mit der traditionellen Ikonographie mixen, gibt es auch mehrere, die deutlich ihre Kritik an westlichen Tendenzen artikulieren. Vier Gemälde von Chi Youhan sehen aus wie monumentale Geldscheine, die Protagonisten der Kuturrevolution scheinen nunmehr Helfershelfer von Kapitalismus und Korruption zu sein. Auf einem Bild von Wang Guangyi sind drei kommunistische Patrioten eng verquickt mit einem amerikanischen Produktnamen.

Und der große Vorsitzende Mao-Tse-Tung? Auch der bleibt nicht verschont, obwohl sein Bildnis eigentlich tabu ist. Ein Maler zeigt Mao mit einem Doppelgesicht, ein anderer dekoriert das Konterfei mit vielen Blüten, Sternen und anderen huldigenden Symbolen, verzerrt und trivialisiert ihn damit zugleich.

Schreiender Mann

Schon in der großen Kölner Ludwig-Schau „Unser Jahrhundert" war Fang Lijuns eindrucksvolles Bild „Gruppe Zwei, Nr. 2" zu sehen: aus einer Reihe von stumpfsinnig und uniform daherschreitenden Männern scheint einer herausgetreten zu sein und hat seinen Mund zum Schrei geöffnet. Warum, bleibt rätselhaft in diesem ansonsten sehr präzise gemalten Bild.

Auf den Fotorealismus westlicher Prägung greift Yu Hong zurück, übrigens die einzige Frau in dieser Ausstellung: Über eine Gruppe junger Menschen, ihren Schülern an der Kunstakademie, setzt sie ironisch einen mit Blumen geschmückten Strahlenkranz.

Einige der Arbeiten besinnen sich auf die große Tradition der Kalligraphie. Kurios zwei Werke von einem Künstler namens Ai Wei Wei: gerahmte Kuhfell-Stücke, die von weitem wie schwarz getuschte Landschaftszeichnungen aussehen. Ein Stipendiat der Heinrich-Böll-Stiftung hat ein Gedicht des Kölner Schriftstellers in moderne kalligraphische Zeichen und Piktogramme umgesetzt, die an Bilder von Miro oder Klee erinnern. Noch deutlicher der Sprung in die Neuzeit bei Xu Tan: auf vier Holzplatten mit chinesischen Landschaftsbildern und Schriftzeichen hat er fünf bunte Spielzeugautos und eine Lokomotive gestellt.

Newspaper article about the exhibition of newly acquired artworks from China at the Ludwig Forum in Aachen.
"Double Mao and a Naked Venus," Aachener Nachrichten, 29.3.1996

AUSTRIA

The Ludwigs' premiere as international benefactors took place, in many ways, in Vienna. The city was the recipient of the first donation of part of their collection outside Germany. The model of a foundation with the aim of securing ongoing acquisitions and promoting projects was also put into practice for the first time in Austria—a model that would later prove its worth in two other countries.

Two people provided the impetus for the Ludwigs to test out their international ambitions in Vienna. One was the president of the Vienna Künstlerhaus (Austrian Society of Visual Artists), Hans Mayr; the other was the Austrian art historian **Hermann Fillitz**, a friend and confidant of the couple, who served as a professor at the University of Vienna from 1974. Their first coup came to fruition on March 7, 1977: the exhibition *Sammlung Ludwig, Aachen – Kunst um 1970. Art around 1970* opened in the Vienna Künstlerhaus, showing a cross section of contemporary art and comprising around one hundred works from the Ludwig Collection. The exhibition took place at the invitation of Hans Mayr and became a huge public success. Talks regarding a long-term loan of works from the Ludwig Collection to the Austrian state, initiated in large part by the minister of science and research, Hertha Firnberg, began while the exhibition was still running. To this end, a loan agreement was finalised on February 21, 1978. 151 works of art were to be loaned for an initial period of five years, forming the basis for a new museum of modern art in the Austrian capital.

The baroque Palais Liechtenstein, in the ninth district, was extensively renovated for the exhibition of the loaned works. As part of the Palais's opening on April 26, 1979, the 20er Haus in the Schweizergarten, which had housed the Museum des 20. Jahrhunderts (Museum of the Twentieth Century) since 1962, became a branch of the newly-founded Museum moderner Kunst (Modern Art Museum). The inaugural director of the museum was **Dieter Ronte**. Between the signing of the contract and the opening of the museum, the Ludwigs continuously expanded their list of permanent loans. Through Peter Ludwig's mediation, the museum also acquired the contemporary art collection of Wolfgang Hahn, a Cologne art restorer.

With the establishment of the Österreichische Ludwig-Stiftung für Kunst und Wissenschaft (Austrian Ludwig Foundation for Art and Science) in January 1981, largely owing to the decisive actions of Hans Mayr and Hermann Fillitz, 129 of the works that had previously been on loan were transferred to the foundation's ownership, as such becoming permanently bound to the museum. Besides the maintenance of the donated works, the foundation's aims were the continual expansion of the collection through acquiring new works, their academic analysis, and the promotion of exhibitions.

On the occasion of the Ludwigs' donation of ninety-nine more works in 1991, the museum's name was changed to the Museum moderner Kunst Stiftung Ludwig (Modern Art Museum Ludwig Foundation). One year earlier, the Hungarian Lóránd Hegyi had been appointed director of the museum. After Peter Ludwig's passing in 1996, Irene Ludwig took over the role of chairperson of the Board of Trustees; she was supported by, among others, **Gottfried Toman**, the foundation's managing director at the time.

In 2001, following discussions which had gone on for years, mumok, as the Museum moderner Kunst – Stiftung Ludwig Wien had come to be known, moved into the newly-constructed MuseumsQuartier in Vienna, which had been designed by the architectural firm of Ortner & Ortner BAUKUNST. A quick look through the Vienna museum's letterheads from the years 1981 to 2001 reveals the museum's genesis to have been an incredibly variable and dynamic process. Like the museum, the Österreichische Ludwig-Stiftung für Kunst und Wissenschaft remains successfully active to this day.

A conversation with **Dieter Ronte** about Peter and Irene Ludwig's work in Vienna, which culminated in the founding of the Museum moderner Kunst Stiftung Ludwig, also known as mumok, and the Österreichische Ludwig-Stiftung für Kunst und Wissenschaft

The interview was conducted in Cologne on April 15, 2016.

PROF. DR. DIETER RONTE (b. 1943, Leipzig) studied art history, archaeology, and Romance studies in Münster, Pavia, and Rome. From 1971 to 1979, he worked at the Wallraf-Richartz-Museum in Cologne. Later, he was a research assistant at the Museum Ludwig before becoming the head of its Graphic Arts Collection. In 1979, he moved to Vienna to serve as the director of the Palais Liechtenstein and the 20er Haus, which was renamed that year to the Museum moderner Kunst, later becoming the Museum moderner Kunst Stiftung Ludwig (Modern Art Museum Ludwig Foundation) or mumok. From 1989 to 1993, he was the director of the Sprengel Museum Hannover, after which he became director of the Kunstmuseum Bonn (Bonn Museum of Modern Art) until 2007.

Peter Ludwig was a man who had a huge influence on my life, and without him my life would probably have been very different. … But were it not for him, today's society would have far less energy. It would have been a tremendous loss had he not existed.

REGINA WYRWOLL I would like to begin our conversation by asking how you came to Cologne.

DIETER RONTE In 1971, I became a research assistant at the Wallraf-Richartz-Museum in Cologne. For five years, I was the right-hand man of the then director-general of Cologne's museums, Gert von der Osten, and of his successor, Gerhard Bott, from 1975. Together, we oversaw the integration of the Ludwig Collection into the museum. In 1976 or 1977, I took over the Graphic Arts Collection. The majority of my time was spent, however, managing the planning—with a focus on the visitor's experience—of the new Museum Ludwig and Philharmonie development, located right by the main railway station. That was my real job.

I arrived in Cologne shortly before receiving my doctorate. I had been lucky enough to receive a scholarship from the Institute of Art History in Munich and wanted to use it to study Nazarene sculpture. Gert von der Osten was responsible for selecting the candidates from North Rhine-Westphalia. We had a chat and he asked, "What do really want to do for a career?" I answered, "I want to work in a museum! Since I was sixteen years old I've wanted to be the director of a museum of modern art." Von der Osten replied, "You'll get the scholarship, but why don't you come to work with me instead?" … And that's how I ended up in Cologne.

RW When did you first meet Peter Ludwig? What kind of impression did he make on you?

DR I met Ludwig for the first time in 1971. To me, he was *the* collector. The museum had doubled its visitor numbers, as every visitor was counted a second time if they went upstairs to the Ludwig Collection—the "Rhenish count." Ludwig was a wonderful man when he taught, which he did for over ten years at the Department of Art History at Cologne University. When he came to the museum with students, I was often there, and I adopted much of his outlook. Coming from a home where we only collected abstract art, I was of course caught completely off guard by suddenly being confronted with Pop Art—Robert Rauschenberg and other Pop artists. These were unbelievably important experiences for me. Peter Ludwig was a man who had a huge influence on my life, and without him my life would probably have been very different.

RW Ludwig provoked a lot of opposition. But there were a few people in Cologne who were well aware of the value of what had fallen into their laps in the form of Ludwig and his collection.

DR Wolfgang Hahn, the then head of restoration at the Wallraf-Richartz-Museum, and later head of the restoration workshop at the Museum Ludwig in Cologne, was himself a collector and knew very well to appreciate Ludwig and his collection. As did Kurt Hackenberg, the former councillor for cultural affairs, who set the tone for cultural politics in Cologne between 1955 and 1979. You also have to include in this group Gert von der Osten, director-general of the Cologne museums from 1960 to 1975. I learned a great deal from him too. He was an accomplished and open-minded museum administrator. The Ludwig Collection undoubtedly gave him no pleasure on a personal level, but he could see that it was an incredible boon for the museum, with which it could look toward the future. I admired the fact that he considered the works in the Ludwig Collection in the 1969 publication *Kunst der sechziger Jahre. Sammlung Ludwig im Wallraf-Richartz-Museum Köln* (*Art of the 1960s: The Ludwig Collection at the Wallraf-Richartz-Museum in Cologne*), while still revealing his perspective as an art historian who would prefer to look at Lovis Corinth or the artists from the Netherlands. At any rate, he made an effort to engage with contemporary art. This was, unquestionably, more difficult for him than for Horst Keller, who was director of the Wallraf-Richartz-Museum at this time. It was admirable that von der Osten, as the director-general, said, "I stand by this, we'll present it to the public, and I will give it some personal thought."

RW Did you have any interactions with the councillor for cultural affairs?

DR Of course. He was a great man. Let me tell you a story: I had applied for a job as a research assistant in Kaiserslautern, because I wanted a permanent position. Hackenberg came to me and said, "You're not leaving, you'll stay here and I'll make sure that you get a permanent position." He was an unusual man who always had a unique way of thinking. Here's another example: I travelled to America with the architects who would design the Museum Ludwig and the Philharmonie, along with some of the Cologne city councillors. We travelled all over the place, looking at concert halls, the architecture of new museums, and so on for research. When we returned, there was trouble with the Committee for Cultural Affairs because they felt that the architects should have paid for their travel out of their own pockets. Hackenberg said, "The architects were not guests of the city, the trip was a gesture on the part of the city!" That was typical for him. Or another story pertains to Hans Mayr, president of the Vienna Künstlerhaus, who played an important role in the Österreichische Ludwig-Stiftung für Kunst und Wissenschaft (Austrian Ludwig Foundation for Art and Science) in Vienna and wanted to become the director of the Kölner Kunsthalle. Hackenberg told him, "You know what, Mr. Mayr, we're already scoundrels ourselves." Only Hackenberg could say things like that.

RW I have heard that Irene Ludwig in particular could never warm to Hans Mayr because he spoke in such a strong Viennese dialect.

DR Absolutely. Mayr was married, but it was rumoured he had a mistress here in Cologne. That was his emotional connection to Cologne.

During that time I often visited artist's studios. … That was also a habit that I picked up from Ludwig, in order to foster my curiosity. You always have to be prepared to challenge your own way of thinking.

RW What was museum work like in those days?

DR It was different to what it's like today. Two days out of the week we handled administrative matters. On the other days we did research, went to the library or the archives. During that time I often visited artist's studios, something that museum staff rarely do today, but which I believe is extremely important. That was also a habit that I picked up from Ludwig, in order to foster my curiosity. You always have to be prepared to challenge your own way of thinking … As soon as you think, "Now 'I' know how the system works," they make clear to you that it works another way—and the young artists are usually right about such things. Of course, the same thing happened to Ludwig's adversaries, much to their embarrassment. They accused him of always turning up with something new, for example with Soviet or East German art. They thought or said: "What's this got to do with us? That's the sort of thing Henri Nannen can show in his museum in Emden!" On his seventieth birthday, Nannen presented the City of Emden with his collection; in 1986, he opened an art gallery that had been built specifically to house it. In short: *typical* museum work was, in principle, much calmer than today.

RW Back then, did you also volunteer to organise exhibitions at the Wallraf-Richartz-Museum?

DR In 1971 and 1972, together with Johann-Karl Schmidt, who later went to Stuttgart and founded the Kunstmuseum (Museum of Art) among other things, I presented the children's exhibition *Hurra!? Vom Unsinn des Krieges* (*Hooray!? On the Insanity of War*). It was a huge success. In 1969, Peter Ludwig had acquired *The Portable War Memorial* (1968)—a work by Edward Kienholz that is exactly what the name suggests—and it formed the centrepiece of the exhibition. The way we wrote the catalogue texts, which we did with the head curator Horst Vey, was typical of museum work back then. Vey would always say, "These texts are too leftist, too political, you can't use them." So we sat down and worked on them some more … and the same thing repeated three times in a row. Finally, I took *Der Große Ploetz* and copied the story from that classic historical encyclopaedia. Vey's reaction was, "No, that's unacceptable!" And I replied, "Mr. Vey, in that case you have to ban *Der Große Ploetz*, because that's word for word what you just read." Vey went to von der Osten who then called me in and said, "Mr. Ronte, there are six questions regarding your catalogue that I would like you to answer." So I answered them for him. Then he said, "I don't always agree with you, but if it results in a political uproar, I will support you." That was von der Osten! This would become a fundamental lesson for my entire career from then on.

Ludwig kept a very tough schedule. He got up at six in the morning, devoted some time to his collection, and then he went to the office.

RW Did Ludwig interfere with the work of the museum?

DR If it was about the museum and about the foundation, of course Ludwig was aware of everything. I was the general director's right-hand man, and it all came across my desk every day.

RW And what was that like?

DR Exciting, unbelievably exciting.

RW What was it like to deal with Peter Ludwig? He was, after all, a very successful businessman.

DR He was tough. Very direct. Very open. But let me jump a couple of years in the future, to Vienna. It must have been 1986 or 1987, and Ludwig called me out of the blue one evening and said, "My dear Ronte, I would like you to exhibit the Soviet artists from my collection in the 20er Haus." I answered: "No. You have a contract with the Künstlerhaus, with Mr. Mayr, and that's where you should hold the exhibition. I won't show it, especially as it doesn't fit our programme at all." He was extremely angry and grew very abusive, and I hung up. The next day he apologised, but from then on we had a very strained relationship, and there was no going back to the way it had been.

RW It must have been the same in Cologne. Ludwig held a gun to people's heads, didn't he?

DR Yes.

RW You arrived at the Wallraf-Richartz-Museum in 1971. Did you have anything to do with the catalogue for the 1969 exhibition *Kunst der sechziger Jahre. Sammlung Ludwig* (*Art of the Sixties: Ludwig Collection*)? Unbelievably for this time, five editions and thirty-thousand copies were printed.

DR The catalogue had just been published when I arrived. Wolf Vostell was commissioned to do the design. The city wasn't willing to finance the catalogue, so Peter Ludwig did it. That was a huge financial mistake by the museum administration and Hackenberg. He could have found the money. But everyone thought that no one would buy it because it's such an unusual catalogue. Ultimately it was a hit, and in fact, it made Ludwig and his collection world famous.

RW When you arrived at the museum, the new building—now the Museum Ludwig—hadn't been built, and there was no collection belonging to the city.

DR The works in the museum were all only on loan. At that time, the question was, where to build a new museum? A number of sites in Cologne were discussed—the Heumarkt, for example. Hackenberg was very astute at dealing with politics, he was incredibly good at it. Suddenly focus fell on the cathedral, right in the centre of Cologne. It was the perfect location. But the construction site was problematic, as it was on a steep slope. We launched an architectural design competition in which many well-known architects took part, like the British James Stirling, who had built the Neue Staatsgalerie (State Gallery) in Stuttgart. Surprisingly, the winners were the Cologne architects Peter Busmann and Godfrid Haberer. And then the fighting started. Ludwig stayed out of it. He left it up to the museum. We then undertook many trips with the architects in order to look at new museum buildings and concert halls; we went to Berlin, Finland, and, as I mentioned before, the US.

RW Public opposition grew because the costs inevitably increased. Isn't that correct?

DR Yes, but it has to be said that Cologne had previous experience with museums and their construction. It wasn't the first building that had been put up since the war. Cologne was still doing relatively well back then. There was greater consensus at the time than there is today. That was also partly due to Hackenberg. Hackenberg was the type of person who liked to keep several plates spinning at once. You have to go from one to the other and keep each of them spinning so that none of them fall. He could do that. That was how he saw himself, by the way, that image was his own description. We had umpteen planning meetings with the architects, discussions with the city councillors, with people from the Department for Cultural Affairs, with acousticians about the planned concert hall, and so on and so on. It was exhausting.

RW Were you ever invited to the Ludwig's private home in Aachen during your time in Cologne?

DR Yes. often. And also to their holiday house in Kastanienbaum on Lake Lucerne. It was always very relaxing. I'll never forget my first time in Lucerne. I went with my museum colleagues to visit an exhibition, and then we all met with the Ludwigs at their holiday house. They made burgers for us in the garden. At eleven, Peter Ludwig said, "Irene, we're going to bed, it's eleven o'clock." Then they left us alone. It was exactly the same in Aachen as well. Ludwig kept a very tough schedule. He got up at six in the morning, devoted some time to his collection, and then he went to the office. I was always amazed that he stuck so strictly to his schedule. It was incredible.

"Mr. Director, we have been given the job of moving you." That's how I found out I had the job.

RW When did you leave Cologne?

DR At the end of August 1979. On September 1, 1979, I started work in Vienna at the Palais Liechtenstein, better known under the name 20er Haus, as the successor to Alfred Schmeller.

RW Who brought you to Vienna?

DR I've never applied for a job in my life, somebody always rang me, but for Vienna you could say that I applied indirectly. Mayr, president of the Künstlerhaus, contacted me about the job and I sent him my information. They were looking for someone who knew the Ludwig Collection. At that time in Austria, there were very few people who had an interest in contemporary art. It took a while before Hertha Firnberg, minister of science and research in Bruno Kreisky's cabinet, agreed to hire me. It was, of course, a federal museum. I was only thirty-six years old at the time, and they asked why they should hire a German, and especially one so young. But they didn't have anyone else, so I got the job. One evening in Cologne I received a call. It was the Vienna trucking company Zdenko Dworak, who informed me, "Mr. Director, we have been given the job of moving you." That's how I found out I had the job. The next day the ministry called me and said, "Congratulations, we look forward to working with you." That's Vienna!

RW What was your work in Vienna like?

DR After the exhibition of his collection at the Künstlerhaus in 1977, Ludwig was asked if he would like to provide works for a museum in Vienna. Negotiations went back and forth for a while. Vienna wondered, "Do we really need it?" They're still asking themselves that today. And then they showed him the Palais Liechtenstein in the ninth district, the baroque Garden Palace of the princes of Liechtenstein from Vaduz. At the time, it displayed the state art collection of Liechtenstein, which is now in a new museum in Vaduz. Incidentally, until 1967, the *Portrait of Ginevra de' Benci* (1474–1478) by Leonardo da Vinci hung there. In 1967, Prince Franz Josef II of Liechtenstein sold it to the National Gallery of Art in Washington for five million US dollars. Ludwig looked over the Garden Palace and said, "I will fill this building!" Intensive negotiations took place, and then the Palais Liechtenstein was converted to accommodate the Ludwig Collection. The conversion took place during 1978. While this occurred, Mayr had the task of managing the establishment of the Museum moderner Kunst. The position of the future director had already been advertised and was to go to me. My office was in the Palais Liechtenstein. And the 20er Haus had just been repurposed to be our exhibition space. It actually still housed the modest Austrian collection of contemporary art, which had been amassed since 1962 by the founding director of the 20er Haus, Werner Hofmann.

RW Hermann Fillitz has said that everything was built on top of the work of Mayr, who was the head of the Künstlerhaus in Vienna.

DR Mayr was unbelievably tenacious.

RW Why was Ludwig, and Irene Ludwig especially, sceptical of him for so long?

DR Mayr was a no-nonsense photographer with a photographic business that specialised in experimental photography, but he was also a very, very clever negotiator, very hardheaded. He woke the Künstlerhaus from its slumber with, among other things, the Pop Art exhibition *Kunst um 1970. Art around 1970* in 1977, composed of works from the Ludwig Collection. He had discovered in the Künstlerhaus's documents that the president of the Künstlerhaus held ministerial status. It was a royal institution, after all. As a result he had direct contact to Minister Firnberg and could advocate for his positions in a completely different way from others. This was the situation that Peter Ludwig encountered. He understood that it presented a great opportunity for him.

RW How did Ludwig come to grips with the Imperial and Royal bureaucracy in Vienna?

DR I think he simply ignored it. He left dealing with it up to Mayr. Fillitz—who was then head of the Kunstkammer des Kunsthistorischen Museums Wien (Kunstkammer at the Museum of Fine Arts Vienna) and became director of the museum in 1982—and Mayr then set up the mumok.

RW You didn't have any problems as a German in Vienna?

DR Of course I did! For the first two years there were almost daily attacks on me in the newspaper, most of them below the belt. There was a personnel manager at the time in the Ministry of Science who said to me, "As a German, I would give you three pieces of advice if you come here: First, if the sun is shining, call the museum and tell them that you won't be in that day." I asked him, "Why?" He answered: "You can't afford to make any mistakes that day. Second, if something is successful, never say that you did it. And third, when someone writes something about you which isn't true or that annoys you, never deny it." That was the most important advice of all! After two years, the press' savaging of me abruptly stopped. But nasty things continued to happen. The Gesellschaft der Freunde der bildenden Künste (Society of Friends of the Fine Arts) had sent out invitations for the farewell reception of Dr. Dieter Ronte, who was apparently going to Durban, South Africa, to work as a curator. Subsequently, journalists called me asking, "Why are you leaving now?" I was astonished: "I'm not leaving!" "But I'm holding the invitation in my hand." And I answered, "Well, then my appointment in Durban has probably been rescinded, because nobody was supposed to know about it." Things like this happened nonstop. Or I would receive a summons to appear before the regional court on a charge of aiding and abetting denigration of the Catholic Church. But I also liked it somehow, it was fun.

But Beuys was always laden with theory. His work had nothing to do with Rudolf Steiner. It's simply another kind of art. Ludwig didn't like it.

RW Did you discuss your programme for Vienna with Ludwig?

DR No. He didn't interfere with the exhibitions in the museums. He might make suggestions. The blowup between us happened because of one of his suggestions, to organise an exhibition of Soviet art in the Palais Liechtenstein. Our relationship remained professional, we would still greet each other and speak. The meetings of the Österreichische Ludwig-Stiftung für Kunst und Wissenschaft were all very cordial. But the warmth was gone.

RW You shared a lively correspondence with Ludwig, exchanges that were exceedingly polite and friendly.

DR Always very professional, yes.

RW Can you recall any personal experiences?

DR Quite a few. When we had meetings of the Österreichische Ludwig-Stiftung für Kunst und Wissenschaft, I always visited Ludwig beforehand at the Hotel Imperial. We would sit and drink coffee. In Vienna, they always put out nuts on the table. Ludwig dug in, and Irene smacked his hand and said, “Peter, that’s enough!” Or during a meeting, when Irene Ludwig was against one or another purchase, Ludwig would suddenly jump in: “Irene, put a sock in it, it’s not your money.” And that was the end of that. He would show that side of himself.

RW Were there artistic viewpoints that neither of them wanted represented in the collection?

DR If you look at Irene and Peter Ludwig’s collecting, there is one oeuvre that is underrepresented in Cologne, one that is possibly the most important for the fine arts in Germany after 1945: that of Joseph Beuys. Ludwig just couldn’t handle his work. I tend to believe that it was because Beuys positioned art in a kind of social compact. Ludwig, who came from Picasso and from abstract art, was against that. Pop Art, too, had this liberal character. It was first theorised in Europe, not in America. But Beuys was always laden with theory. His work had nothing to do with Rudolf Steiner. It’s simply another kind of art. Ludwig didn’t like it. That’s why there are very few pieces of his in the collection, only around forty works. Today, they can be found in Vienna and Cologne.

RW There is some conjecture—and it’s all just conjecture—that Irene Ludwig sometimes put the brakes on her husband.

DR I could believe that. But that was something that never involved me. If you look at the collection in Vienna, you have to keep in mind that the purchase of the Wolfgang Hahn Collection introduced the side of modern art that Ludwig hadn’t collected.

RW They were in close contact, maybe even friends.

DR Hahn and Ludwig? I don’t think Ludwig would have come to Pop Art without Hahn. I think the decisive impetus to collect Pop Art came in 1968 when Wolfgang Hahn was on a trip to New York and Peter Ludwig met him there. That’s typical Ludwig: once the spark was there, then he really got stuck in. Of course, the entire gallery scene in Cologne benefitted from Ludwig’s commitment. The ideas of the foundation and the Ludwig Collection and the Museum Ludwig in Cologne ultimately fostered an enormous vibrancy, affected the art market, and so on. It all has to be seen as part of an interconnected web. Then you realise that this man from Aachen had set off an aesthetic bomb in the city, a stunning "big bang" for Cologne.

RW I have the impression that something similar occurred for Vienna through the Österreichische Ludwig-Stiftung für Kunst und Wissenschaft and the purchase of the Hahn Collection.

DR Yes. When I arrived, the Hahn Collection had already been purchased. Two books were released to mark the occasion of the opening exhibition at the newly founded Museum moderner Kunst in the Palais Liechtenstein in 1979, which included works from both the Ludwig and the Hahn Collections. That had a huge effect on the galleries. Let me give you an example. The artist Rudolf Hausner called me and asked, "Can you write something for me for the Künstlerhaus?" I wrote a text for him in which I attempted to place his art in an international context. He called me again and told me that he didn't want to print this text. I replied, "Rudi, don't worry about it, I'll print it after you die." He didn't find that funny. But his work was ultimately placed in a different context by, for example, the fact that a large painting by Hausner was on display in the Palais Liechtenstein alongside works by Paul Sarkisian, Franz Gertsch, and Chuck Close. The Palais Liechtenstein managed to create a mixture of the international and the Austrian, but the Austrians have probably still not understood it. They always wanted to see Austrian art in isolation. When I was leaving Vienna, I spent an hour explaining to the then minister of science and the arts, Erhard Busek, a member of the ÖVP (Austrian People's Party) and a very important figure, how the museums in Vienna needed to be restructured. I said to him: "If you move the mumok to the Messepalast, you will create a museum with a collection that covers the period from 1900 to the present, directly opposite the Kunsthistorisches Museum. Until Peter Ludwig's time, Austrian art has almost always been presented in Vienna without an international context." And he replied, "This has been one of the most fascinating hours I have had as a minister." Fourteen days later, my assistant called me and said, "It's not politically feasible." And that was that! Today there are numerous institutions, but nowhere where the finest works can all be seen together within a shared framework. In my opinion, the impact of Austrian art continues to suffer to this day from the fact that it remains stuck in its own little world.

RW Let's get back to your museum work. I was astonished to see in the archives that in the early days of the museum, Peter Ludwig was very closely involved with some of the loan requests. Requests were made and he was always the one who made the decision. For example, he would come to you and say that a particular work had to be sent to this or that place. How did it come to be that he was so deeply involved in logistics?

DR That's why Ludwig had to get up so early, that was his museum time. He enjoyed it. Art was his passion.

Hungary was different to the other Eastern European countries. A more liberal form of communism existed there. You might recall phrases like Goulash Communism.

RW During your time as director, the Ludwig Múzeum in Budapest was founded. How did that work out?

DR One of the first exhibitions that I curated with works from both the Ludwig Collection and from the Palais Liechtenstein was at the Műcsarnok, the Budapest Kunsthalle, in 1983. On July 8, 1983, the exhibition *EGYETEMES MÜVESZET 1960 UTÄY (Universal Art Since 1960)* opened with a speech by Hertha Firnberg, among other things. It was the first large-scale, international exhibition in Budapest in which Pop Art, including works by Roy Lichtenstein, could be seen. I had received an invitation from Budapest—as soon as I had arrived in Vienna, I had been invited to join the jury of the Biennial for Small Sculpture in Budapest. It allowed me to quickly make connections. Artists like Dóra Maurer and Tibor Gáyor didn't live in Budapest, but in Vienna, as did János Megyik. Many of the artists that now live in Budapest were living in Vienna then. We decided to invite Peter Ludwig to Budapest, and he and his wife came. Ludwig quickly realised that he could accomplish something in Budapest and initiated talks.

RW But wasn't it Mayr and Firnberg that set it in motion?

DR No. Fillitz was the museum's most important advocate. He had known both the Ludwigs since the 1950s in Cologne, where he worked together with the Museum Schnütgen and met the Ludwigs through its then director, Herrmann Schnitzler. Firnberg saw the Budapest initiative as competition for Vienna, as did Mayr. The artist Dóra Maurer was also very committed to it.

RW That was possible in Hungary?

DR Hungary was different to the other Eastern European countries. A more liberal form of communism existed there. You might recall phrases like Goulash Communism.

RW Let me see if I understand this correctly: your exhibition *EGYETEMES MÜVESZET 1960 UTÄY (Universal Art Since 1960)*, which included works from the Ludwig Collection, was shown in the Műcsarnok, and that was the context in which negotiations began?

DR That's right. Ludwig liked the city. It really is a fascinating place.

For example, in Vienna, when he saw the baroque Palais Liechtenstein, he would say, "And that's mine!" He was speaking figuratively, of course.

RW Is it possible that Ludwig was fascinated by the Imperial and Royal pomp, by the splendour of the Austro-Hungarian monarchy?

DR I don't know if Ludwig even understood the whole Imperial and Royal idea. I don't believe he had any business connections to Hungary either. Nor did he have any to Austria as far as I know. The former GDR was another story, however, as was Russia. No, he just had fun with it. For example, in Vienna, when he saw the baroque Palais Liechtenstein, he would say, "And that's mine!" He was speaking figuratively, of course. One of Peter Ludwig's strengths was that he could think purposefully, to put it mildly. This radical orientation toward success was something, I believe, that always defined him.

RW How often did Ludwig visit Vienna?

DR Once a year for the foundation's board meeting. He might also have sometimes come again for an exhibition opening, but usually just the one time.

RW Did you have anything to do with any of the other Ludwig museums?

DR Well, we worked together with Marc Scheps, who was director of the Museum Ludwig in Cologne from 1991 to 1997, and with the museum in Aachen too. But the exhibition programme in Vienna was largely kept separate from those other Ludwig projects. That was how I wanted it.

RW What was your concept for Vienna, and how did you implement it?

DR My idea was simply to show Vienna a modern museum for once, with tours and museum education—an internationally active museum. I quickly realised that there was a tremendous need to exhibit Austrian artists. Maria Lassnig had *never* had an exhibition, Christian Ludwig Attersee had *never* had an exhibition, Hermann Nitsch had *never* had a museum exhibition, Cornelius Kolig and others had *never* had one. I exhibited all of these artists and also curated themed exhibitions. For example, I'll tell you a story that's typical of Vienna: Erwin Melchert suddenly published a three-quarter-page hatchet job in the *Kronen Zeitung* newspaper, questioning why we had ever purchased the Ludwig Collection. "We do not need it" … and then he attacked the art. I called the editor, Hans Dichand, who collected art himself. I said, "Mr. Dichand, you can rail against me in your newspaper, you can rail against Firnberg, you can rail against my staff, but it is unacceptable to try to destroy the art." Dichand answered: "Write a response, one page. I need the text by one p.m." It was eleven. Dichand got his article and printed it as it was. A few days later he called me: "You can have a regular column." That's also typical of Vienna. I said: "No thanks, my focus is the museum. I don't want to write a column, it's not going to happen." Then the air was clear again, and we organised the exhibition *Faszination des Objekts* (*Fascination of the Object*) out of the Hahn Collection, which was held in the mumok in 1981. I experienced many reactions like that, time and time again.

RW The Hahn Collection was a stroke of luck for the museum, wasn't it?

DR The Hahn Collection was an absolute godsend, as the Actionist works in the collection allowed us to draw connections to Viennese Actionism. I began to build a photographic collection, as there wasn't already one in Vienna. Together with the Österreichische Ludwig-Stiftung für Kunst und Wissenschaft, we purchased the *Blauen Bücher* (*Blue Books*).

RW What do you mean by that?

DR There were these photographic volumes, the *Blauen Bücher*, published by Karl Robert Langwiesche. In 1986, we purchased the archive of around thirteen thousand vintage prints by well-known photographic artists of the 1920s to 1940s, which were the master copies used to print the books.

RW Your professional relationship with Ludwig didn't change in spite of your disagreement about the exhibition of Soviet art?

DR No, Ludwig was too clever for that. It would have ruined everything. He also accepted that I bought and exhibited works from the Vienna School of Fantastic Realism, even though he was certainly no fan of this artistic movement. Ludwig tolerated such things, which I think is good.

RW Can you tell me what kind of social status the director of the Palais Liechtenstein had during your years in Vienna?

DR A very good one. In Vienna they say, "Oh, the *director* is coming." You are at the top of the pile, both at work and in society. It is, after all, a federal museum. When searching for a name for the museum, I conferred with the minister. She wanted to call it the Museum for Modern Art. I asked her, "Will there also be a Museum Against Modern Art?" In the end it was called the Museum moderner Kunst.

RW Ms. Firnberg had put a lot of effort into acquiring loans and donations from the Ludwig Collection and was also responsible for the purchase of the Wolfgang Hahn Collection, both of which were controversial decisions. What was she like?

DR Curious, very assertive, but she could also be very helpful. I'll give you a small example: I purchased a work by Yves Klein because of Hahn, as he had been promised that a Klein would be added to the collection. It wasn't particularly expensive either. I wrote to the ministry several times asking for approval, but nothing happened, there was no response. Nor was there to other requests. Then, out of the blue, a privy councillor called me: "Director, congratulations, she signed it." I said, "She is a wise woman!" To which he replied, "True, but I am calling to warn you urgently not to buy the painting." So I wrote a glowing letter to the minister. She required it to justify, in a manner of speaking, her approval. She was happy with that. That's Vienna, politics of the highest order!

RW When did you leave Vienna and why?

DR 1989. I am the kind of person that likes to move around and I felt, after ten years in Vienna, that I had learned all I could. I no longer believed in the conversion of the Messepalast to the MuseumsQuartier, where the mumok was supposed to move to and which had already been in the works for three years. I thought that the plan had been talked to death and that it was no longer viable. Indeed, the MuseumsQuartier wasn't completed until 2001. And Hanover had offered me the opportunity to oversee the second phase of construction of the Sprengel Museum. I have always wanted to build. I've advised many architects, been on a lot of juries. I wanted to be deeply involved in a construction project and to design a building from the beginning. So I went to Hanover, but realised after four years that it wasn't the city for me, even though I had grown up in Lower Saxony. Then came the enquiry from Bonn about working at the Kunstmuseum Bonn, one of the finest museum buildings that I know of. I stayed there as director until 2007.

RW How do you view Peter and Irene Ludwig today, after so many years?

DR With the benefit of hindsight, one could say that it was the times that allowed him to be so successful. It would probably no longer be possible today. But were it not for him, today's society would have far less energy. It would have been a tremendous loss had he not existed. An incredible achievement!

RW Professor Ronte, thank you for taking the time to talk to us.

A conversation with **Hermann Fillitz** about the establishment of the museum and foundation in Vienna, twenty years of collaboration, and forty years of friendship

The interview was conducted on February 12, 2016, at the Austrian Academy of Sciences in Vienna.

PROF. DR. HERMANN FILLITZ (b. 1924, Vienna; d. 2022, Vienna) wrote his dissertation in 1947 about the history of the form and style of the German imperial crown. From 1958 to 1964, he was the head of the Kunstkammer at the Kunsthistorisches Museum (Museum of Fine Arts) in Vienna, and from 1965 to 1967 head of the Austrian Cultural Institute in Rome. As professor of art history at the University of Basel from 1967 to 1974, he focussed on the subject of modernism. From 1974 to 1994, he was a full professor at the University of Vienna. In the years from 1982 to 1990, he was both general director of the Kunsthistorisches Museum and head of its Gemäldegalerie (Picture Gallery), where he spearheaded its modernisation and restoration. As an advisor to Peter and Irene Ludwig, Fillitz was among those who paved the way for the Museum moderner Kunst Stiftung Ludwig (Modern Art Museum Ludwig Foundation), or mumok, in Vienna.

They began to collect very early on—they had the means to do so, after all.

REGINA WYRWOLL Thank you very much for sharing your experiences with Peter and Irene Ludwig with us. When did you first meet the couple?

HERMANN FILLITZ My wife and I had known Peter and Irene Ludwig since the second half of the 1950s. At that time, the Ludwigs primarily collected works of medieval art. They were advised by Hermann Schnitzler, who served as the director of the Museum Schnütgen in Cologne from 1953 to 1970 and was a friend of theirs. I also knew him well, and that's how the connection to the Ludwigs came about.

RW Would you see the Ludwigs in Cologne or in Aachen?

HF Both. I was frequently in both Cologne and Aachen. Back then, during the reconstruction period, there were a lot of conferences, as well as personal invitations, about specific subjects. It was in this context that my friendship with Schnitzler and relationship with the Ludwigs developed, among others. The strangest encounter with Peter Ludwig took place in Vienna in 1963. Ludwig was in the process of acquiring the famed ivory *Harrach Diptych* (c. 800), made by the Court School of Charlemagne, from Countess Stephanie Harrach. The countess made clear to him that I shouldn't know anything about it—I had once asked her about the whereabouts of the diptych. Of all people, Ludwig ran into my wife and I on his trip. It was the only time I ever saw him disconcerted.

RW We want to preserve personal memories of Peter and Irene Ludwig for the foundation. Let's begin with their house in Aachen. What did it look like in the 1950s?

HF Much the same as it does today. They began to collect very early on—they had the means to do so, after all. They added to their house in south Aachen using ruins from the war that were then available—that's the story they told, in any case. When we got to know them, there were already some collector's pieces in the house. For example, Ludwig had bought the glass windows of the parish church of St. Lorenzen, in the parish of Bruck an der Mur (Styria), which were then integrated into the house's entry area.

RW The Ludwigs also incorporated Dutch tiles from the eighteenth century into their house. Could these be seen at the time of your visit?

HF Those came bit by bit and were added gradually. Ludwig purchased them over time and brought them from the Netherlands. No, no—the tiles came bit by bit.

RW And the collection of beautiful Meissner porcelain from the eighteenth century?

HF Those pieces also came gradually.

RW In other words, the interior furnishing grew steadily over time.

HF Yes. But then, in the 1960s, came the turn to modernism, to contemporary art.

RW How do you explain this transformation in Peter and Irene Ludwig's collecting interests?

HF Let's put it this way: classic modernism was always present in Irene Ludwig's family home. Her parents, Franz and Olga Monheim, collected such work. So she grew up with modernism, she inherited it. Peter Ludwig, on the other hand, wrote his doctoral thesis in Mainz with Professor Friedrich Gerke about Picasso. It was the first dissertation in Germany about Picasso—a real sensation. Peter and Irene met each other at the Johannes Gutenberg University. Irene studied art history and archaeology. So the predilection for modernism was already there, but how they came to contemporary art, and, in particular, American contemporary art, I don't know for sure. What was always said was that all of a sudden, the spark was there. In any case, it must be recognised as their true achievement.

RW You were the general director and head of the Gemäldegalerie at the Kunsthistorisches Museum in Vienna, one of the most beautiful buildings in Europe, or indeed the world!

HF As a building it is quite beautiful, but it is almost entirely unsuitable for a museum.

RW Yes, but it has a fantastic collection.

HF People don't see the problem. The two buildings, the Naturhistorisches Musuem (Natural History Museum) and the Kunsthistorisches Museum, were not built to be museums. At the time they were totally out of date, as they remain to this day. They are monuments to the imperial house's services to science and the arts, which is why, for example, they have these monumental flights of stairs. As buildings, they are of course among the finest constructed in the late nineteenth century. As early as 1919, an anonymous text was published. It was, in all likelihood, written by the lord chamberlain, Count Karl Lanckoroński, who was responsible for the museums. In his letter, he wrote to the effect that the Kunsthistorisches Museum is entirely unsuitable for its art collection. The building should go to the Naturhistorisches Museum, which is far too small. The collections of artworks should be housed in the palaces that have been freed up as a result of the ousting of the Habsburgs! There was a great deal to do: the building had no elevators for visitors when I took over, the opening times were the same as in the time of the monarchy—meaning three or four hours a day—the electric lighting had to be repaired, and much more.

In any case, one day [Hans Mayr] came to me and said: "Every time Peter Ludwig comes to Vienna, he has added on to the list. It's no longer eighty, but now totals almost three hundred works. We won't fit it all into the 20er Haus."

RW Now we come to the appearance of the Ludwigs in Vienna. Hans Mayr, as president of the Künstlerhaus, ultimately brought them there. Was he an artist himself?

HF He was a photographer. There was a photography section in the Künstlerhaus at the time. The Künstlerhaus lived on exhibitions. They exhibited anything and everything, including hot plates, iceboxes, and other such things. They survived on these rentals and receipts. Mayr wanted to make the museum into a modern institution, and that's what brought him to the Ludwigs. As I've said, I had met the couple a number of times before then, and, on one occasion, they told me about the work they were doing all around the world. I asked, "And what about Vienna?" Peter Ludwig could sometimes be very brusque: "Oh, Vienna is utterly boring!" Mayr, however, needed something to jump-start the Künstlerhaus and liven things up. He went to see Peter Ludwig in Aachen a number of times. I know from the two of them that he was turned down on several occasions; Mayr reported that he was shown the door in no uncertain terms four or five times. However, Hans Mayr was an extraordinarily persistent individual. Peter Ludwig realised this and, at some point, took a liking to the persistent Mayr. Irene Ludwig, on the other hand, didn't—she never liked him. Finally, Ludwig agreed to an exhibition that, I believe, took place in 1977 in the Künstlerhaus: *Sammlung Ludwig, Aachen – Kunst um 1970. Art around 1970.* A couple of years later, in 1979, the Museum moderner Kunst opened in the rooms of the Palais Liechtenstein, with a further presentation of works from the Ludwig Collection, mostly Pop Art and Hyperrealist works.

RW A sensation, I imagine.

HF Yes, it was the spark that lit the fuse. At the opening, I stood behind the lectern with Irene Ludwig. In a speech delivered to Austrian political representatives, Mayr said, "Minister, you must ensure that these works remain in Austria!" And Irene said to me, "So, what do you make of this cheeky fellow!?" It was clear that a new idea had grown in Mayr's mind, namely that the 20er Haus—a glass pavilion owned by the federal government and then used as a kind of museum of the twentieth century—could be revitalised with Ludwig's loans, as almost nothing could otherwise be done there due to budgetary constraints. Today, the building is known by the name Belvedere 21 and is a venue for art, performances, music, lectures, and discussions.

RW That was a splendid idea. What kind of person was Mayr?

HF Unfortunately, he has been repeatedly bad-mouthed. He is said to have come from a well-off Viennese family. However, he spoke in an awful slang dialect, which he had picked up from artists. That was one of the reasons why Irene Ludwig couldn't warm up to him. But he was a farsighted man who wanted to persuade the Ludwigs to lend a large number of objects from their collection to Vienna. To this end, he required a committee of advisers, to which he appointed me—it was always good to have a professor from the university on such a committee, and all the more so when the professor was a friend of the Ludwigs. Over the course of the negotiations, Peter Ludwig's interest in Vienna grew. Minister Hertha Firnberg, the first Austrian minister of science, played a major role in this through the awarding of titles and honours. On her initiative, Peter Ludwig received the Austrian Decoration for Science and Art in 1978; previously, in 1976, he had been made an honorary member of the Vienna Künstlerhaus. Two years later, in 1981, the Österreichische Ludwig-Stiftung für Kunst und Wissenschaft (Austrian Ludwig Foundation for Arts and Science) was founded, through which parts of the Ludwig Collection were permanently donated to Vienna.

RW In 1978, the minister purchased the collection of the Cologne collector Wolfgang Hahn.

HF Hahn was head of restoration at the Wallraf-Richartz-Museum and later led the restoration workshops at the Museum Ludwig in Cologne. In this role, he accompanied the transfer of the works from the Ludwig Collection to Vienna. During this process, Hahn began talking to Mayr and confided that he wanted to sell his collection to the City of Cologne, but the negotiations had stalled. With this information, Mayr went straight to Minister Firnberg and proposed to purchase the Hahn Collection: "See here, let's snap it up, let's buy it!" We had already begun planning the installation of the Ludwig Collection in the Palais Liechtenstein. The Hahns were in Vienna at the time and negotiated with Firnberg. We were completely surprised by the purchase. I was present at a dinner at the Hotel Sacher where it was discussed once more. Hahn asked his wife, "What do you think, do you agree?" … And that was how the Hahn Collection came to Vienna. We also then had to work out how we could accommodate it at the Palais Liechtenstein, as everything had been planned without it.

RW Interesting! So the Ludwig Collection was supposed to go to the 20er Haus?

HF It was initially only about the idea of the Museum des 20. Jahrhunderts (Museum of the 20th Century) and finding a way to stimulate it, as it had been unable to develop, mainly due to its extremely tight budget.

RW Once more, to clarify: When did the Palais Liechtenstein come into play?

HF For the first contract with Ludwig, four men went to Aachen and negotiated with Peter Ludwig. It was a museum commission consisting of Franz Mairinger, the rector of the Academy of Fine Arts in Vienna, Alfred Schmeller, the director of the Museum des 20. Jahrhunderts, Kurt Ingerl, vice president of the Gesellschaft bildender Künstler Österreich (Austrian Society of Visual Artists), Vienna Künstlerhaus, and John Sailer, president of the Galerieverband Österreich (Gallery Association of Austria), Vienna. Mayr and I were also involved. Irene Ludwig only joined us later on. There, we agreed upon a list of eighty artworks that were to be exhibited in Vienna. Afterwards, there were things that needed to happen and be arranged, about which I, at least, didn't know anything, and I don't believe Mayr did either. In any case, one day he came to me and said: "Every time Peter Ludwig comes to Vienna, he has added on to the list. It's no longer eighty, but now totals almost three hundred works. We won't fit it all into the 20er Haus." However, there was a passage in the contract stipulating that all of the loan works had to be exhibited within one year, otherwise the contract would be invalid. Accordingly, an extension to the museum building had to be considered. I'm not sure why these considerations came to nothing—the relevant negotiations were led by Mayr who only told me bits and pieces about them; for example, the city government refused the extensions because it would have required the removal of surrounding shrubs and bushes. The city was worried about having problems with environmental groups. There were also draft designs created by the architecture firm Schwanzer, who had designed the original building. I don't know why these didn't receive any attention. It was in this context that the director of the Liechtenstein's administration offered the usage of the Palais Liechtenstein, which was standing empty at the time. I had to compile an advisory report for the ministry. In it, I wrote that this should only be a temporary solution, for ten years at the most. It ended up being twenty.

RW Good. So now we've come to the Palais Liechtenstein, which was opened in 1979 and which, together with the 20er Haus, formed the Museum moderner Kunst.

HF The opening was supposed to take place in autumn 1979. There was an election that year, which was brought forward from October to May. Minister Firnberg insisted on the opening taking place before the election, as she couldn't know if she would still be in the government afterwards. That was a major blow, as we had to open four or five months earlier than we had planned. Mayr made it happen, and I worked very hard on it too. We both spent Easter Sunday at the museum cleaning the rooms so that the tradespeople could carry on with their work on the Tuesday after Easter. I can still see Mayr standing in front of me in his orange overalls. We pulled it off! I can still see a nervous Peter Ludwig in front of me, too, asking if there would be enough people attending the opening … At the opening, on April 26, 1979, the hall was overflowing.

RW How did the Viennese press react?

HF Well … as is usual in Vienna, it was ferociously attacked from the start. At the opening, however, everyone was very positive. In Vienna, everything is always intensely politically charged, and as Minister Firnberg was from the social-democrat side, the conservatives attacked us. It was the same when she wanted me to take over at the Kunsthistorisches Museum. Hardly a day went by when there wasn't an article criticising me in the press. There was even an article in the Catholic weekly paper *Die Furche*, which I had written for myself when I was a student. It was titled, "Kunstgeschichte als Gunstgeschichte" ("Art History as a Story of Favouritism"). They wrote, "If Firnberg is going to make one of her favourites the director of the museum, then it shouldn't be Professor Fillitz, who has never spent a day of his life at the museum." They didn't mention the fact that I had worked there for seventeen years. The editor-in-chief declined to print a correction. The attacks only came to an end when, in a personal conversation, the then head of the Austrian People's Party, Alois Mock, gave the order for them to stop. These attacks were entirely based on the assumption that since Minister Firnberg had appointed me, I must be her political ally—my professional abilities were never discussed.

The art world saw it as an opportunity. In a city that had never spent money on modernism, there was suddenly money available.

RW How did the national foundation come about?

HF That's the next point. Dieter Ronte, from the Wallraf-Richartz-Museum in Cologne, was one of the applicants for the position of director at the Museum moderner Kunst, a position that was open because Alfred Schmeller, the director of the 20er Haus, was retiring. Ronte was announced as the successor and took over as director on the day after the opening. Our presentation was intended to show both the abundance and the variety of the loaned works. The aim was to showcase what the acquisition of the Hahn Collection and the loans from the Ludwigs brought. That means we exhibited as much as possible. It was very positively received. The next good idea then came from Mayr ... The Museum des 20. Jahrhunderts had been established in 1962, and the founding director was Werner Hofmann, who left for the Hamburger Kunsthalle in 1969. At first, he had been given a very good budget and collected well. The budget, however, increasingly diminished.Mayr didn't want the Museum des 20. Jahrhunderts, which was once again so well-stocked, to face the same problem again, so he came up with the idea of a foundation. Mayr said: "What do you think about the idea of the Ludwigs donating a portion of the works that are currently here on loan under the condition that the state contribute financially? And that would form the basis for the foundation?" And it worked! Peter Ludwig agreed immediately. Minister Firnberg, who had a very good relationship with the then finance minister, Hannes Androsch, ensured that a contract lasting for over fifteen years was agreed to. Ludwig donated 129 works of art, and the state paid a set amount into the foundation's coffers every year, so that a sufficient amount of capital amassed for the museum to make use of, even if the state later reduced its support. The contract was later extended to 2010. That's what came of Mayr's basic idea: the Österreichische Ludwig-Stiftung für Kunst und Wissenschaft.

RW But the unusual thing about this particular foundation is that the Österreichische Ludwig-Stiftung doesn't just fund one museum—it serves all the federal museums in the country.

HF That was the compromise that Minister Firnberg had to accept. Mayr's original idea was for the foundation to concentrate on the Museum moderner Kunst. But in typical Viennese style, everyone had their say … indeed, the whole of Austria. If you look at the original contract from back then, it discusses the support and promotion of art in Austria. It became a cumbersome undertaking: an artistic advisory board was appointed that always met before the Board of Trustees and made recommendations to them. The general secretary of the foundation at the time, Privy Counsellor Gerhard Sailer, fought for years to finally do away with this advisory board.

RW The chairperson of the advisory board was the sculptor Oswald Oberhuber, right?

HF Yes, it was Ossi Oberhuber. He was on the black team then, that is he belonged to the Austrian People's Party, and was very influential. He also, by the way, had a very good relationship with Minister Firnberg. He was the rector of the University of Applied Arts and was the driving force. Many acquisitions can be traced back to him.

RW Did Oberhuber have a good relationship with Peter Ludwig?

HF I can't say, as Ludwig was never present at the Board of Trustees meetings.

RW Were you a member of the Board of Trustees from the beginning?

HF There were four people nominated by the Austrian government and four by the Ludwigs. Peter had called me: "I would like you to come onto the board so that there is also an Austrian on the board from my side, and it doesn't look like we are dominating from Germany." There were Peter and Irene Ludwig—who together had one vote—Franz Meyer, the former director of the Kunstmuseum Basel (Basel Museum of Art), Hans Mayr, and myself. On the Austrian side, there were always two ministers, the minister of science and the finance minister, but only one of them came to the meetings … and then there were two section heads.

RW How did Vienna react?

HF At the time, positively. The art world saw it as an opportunity. In a city that had never spent money on modernism, there was suddenly money available.

RW What's special about the Österreichische Ludwig-Stiftung is that it has played a decisive role in changing the scene in Vienna as a whole, which is to say that it has had a spectacular effect.

HF Absolutely. But there was then an unfortunate development, which we in the foundation also lamented. In Vienna, there has never been a clear "division of labour" between the museums. What we actually wanted to create in Vienna was something like the Centre Pompidou, but that didn't work out. I mean that there's the Albertina, which collects contemporary art, but so does the Belvedere, and so on. In other words, today we have four or five museums that all have a similar focus.

RW Which directors did you experience during your time at the foundation?

HF The first director of the Museum moderner Kunst was, as I already mentioned, the German Dieter Ronte. Then came the Hungarian art historian and curator Lóránd Hegyi, who was followed by the Austrian artist Edelbert Köb.

RW Let's come to the subject of Peter Ludwig's vanity. Can you recall any stories about that?

HF Peter Ludwig once offered to donate the works from his collection that were on loan in Vienna if, in return, the University of Vienna awarded him an honorary doctorate. Years earlier, when I was still a professor there, he had donated his collection of antiquities to Basel and received an honorary doctorate from the university. He suggested to do the same thing in Vienna.

RW So does that mean he received an honorary doctorate in Vienna?

HF No, he didn't. I was given the task, as a professor, of advocating for it. So I went to the rector of the University of Vienna, Richard Georg Plaschka, who didn't see any problems in terms of the university's statutes. Minister of Science Firnberg also had no objections. Then, at a faculty meeting, the dean ranted, "It's an insult to the university, this rubbish, this modernism." My colleague Renate Wagner-Rieger, professor of art history at the university, stood up and countered, "The faculty already made a mistake, when it turned down four Gustav Klimt paintings for the ballroom." But it was to no avail, and the proposal was declined. Ludwig was angry and called me incompetent, it was a really awkward moment. I still have a letter from him that shows how he raged at the time. He was really furious with me. Hans Mayr smoothed everything over.

RW How?

The Ludwigs set themselves apart from other collectors because they didn't collect for themselves, but only for the public, right from the start.

HF I can't remember exactly.

RW Didn't you find Peter Ludwig to be a little too vain?

HF Leave out the word "little" and then you would be right. He said it himself: "Yes, I am vain!"

RW Did you ever talk about art with Peter and Irene Ludwig, about paintings or about Pop Art, for example?

HF Oh yes. I would almost say more with her than with him. I often discussed art with her. One example would be at the first exhibition, which was put together, as I said previously, very quickly and not according to any particular aesthetic principles, but instead so as to show as much as possible. Irene came by—I have two or three specific artworks in mind—and said, "No no, you have to hang that differently."

RW Do you believe she had a big influence on how the house in Aachen was furnished?

HF Yes. I believe she was very involved in the background.

RW What were Peter Ludwig's most prominent characteristics?

HF He was, of course, a go-getter, and he was a very dynamic businessman. The Ludwigs set themselves apart from other collectors because they didn't collect for themselves, but only for the public, right from the start. He wanted to make a difference on a global scale. He wasn't the kind of collector who surrounds himself with works that he loves, that he treasures. Instead, he wanted to achieve something with art for the international public. That's what fundamentally separated the Ludwigs from everyone else we know as collectors.

RW What kind of impact was he hoping to make?

HF Maybe a change of consciousness.

RW So his idea was one of cultural politics?

HF Absolutely. I still often read the preface of the catalogue for the exhibition *Kunst der sechziger Jahre* (*Art of the Sixties*), which was shown in 1969 at the Wallraf-Richartz-Museum in Cologne. In it, he outlined a commitment to the task of collecting. It should be reprinted. He said something to the effect of: "As a private individual, I can buy, unlike a museum director, whatever I like. And that which proves to be lasting is that which must be handed over to the public." So his fundamental idea was always to make the collection available to the public. The larger the collection became, the more his awareness grew that he could, if you will, use his collection for political purposes. One example is that he took his collection to East Germany.

RW How did you perceive his path to Eastern Europe?

HF I thought it was very important. I had the impression that, by going there, he wanted to open up the East intellectually—or, let's say, to significantly contribute to its intellectual opening up. He stimulated the people there. There was also the fact that, in the contracts for both East Berlin and Budapest, it was stipulated that the works had to be exhibited. The Ludwigs had something of a sense of mission.

RW Ludwig's almost world-encompassing activities were a step in the direction of globalisation. Did he want to bring about globalisation in today's sense, or did he have something else in mind when he collected numerous works of art from different cultural backgrounds?

HF Globalisation is a broad term, which is, justifiably, controversial today. Back then, Ludwig was entirely open to the fact that every epoch has its art, National Socialism included. That was highly controversial, but Ludwig's standpoint was that every epoch has its art, and whether one sees it positively or negatively, it is the expression of that epoch. And he was right. He expressed this point of view many times in our conversations.

RW Could you describe that idea in more detail?

HF Let's put it this way: every political epoch has a reflection—a reflection in art. So, in those years, Ludwig wasn't really collecting works of art, but documents. Objects that documented something about political epochs—about social situations—and which captured some aspect of them. We talked about this at the beginning of the 1990s, when he was already an established collector. He wanted to juxtapose authentic documents. This idea had developed in him over many years. It had nothing to do with what we understand as globalisation today, which is more about levelling down.

RW Ludwig was a businessman: he traded in cocoa, he produced chocolate. What did art mean for him?

HF Art was essential. Everything else was just a means to an end of collecting.

RW When did you last see the Ludwigs?

HF Peter died completely unexpectedly in 1996. I went to Aachen for the requiem mass. I can still remember the way Irene hugged me and cried. She was very emotional, we had a very close friendship. I saw Irene Ludwig for the last time in Vienna, at a Board of Trustees meeting. She didn't feel well and flew back to Germany early. That was the last time I saw her.

RW Thank you very much for taking the time to talk to us, Mr. Fillitz.

A conversation with **Gottfried Toman** about the formation and work of the Österreichische Ludwig-Stiftung für Kunst und Wissenschaft and the role played by Irene Ludwig

The following interview was conducted on March 22, 2019, in Vienna at Café Prückel, a quintessential Viennese coffeehouse.

DR. GOTTFRIED TOMAN (b. 1955) studied jurisprudence, history, and politics at the University of Vienna and received his doctorate in jurisprudence in 1981. Until the end of 2020, he worked as a lawyer for the Finanzprokurator (finance prosecutor) in the Federal Attorney's Office of the Republic of Austria, where he was responsible for legal cases in the fields of art and culture, among other duties. In addition to conducting numerous contract negotiations and court cases, some of them in the US, he was instrumental in setting up a cooperation agreement between the Republic of Austria and the Friends of the Schindler House for the establishment of the MAK Center for Art and Architecture, Los Angeles in 1994. He taught law at the Academy of Fine Arts in Vienna and was the chairperson of the Supervisory Board of the Österreichische Nationalbibliothek (Austrian National Library) for fifteen years. In 2002, he became managing director (general secretary) of the Österreichische Ludwig-Stiftung für Kunst und Wissenschaft (Austrian Ludwig Foundation for Art and Science), where he continues to serve as chairperson of the management board.

I admire the Ludwigs because they lived according to the motto: "We have the means, we have the interest, and we want to create something lasting through art and the encounters it facilitates."

REGINA WYRWOLL Dr. Toman, thank you very much for talking to us about the Österreichische Ludwig-Stiftung für Kunst und Wissenschaft's work with Irene Ludwig, where you have worked since 2002. Is this job your main occupation?

GOTTFRIED TOMAN No, I work at the Finanzprokurator, which is part of the Federal Attorney's Office for the Republic. My predecessor at the foundation was a colleague of mine from the Finanzprokurator; he had the idea to create the Austrian foundation when the Ludwigs came to Austria at the beginning of the 1980s. After it was founded, he was appointed its general secretary. That title is somewhat misleading as the job is effectively that of the foundation's managing director. I succeeded him in 2002.

RW What was his name?

GT His name was Dr. Gerhard Sailer. He was president of the Federal Monuments Office for many years, and he contacted me in mid-2001. I had had contact with him on a professional level after providing legal representation for the Federal Monuments Office. I was sceptical at first about getting involved; I felt that there were so many other things which kept me busy outside of my main job, especially as I also held a teaching position at the Academy of Fine Arts in Vienna. I was also not fully informed about the quantity of work at the foundation. Sailer took me to a foundation meeting on November 11, 2001, where I first introduced myself and then quickly agreed to join. What I had not anticipated was that Sailer would die six weeks later. Suddenly I was in charge of a quite complex foundation about which I knew very little. However, Sailer had a very helpful daughter who had gathered together all of the paperwork. I received all of that from her and gradually grew into the role. It was fascinating for me to see everything that the foundation had achieved in the previous two decades in Austria. I never knew Professor Peter Ludwig, as he had died in 1996. As a result, his wife was the one that I worked with and the one that

I admired. I believe Peter Ludwig was a very powerful and power-conscious personality—it must not have been easy for her.

She very much had her own ideas. A meeting without specifically considering a purchase was unthinkable for her.

RW From your perspective, what were the problems that she faced?

GT After her husband's passing, Irene Ludwig had to define a new position for herself and move out of his shadow. Suddenly, she became the centre of attention of all their foundations and museums. I can imagine that it was very challenging for her.

RW Did you get to know Irene Ludwig well?

GT I had a number of opportunities to get to know Professor Irene Ludwig well. I also went to her house in Aachen a few times. She chaired the Board of Trustees of the Austrian foundation and as such was often in Vienna. I was fascinated by how she was always interested in doing something concrete, in making something happen for art, in acquiring quality art. When it came to questions of quality, she highly regarded expert opinions, but also attached importance to her own opinions. It was important to her to give a certain impression: "Considering this work is sensible, we should do something here, we should buy this." I think there was something very personal about how she went about her work.

RW You mean that she had her own ideas about what the foundation should acquire?

GT Yes. She very much had her own ideas. A meeting without specifically considering a purchase was unthinkable for her. I appreciated her approach very much, because modern art always has something experimental about it. You never know for certain whether it will end up being something: whether it's of value or will turn out to be nothing. When in doubt, her attitude always was, "Let's just give it a try." I appreciated that because I know fully well that it was accompanied both by a willingness to take risks and by a great esteem for modern art and its all of its varied developments.

RW How often did these meetings take place?

GT We had a board meeting once a year, and Mrs. Ludwig always came to them, with a few exceptions. At one point her relationship with Austria came under a bit of a cloud. I believe it was because she felt that she wasn't being treated in the proper fashion.

RW Irene Ludwig came from a family of industrialists in Aachen, which had close connections to the CDU (Christian Democratic Union of Germany).

We provide works of art for the museums which they would be unable to afford themselves.

GT I'm very grateful that I managed to do something back then, with the help of the then Austrian minister for education, the arts, and cultural affairs, Dr. Claudia Schmied. We ensured that the German Peter and Irene Ludwig Foundation maintains permanent representation on the Board of Trustees of the Österreichische Ludwig-Stiftung. Let me be frank. My aim was to prevent the possibility of political interference along the lines of: "Well, we could change the purpose of the foundation, we could change the name, we could change its mission, we could change its acquisition policy." I am thankful that it was possible to encourage Dr. Schmied and Mrs. Ludwig to alter the articles of the foundation to stipulate that, in the event of Irene Ludwig departing at some point in the future, the German foundation would always be represented on the board of the Austrian foundation. This ensures that the foundation's mission cannot be changed without the agreement of the German foundation, as unanimity is required for the articles to be altered. This still appears to me to be an essential guarantee that both the purpose and concept of the foundation, and by extension the work of Peter and Irene Ludwig, will be continued in the future.

RW From 1981 to 2010, a period of thirty years, the Austrian state paid a certain amount into the foundation each year in order to bestow the foundation with enough funds to become independent. That was what had originally been agreed to in 1981.

GT Yes.

RW Is the amount sufficient? Is the foundation able to fulfil its mission?

GT The sums paid by the state matched the Ludwig Collection's contribution of 129 works of art to the foundation. The foundation hasn't received subsidies from the state since 2010 and now must "take care of itself." Thanks to our amassed funds, we are well able to currently allot money according to the foundation's mission. Of course, at some point there will be a question of whether it remains sufficient to continue our operations.

RW How much money has accrued since 2010? A sum in the tens of millions?

GT I'd rather not put an exact number on it. Maybe I can put it like this: The foundation's articles stipulate that the amount required for the foundation to be self-sufficient is around 8.5 million euros. That figure is currently exceeded by a considerable amount. And it's true to say that we are in the range of tens of millions. Of course nothing can be ruled out, but assuming that things go as expected and that interest rates will change again, the foundation will be able to fulfil its mission for many years to come. Currently, we spend around 900,000 euros per year, principally for new acquisitions. And given that there is relatively little state funding for acquisitions, we function as a guarantee that acquisitions can be made at all in Austria, especially for federal museums and particularly the Museum moderner Kunst Stiftung Ludwig Wien (Modern Art Museum – Ludwig Foundation Vienna), or mumok for short.

RW When you provide funds to other institutions for new acquisitions, does the foundation then own the works?

GT We don't buy for the museums, we buy for the foundation. The museums provide us with recommendations for purchases, and the foundation has final say. These acquisitions are then given to the museums in the form of permanent loans. The idea is a relatively simple one: we provide works of art for the museums which they would be unable to afford themselves and, in return, on the basis of the loan agreement, we have no "maintenance" costs, by which I mean custodianship, security, insurance, restoration—all of that is the responsibility of the museums. Through this arrangement, we currently own around nine hundred works.

RW Who makes decisions regarding the proposals?

GT We have a Board of Trustees. During the period when Irene Ludwig still chaired the foundation, there were four German and four Austrian representatives. That has since changed, and there are now seven Austrian representatives and a single representative of the German Peter and Irene Ludwig Foundation. There is, however, a condition that states that changes to the foundation's articles can only be passed by unanimous agreement. Those sitting on the Board of Trustees are chosen via a political process, but I must emphasise that decisions are made with great care, and attention is given to ensuring the board includes members who are specialists in modern art. In addition, there was a change to the law regarding foundations in 2015, which requires that there must be two executive management positions that head a foundation. I come from the economic, legal side of things. Because of this, I stressed the importance of the second person coming from the art world—namely from the field of academic research. The individual we chose is Professor Doctor Sabeth Buchmann, who teaches modern and postmodern art history at the Academy of Fine Arts. For many years, she was a member of the Board of Trustees and now has an executive role.

RW It's clear from what you've said that the foundation plays an important role in Austria.

GT Yes, definitely. However, one thing needs to be said: I think that it's likely nothing would have come of setting up a foundation without the impetus provided by the Ludwigs, together with the then minister for science, Dr. Hertha Firnberg, and Professor Hans Mayr from the Künstlerhaus, in connection with Mr. Sailer's idea for a foundation. I want to be clear about that, because I believe that in Austria during this time, there was little recognition of the potential of such an idea. A journalist at the time described the art scene as "comatose."

And another thing, the thing that fascinates me the most, is that the life's work of the Ludwigs and their foundations has radiated outwards to Beijing, Shanghai, and St Petersburg. But the real achievement was the establishment of a foundation in Havana. It is one of very few foundations in Cuba that is based on Spanish civil law, which was still in effect there at that time.

He declared that he needed art to recover from work and work to recover from art. I think there is a great deal of truth in that. The Ludwigs were the right people at the right time.

RW The Fundación Ludwig de Cuba is not a museum. It is active in a broader sense, through artist exchange programmes and art education.

GT That's right. I visited the foundation once a couple of years ago. I admire the Ludwigs because they lived according to the motto: "We have the means, we have the interest, and we want to create something lasting through art and the encounters it facilitates." This was always accomplished with a certain willingness to take risks while also remaining prudent.

RW Peter Ludwig was a preeminent businessperson. He understood risk.

GT He declared that he needed art to recover from work and work to recover from art. I think there is a great deal of truth in that. The Ludwigs were the right people at the right time.

RW Let's return to Irene Ludwig. What was it like the first time you met her?

GT It must have been 2002. I flew to Cologne, was picked up by her chauffeur, and driven to this splendid property in Aachen. I was impressed by two things: first, the generosity of the house, and second, her personality. Irene Ludwig was a warm-hearted, charming person who was interested in people and—above all—who listened. You always had the impression that she was interested in both the conversation and the person she was talking to. I visited her in Aachen, I believe, four or five times. I can still picture us sitting together in her house, in the superb library with green leather armchairs, with her sitting on the bench that had a wonderful view of the garden. I was there together with Professor Dr. Hermann Fillitz too, once or twice. It was immediately clear how friendly their relationship was. He was one of the "founding fathers" of the Österreichische Ludwig-Stiftung für Kunst und Wissenschaft and was a very important figure for the Ludwigs and for their relationship to Austria. The other thing that struck me was Irene Ludwig's eagerness to experiment, according to the principle: "Let's buy something that's a bit of a risk, rather than let a chance that we might regret later pass us by." That was something that set her apart.

RW In the meetings, would she make quick decisions like her husband, or would she take some time to think about things?

GT I remember that she always wanted to discuss things, but at a certain point she regarded the subject as settled and agreed upon: "Good, that's what we'll do." That's also clever in a business sense—not to let the discussion get out of hand, but to ensure there is a final decision.

RW Did Irene Ludwig ever say "No?"

GT That's interesting. I can only recall two discussions where we were unable to reach a unanimous decision under her leadership. At the end of the day, she always strove to achieve a consensus in which the various suggestions for acquisitions were taken into account—even if it was at the cost of going over budget. That attests to her solution-oriented approach. The meetings had a structure: I presented the general business topics, and then she opened the discussion of acquisitions and we had a *tour de table*, going through each museum that had made a submission. And after that there was a second discussion: "Where do we have clear majorities? Where are there differences of opinion?" She did that with great aplomb. She was naturally authoritative.

RW When she died in 2010, did you attend the funeral?

GT I attended her eightieth birthday celebration, which was also attended by the then premier of North Rhine-Westphalia, Dr. Jürgen Rüttgers. And I was at her funeral in Aachen in the cathedral and in the Church of St. Paul. It made a deep impression on me and greatly moved me, not least because it also made clear to me what an important figure she was, both for Aachen and for art.

RW Dr. Toman, thank you for taking the time to talk to us.

"Aachener Volkszeitung" AUS DEM KULTURELLEN LEBEN 5. Jan. 1979

Leihgaben aus Aachen setzen an der Donau vieles in Bewegung

Ludwig-Werke wirbeln Wien auf

Palais Liechtenstein als vorläufiges Domizil für die Kunst der Moderne

VON KLAUS GRUBER

Wien. – Wie immer man über Popart denken mag: Der deutsche Kunstsammler Peter Ludwig hat etliches in Bewegung gebracht, als er im Frühjahr 1977 einen Teil seiner bekannten Aachener Sammlung in Wien ausstellte und der österreichischen Regierung anbot, 120 Kunstwerke auf unbestimmte Zeit in der Donaustadt zu belassen. Voraussetzung war die Bereitstellung geeigneter Räume. So gern man in Wien den Impuls für eine große Lösung genutzt hätte: So viel Geld war nicht aufzutreiben. Also beschied man sich vorerst mit einer kleinen.

Die große Lösung wäre die Einrichtung eines umfassenden Museums der Kunst des 20. Jahrhunderts im bisherigen Messepalast gewesen. Der langgestreckte, geräumige Barockbau – einst die kaiserlichen Hofstallungen – schließt das große Museums-Areal bei der neuen Hofburg ab, in dem schon die meisten Bundesmuseen untergebracht sind. Gibt man jetzt das wenige vorhandene Geld für ein Provisorium aus, kann niemand wissen, wann es zu dieser logischen und sinnvollen Lösung kommt.

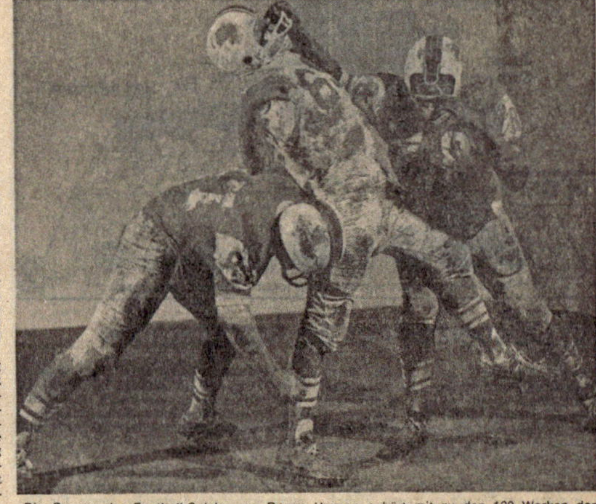

Die Gruppe der Football-Spieler von Duane Hanson gehört mit zu den 120 Werken der Sammlung Ludwig, die den Weg von Aachen nach Wien angetreten haben. (Foto: Archiv)

Es wurde nun aber erst einmal beschlossen, das spätbarocke Palais Liechtenstein, das bisher für mancherlei Ausstellungen nur unvollkommen genutzt wurde, für die moderne Kunst zur Verfügung zu stellen. Hier sollen nicht nur Ludwigs Dauerleihgaben, sondern auch die meisten Bestände aus dem bisherigen Museum des 20. Jahrhunderts unterkommen, das in dem einstigen Pavillon der Brüsseler Weltausstellung von 1958 etwas zentrumsfern am Wiener Südbahnhof nicht gerade überlaufen ist. Man will den Pavillon dann entweder für andere Zwecke nutzen oder für Wechselausstellungen, Film- und Foto-Dokumentationen, Aktionen oder schlicht für die Plastiken des 20. Jahrhunderts. Ein Direktor für beide Häuser zusammen wird noch gesucht.

Außer einer Reihe von Österreichern, unter denen kaum sehr überzeugende Persönlichkeiten zu finden waren, bewarben sich auch die Deutschen Dieter Ronte, Thomas Deecke und Manfred Schneckenburger, dazu ein Holländer und zwei Auslands-Österreicher. Schon wurden in Wien Stimmen laut, die darauf drängen, daß ein Österreicher zum Zuge kommt. Dabei täte, wie das Beispiel Peter Ludwig zeigt, der bildenden Kunst in Österreich etwas frischer Wind, etwas Erfahrung von Leuten, die sich in der Welt umgesehen haben, durchaus gut.

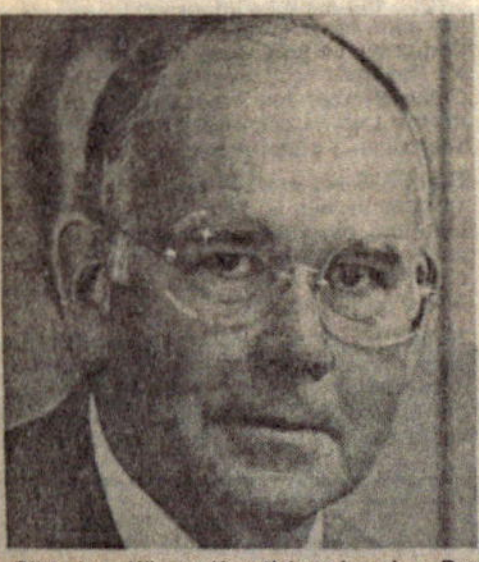

Gibt dem Wiener Kunstleben Impulse: Der Aachener Sammler und Mäzen Prof. Dr. Dr. h. c. Peter Ludwig. (Foto: Hein Call)

Über die Personalfragen hinaus, die sich immer am besten zum streiten eignen, hat der Ludwig-Impuls auch zum Nachdenken darüber geführt, ob der staatliche Kunstbesitz heute noch sinnvoll aufgeteilt ist. Das kaiserliche Erbe wurde ja schon in der ersten Republik etwas provinziell in internationale und österreichische Kunst geteilt. Das „internationale" kunsthistorische Museum endet mit Beginn des 19. Jahrhunderts. Alles spätere wurde – qualitätsvoll, aber lückenhaft – in einer eigenen „Neuen Galerie" zusammengefaßt. Die „Österreichische Galerie" hat im oberen Belvedere 19. und 20. Jahrhundert versammelt und nimmt sich auch solcher Zeitgenossen an, die gerade nicht auf der Kunst-Börse notieren. Kunst des 20. Jahrhunderts besitzen ferner die Galerie der Kunstakademie, das Museum für angewandte Kunst, das heeresgeschichtliche Museum und die graphische Sammlung Albertina.

Ein zentrales Museum des 20. Jahrhunderts, wie es sich manche Experten wünschen, würde alles zusammenfassen, was im Augenblick als qualitätsvoll und prominent angesehen wird. Für eine solche Umorganisierung lassen sich gewiß gute Argumente anführen, aber man würde gewachsene Sammlungen zerreißen und sie weniger attraktiv machen, weil ihnen nur die zur Zeit nicht aktuellen Namen blieben und der riesige Stapel von staatlichen Ankäufen, die mehr aus sozialen Motiven getätigt werden.

Was man sich von einem neuen Mann in einem neuen Museum erhoffen sollte, wäre Orientierungshilfe für solche Menschen, die sich für Kunst, auch für Kunst unserer Zeit, interessieren. Entgegen alten Behauptungen in Wien und anderswo ist es nämlich nicht wahr, daß die Donaustadt rückständig ist, daß hier nichts geschieht. Das Angebot ist riesengroß, aber es geschieht in einer mittlerweile kaum noch überschaubaren Zahl von Galerien, in Museen, in den Gebäuden der beiden führenden Künstler-Vereinigungen: Künstlerhaus und Secession. Das städtische Kulturamt steuert von Zeit zu Zeit die umfassende Ausstellung eines „Klassikers der Moderne" bei (1979 soll es Giacometti sein) und will demnächst nach Zürcher Muster eine große juryfreie Kunstausstellung veranstalten.

Was fehlt, sind die Maßstäbe, ist die Unterscheidung von wesentlich und unwesentlich im internationalen Vergleich, ist ein Wegweiser durch das Vielerlei. Dergleichen ist heute natürlich viel schwerer zu bewerkstelligen als in den sechziger Jahren, da Werner Hofmann das „Museum des 20. Jahrhunderts" aufbaute und auf einer noch spärlichen Kunstszene unbestrittene Autorität sein konnte. Hofmann wurde zur Hamburger Kunsthalle „abgeworben". Warum sollte Wien nicht attraktiv genug sein, um eine ähnliche Persönlichkeit – Ausländer oder Auslands-Österreicher – für eine so reizvolle Aufgabe zu locken?

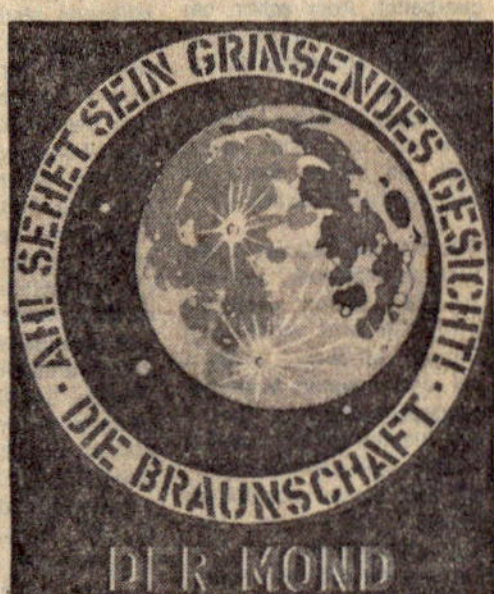

Auch das Acryl-Bild „The Moon (Die Braunschaft)" von Robert Indiana aus dem Jahre 1969 wird als Aachener Leihgabe in Wien zu sehen sein. (Foto: Archiv)

Newspaper article about the exhibition of the first loaned works from the Ludwig Collection at the Palais Liechtenstein in Vienna.
"Ludwig Works Stir Vienna Up," Aachener Volkszeitung, 5.1.1979

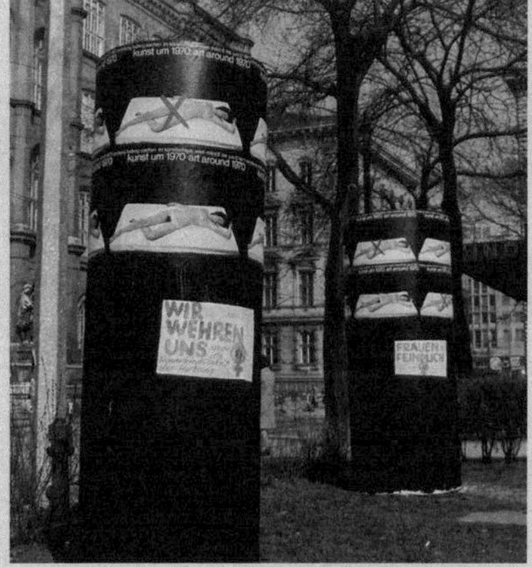

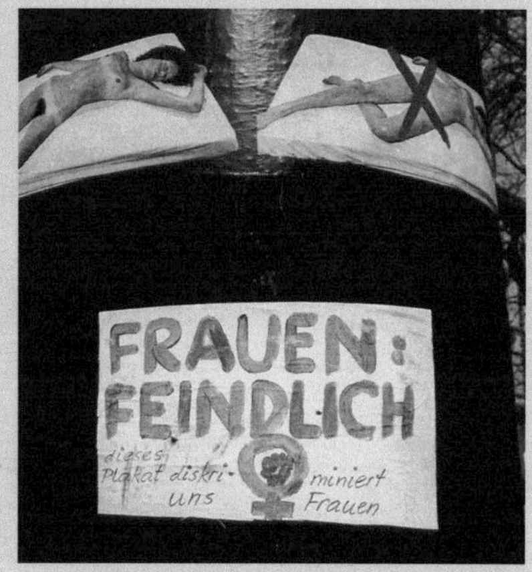

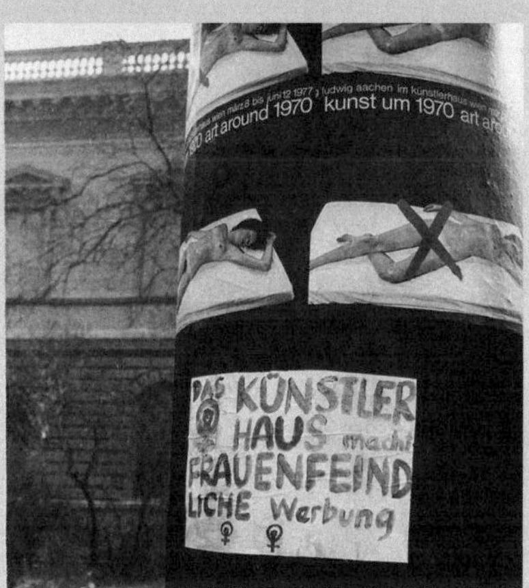

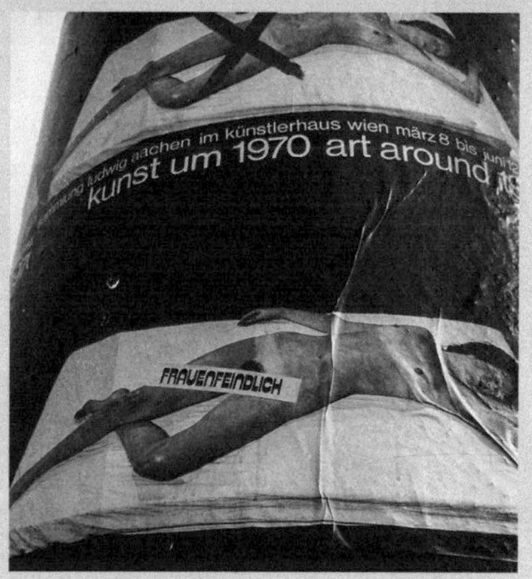

The exhibition poster for *Kunst um 1970. Art around 1970* at the Künstlerhaus in Vienna, 1977, which featured a sculpture by John De Andrea from 1974, provoked a scandal.
Photos: private

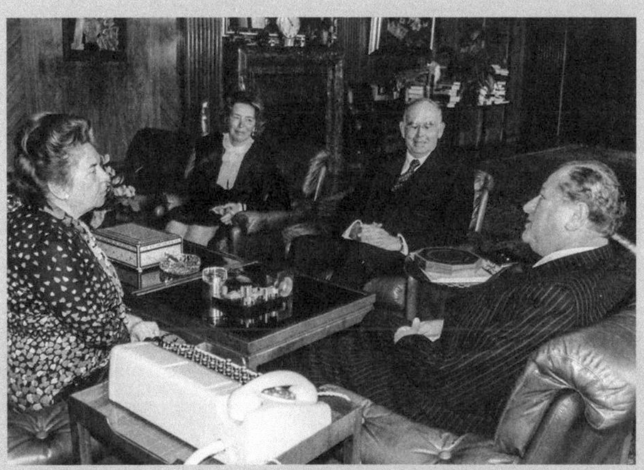

Visiting the Austrian chancellor, Bruno Kreisky, in Vienna, 1978. From left to right: Hertha Firnberg, Irene Ludwig, Peter Ludwig, Bruno Kreisky.
Photo: unnkown

NEUE KUNST:

Ludwig kommt

Einer der weltweit größten Privatsammler bietet den Wienern erstmals einen umfassenden Überblick über die jüngsten Stilrichtungen internationaler Kunst.

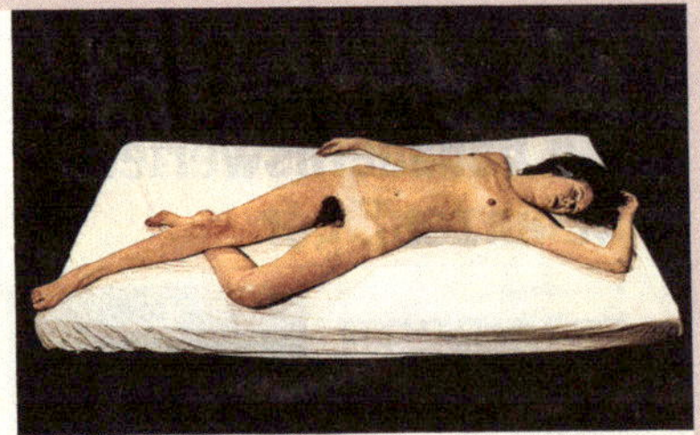

Ein liegender Akt, von John de Andrea naturgetreu aus Polyester und Fiberglas geformt, brachte den Präsidenten des Wiener Künstlerhauses in Pornographieverdacht. Professor Hans Mayr, der mit einer Plakatversion der Liegenden (siehe Farbbild) für die am 8. März beginnende Ausstellung „Kunst um 1970“ werben wollte, wurde von den Geschmacksrichtern des gemeindeeigenen Ankündigungsunternehmens „Gewista“ belehrt, daß sie derlei nicht affichieren würden. Eine zweite Version mit dem Überdruck „Kunstzensur“ wurde gleichfalls nicht akzeptiert. Nun wird ein mit blutroter Farbe übertünchtes Plakat darauf aufmerksam machen, daß „die Weltspitze der modernen Kunst nach Wien kommt“ (Mayr).

Die Ausstellung, vom deutschen Sammlerpaar Dr. Peter und Irene Ludwig zusammengetragen und in der Aachener „Neuen Galerie“ beheimatet, umfaßt 88 wesentliche Werke der Pop-art, von Fotorealismus und Konzeptkunst. Das Künstlerverzeichnis liest sich wie ein Gotha neuester Malerei.

Es bringt Popklassiker wie Andy Warhol, Roy Lichtenstein und Robert Rauschenberg, Love-Sprüche von Robert Indiana und Fahnen von Jasper Jones. Die lebensgroßen Figuren von Duane Hanson und John de Andrea sind ebenso vertreten wie der Verpacker Javacheff Christo und der deutsche Konzeptkünstler Joseph Beuys. Neben solchen Namen, die bei Kennern auch hierzulande Augenglänzen hervorrufen, werden Vertreter des neuen, mit fotografischer Genauigkeit gemalten Realismus gezeigt (für Eingeweihte: unter anderem Chuck Close und Ralph Goings).

Der Versicherungswert der Bilder, denen zu spät gekommene amerikanische Museen schon jetzt nachweinen, wurde von Doktor Ludwig mit 40 Millionen Schilling festgesetzt. „In Wahrheit liegt er aber fünf- bis zehnmal so hoch“ (Prof. Mayr).

Für Ludwig, den 52jährigen Schokoladeindustriellen (Marke: „Trumpf“) und promovierten Kunsthistoriker (Thema: „Das Menschenbild Picassos“), ist das aber nur ein Bruchteil seines Kunstschatzes. Die gesamte Sammlung, für den Experten Peter Baum nur mit jenen „des Kaiserhauses und verschiedener Fürstenhäuser“ vergleichbar, füllt neben der Aachener Galerie auch noch ein Museum in Köln. Zwei weitere verwahren Ludwig-Sammlungen mittelalterlicher Werke und Kunst aus dem vorkolumbianischen Amerika.

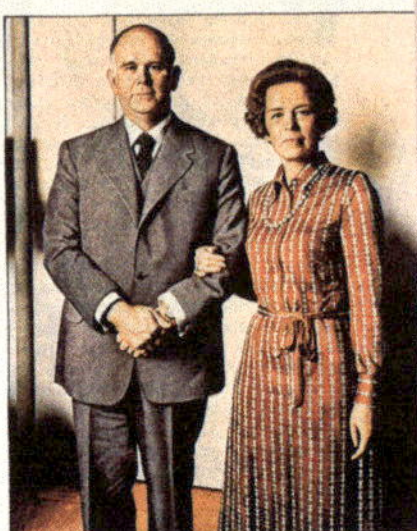

Auf Pop-art und die nachfolgenden Strömungen stürzte sich Ludwig, weil er darin erstmals die Industriegesellschaft künstlerisch verarbeitet sah. Als privater Sammler — der die Öffentlichkeit aber nie aussperrt — kann er eher als die Museen riskieren, neuesten Strömungen nachzujagen und sich dabei gelegentlich auch zu irren.

Mit der Wiener Schau, die auf eine persönliche Bekanntschaft mit dem Fotografen Prof. Mayr zurückgeht, will Ludwig sein internationales Kunstpanorama deshalb vor allem zur Diskussion stellen. Ludwig: „Zustimmung oder Ablehnung sind jedem freigestellt. Unverständnis ist keine Schande.“ ●

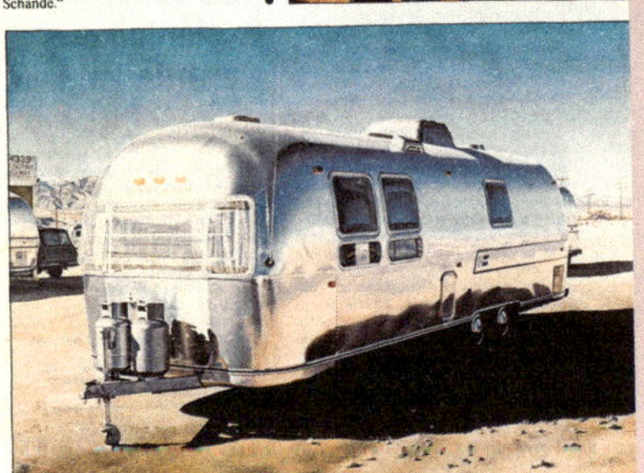

Farbbilder (von oben nach unten): John de Andrea — „Woman on bed“, lebensgroße Polyester- und Fiberglasplastik (1974); Jean-Olivier Hucleux — Porträt des Ehepaares Ludwig, Öl auf Holz (1975/76); Ralph Goings — Wohnwagen, Öl auf Leinwand (1970).

Newspaper article about the exhibition *Kunst um 1970. Art around 1970* at the Künstlerhaus in Vienna.
"Ludwig is Coming," Profil, 1.3.1977

Zu Gast in Wien: Sammlung Ludwig

Minister Firnberg nahm die erste Sendung in Empfang

Der erste Teil jener Leihgaben, die der deutsche Kunstsammler Peter Ludwig der Republik Österreich zur Verfügung stellen will, ist am Freitag in Wien eingetroffen. In einer Lagerhalle neben dem Palais Liechtenstein nahm Wissenschaftsminister Hertha Firnberg die erste Lieferung in Empfang. In dem Palais, das derzeit renoviert wird, werden ab Frühjahr 1979 Teile der Ludwig-Sammlung — eine der bedeutendsten Sammlungen zeitgenössischer Kunst überhaupt — den „Kern“ der Bestände eines neuen österreichischen Museums für moderne Kunst bilden, das durch Objekte vor allem aus dem Museum des zwanzigsten Jahrhunderts ergänzt werden soll.

Als einen „Impuls zur Auseinandersetzung mit der zeitgenössischen Kunst“ bezeichnete Minister Firnberg die Schaffung des neuen Museums, das in dem Barockpalais im neunten Bezirk seine nicht unumstrittene Heimstätte finden soll. Peter Ludwigs großzügige Spende habe die Konstituierung eines solchen Museums überhaupt erst ermöglicht, die moderne Kunst werde damit endgültig ihre Bleibe in Österreich finden. Die Erweiterung der Sammlung durch Bestände des Museums des zwanzigsten Jahrhunderts und anderer staatlicher österreichischer Sammlungen sei außerdem ein erster Schritt zu einem „Museumsverbund“, der — unter der Leitung eines „Generalmanagers“ — Österreichs staatliche Ausstellungen miteinander fusionieren solle, stellte die Ministerin fest.

Aus der Sammlung des Aachener Industriellen und Kunstexperten Peter Ludwig wurden 168 Exponate ausgewählt. Das künftige Moderne-Museum, dessen endgültige Benennung derzeit noch ebensowenig feststeht wie der Name seines Direktors, soll nicht als statische Sammlung geführt werden, sondern rund um die Ludwig-Objekte die internationale aktuelle Kunstszene möglichst variabel repräsen tieren. Auch an die Heranziehung großer Wanderausstellungen mit moderner Kunst ist gedacht.

Mit der Bestellung des neuen Museumsdirektors ist eine Kommission befaßt, die die eingelangten zwanzig Bewerbungen zu prüfen hat. Minister Firnberg wies allerdings darauf hin, daß auch Kandidaten in Betracht kommen könnten, von denen keine Bewerbung vorliegt. Als Konsulent überwacht interimistisch Künstlerhauspräsident Hans Mayr die Auswahl und die Übersiedlung der Ludwigschen Leihgaben.

Photo: „Die Presse“/Blaha

MINISTER FIRNBERG ANGESICHTS NEUER BILDER: WOHLGEMUT

Über das Schicksal des Museums des 20. Jahrhunderts herrscht derzeit noch Ungewißheit. Nach der Giacometti-Ausstellung, die in dem Pavillon im Schweizergarten von Jänner bis April 1979 zu sehen sein wird, soll das Museum einstweilen zwecks Generalrenovierung geschlossen werden — etwa zu demselben Zeitpunkt, zu dem das Moderne-Museum im Palais Liechtenstein seine Tore öffnen wird.

Die bevorstehenden Veränderungen in Österreichs Museenlandschaft entfachen bereits rege Diskussionen. So wird am 10. Oktober in der Galerie nächst St. Stephan ein Forum aus Künstlern und Fachleuten die Frage erörtern: „Museumskrise in Wien?“ khi

Newspaper article about the arrival of the first loaned artworks in Vienna.
"Visiting Vienna: The Ludwig Collection," Die Presse, 7.10.1978

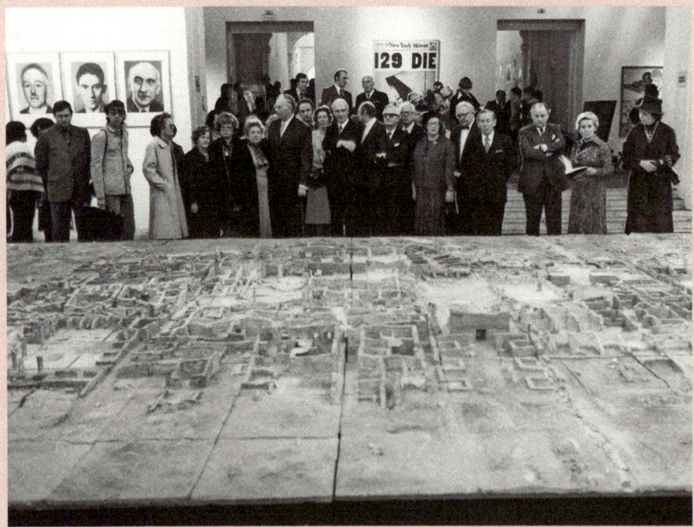

Opening of the exhibition *Kunst um 1970. Art around 1970* at the Künstlerhaus in Vienna, 1977.
Photo: unknown

MUSEUM MODERNER KUNST

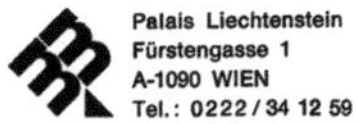

Palais Liechtenstein
Fürstengasse 1
A-1090 WIEN
Tel.: 0222 / 34 12 59

Museum d. 20. Jahrhunderts
Schweizergarten
A-1030 WIEN
Tel.: 0222 / 65 51 21

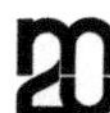

Herrn
Prof.Dr.Dr.h.c.
Peter Ludwig
Schokoladefabrik Leonard Monheim

Deliusstrasse 6
D - 51 AACHEN

Wien, 1980 - 12 - 19
Dr. Ro/Hö

MUSEUM MODERNER KUNST
STIFTUNG LUDWIG

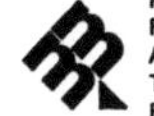

Palais Liechtenstein
Fürstengasse 1
A-1090 WIEN
Tel.: 0222/34 12 59
Fax: 0222/34 52 70

Museum d. 20. Jahrhunderts
Schweizergarten
A-1030 WIEN
Tel.: 0222/78 25 50
Fax: 0222/78 97 39

Herrn
Prof.DDr.h.c.mult Peter Ludwig
Süsterfeldstraße 19o
D-51oo Aachen

Wien, 1992-o5-21
to

MUSEUM MODERNER KUNST STIFTUNG LUDWIG WIEN

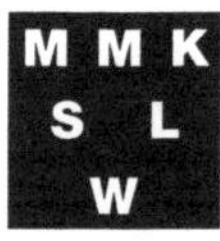

Herrn
Prof. DDr. Peter Ludwig

Eupener Str. 281
D-52076 Aachen

Wien, 10. Dezember 1993

Palais Liechtenstein
Fürstengasse 1
A-1090 Wien
Tel. +43/1/317 69 00
Fax +43/1/317 69 01

Museum des 20.Jh.
Schweizer Garten
A-1030 Wien
Tel. +43/1/78 25 50
Fax +43/1/78 97 39

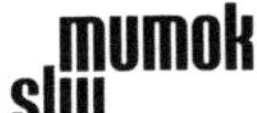

Museum moderner Kunst
Stiftung Ludwig Wien
im MuseumsQuartier

Österreichische Ludwig-Stiftung
Präsident HR Dr. Gerhard Sailer
Säulenstiege
Hofburg
1010 Wien

Letterheads of the Museum moderner Kunst Stiftung Ludwig (Modern Art Museum Ludwig Foundation) in Vienna from 1980 to 2001.

HUNGARY CZECHOSLOVAKIA ROMANIA

Throughout the 1980s, Peter and Irene Ludwig developed a greater interest in Eastern Europe. In the mid-1980s, they met **Lóránd Hegyi**, whose work as a curator in Budapest gave him excellent contacts in, and insights into, the art scene there. In 1987, the Ludwigs proposed to the Hungarian government to establish both a foundation and a museum in Budapest. The director of the Műcsarnok, or Kunsthalle, in Budapest, Katalin Néray, was an important supporter of the project and helped to initiate it. On March 24, 1988, the Ludwig Foundation in Hungary was established. In February of the following year, the exhibition *Kunst heute in Ungarn* (*Art Today in Hungary*), consisting of contemporary Hungarian art, could be seen in Aachen's Ludwig Forum. The Ludwig Collection later acquired thirty-five works from the exhibition, including works by Ákos Birkás, László Fehér, and István Nádler. On June 4, 1991, the Ludwig Múzeum opened inside of the Hungarian National Gallery. The museum's founding was accompanied by a donation of seventy international works and a permanent loan of ninety-five further works from the Ludwig Collection. In December 1996, the museum expanded into additional rooms in the National Gallery. Under the new name of Ludwig Múzeum – Museum of Contemporary Art, its collection of international art was exhibited alongside contemporary Hungarian art. The Ludwig Foundation in Hungary was disbanded in 2006, but the Ludwigs' commitment continues to this day through the activities of the Ludwig Múzeum.

However, not all of the projects initiated by the Ludwigs in Eastern Europe bore fruit, such as in Bulgaria and Poland, where initial talks in the early-1990s failed. Plans for the founding of a museum in Czechoslovakia reached a somewhat more concrete form. In 1987, the exhibition *Zeitgenössische Kunst aus den Sammlungen des Prof. Dr. Peter Ludwig in Aachen* (*Contemporary Art from the Collection of Prof. Dr. Peter Ludwig of Aachen*) took place in Prague in the riding hall of Wallenstein Palace. Organised by the National Gallery Prague, the show was a hugely popular success, receiving extensive coverage in the press. The architect **Iva Haendly-Dassen**, who hailed from what was then Czechoslovakia and lived in Aachen, translated the longer newspaper articles about the show. The Ludwigs maintained close ties with Milan Knížák, the director of the Academy of Fine Arts in Prague, from whom they purchased a number of artworks. The possibility of a collaboration with the National Gallery Prague was discussed during a visit the Ludwigs made to Prague in March 1993, where they met with the then president, Václav Havel, among others. There are very few extant documents describing the exact negotiations, but the founding of a Ludwig museum in Prague seems to have been discussed. A subsequent visit to Prague's Trade Fair Palace may well have been connected to such plans. The building had become part of the National Gallery a short time earlier and, as a result, had been extensively renovated. In the end, however, the founding of a museum never came to pass.

Efforts in Romania were similarly promising in their early stages. The Ludwigs' interest in Romanian art was stirred by, among others, the Romanian architect **Radu Dobre-Sima**, a resident of Aachen. Since 1988, Dobre-Sima had been in close contact with Wolfgang Becker, the director of the Neue Galerie – Sammlung Ludwig (New Gallery – Ludwig Collection), and later of the Ludwig Forum für Internationale Kunst (Ludwig Forum for International Art). In 1993, Dobre-Sima set up a scholarship that brought Romanian artists to the Ludwig Forum. During a trip Peter Ludwig made to Romania in November 1994, where he was accompanied by Dobre-Sima, he made connections with artists and the larger cultural scene. Subsequently, Peter and Irene Ludwig offered the president of the Chamber of Deputies, Adrian Năstase, their support for the founding of a contemporary art museum in Bucharest, pledging to contribute international works of art from their collection. The negotiations were to be handled by Dobre-Sima as the Ludwigs' representative, but the project came to a sudden end with Peter Ludwig's tragic death in 1996. In April 1997, the exhibition *Bukarest nach '89: Kunst aus Rumänien* (*Bucharest After '89: Art in Romania Today*) opened at the Ludwig Forum. The exhibition featured the works that Peter Ludwig had acquired for the collection over the previous two years, including pieces by Mihai Buculei, Dan Perjovschi, Paula Ribariu, and Marian Zidaru.

A conversation with **Lóránd Hegyi** about the founding of the Ludwig Múzeum in Budapest, his time as director of the Museum moderner Kunst Stiftung Ludwig in Vienna, and the exchanges between Budapest and Vienna during this time

The interview was conducted at the Hotel Rosso 23 in Florence on August 7, 2019.

LÓRÁND HEGYI (b. 1954, Budapest) is an art historian and curator. From 1972 to 1977, he studied history, art history, and aesthetics at the Eötvös Loránd University in Budapest. Directly following his studies, in 1977, he worked at the Institute for Art History at the Academy of Sciences. In 1989, on the invitation of its director Katalin Néray, he joined the Műcsarnok or Kunsthalle (Palace of Art) in Budapest, where he was head of its international department. At the same time, he taught at Eötvös Loránd University in Budapest and at University of Graz. From 1991 to 1997, he was the organiser of New Sensibility, a biennial series of exhibitions that presented and theoretically reappraised the current trends in Hungarian art. From 1990 to 2001, he was the director of the Museum moderner Kunst Stiftung Ludwig (Modern Art Museum Ludwig Foundation) in Vienna, serving as successor to the founding inaugural director, Dieter Ronte. Hegyi subsequently moved to Naples and worked at the Museum PAN, Palazzo delle Arti di Napoli. From 2003 to 2017, he was director of the Musée d'Art Moderne et Contemporain (Museum of Modern and Contemporary Art) in Saint-Étienne, France.

That was one of the most fascinating and creative times in my career, because from the beginning of the 1980s, both international and Hungarian contemporary art had a strong presence in Hungary.

REGINA WYRWOLL Mr. Hegyi, could you please describe the social and political climate in Hungary during the era of glasnost and perestroika? Were there many international exhibitions, or did you mainly show Hungarian art?

LÓRÁND HEGYI That was one of the most fascinating and creative times in my career, because from the beginning of the 1980s, both international and Hungarian contemporary art had a strong presence in Hungary. There were many reasons for that. At the time, Hungary was considered a model country for potential democratisation. We had very good relations with Germany, which was primarily fostered by the German *Ostpolitik* policy. In 1984, the Hungarian-born investor and philanthropist George Soros, who had emigrated to the US in the middle of the 1950s, founded the Open Society Foundations in New York, which would expand their activities into Budapest. This umbrella organisation in turn coordinated a number of autonomous foundations and institutions in Central and Eastern European countries that showcased the current trends in art of the time. An example is the Soros Center for Contemporary Arts Budapest in the Kunsthalle. While I was in Budapest, I worked together with the head office of the Open Society Foundations in New York, and I continued to do so later on during my years in Vienna. There were also many international exhibitions of contemporary art, like the 1983 Triennal of Small Sculpture held at the Műcsarnok, the Budapest Kunsthalle. The curator and later director, Katalin Néray, showcased many current styles and pieces there. Important contemporary artists participated in this exhibition, from Günther Uecker to Franz West and Bertrand Lavier, to name just a few. I curated a large exhibition myself in 1985 at the Hungarian National Gallery. It was called *Eclectic* and presented forty-four artistic works from across the spectrum of new developments in Hungarian art. There was always, of course, an official tendency toward censorship. There was a line that could not be crossed, a political rather than an aesthetic one. You couldn't just exhibit anything. Direct political statements against the Soviet Union, against the presence of Russian soldiers or things like that, simply couldn't be shown. But we didn't place any restrictions on ourselves in terms of what we showed. We—myself and some young artists—worked according to this principle. The small Fészek Gallery was a kind of artist's club, in effect a subset of the union of cultural workers from the areas of art, theatre, opera, and film, as well as freelance intellectuals. Its exhibition space was in a very nice building in the city centre, a situation typical for Hungary at the time. We exhibited there, which was very important for us as we could put together the exhibition programme with almost complete freedom.

To put it simply, the primary focus of the Communist Party leadership in the 1980s was to create a survival strategy. It was clear that, sooner or later, a radical turning point would come, and this Soviet-style society would not be able to continue—politically, economically or culturally. The simplest way to demonstrate democratisation, tolerance, and the will to open up was through the fields of art and culture. From the mid-1980s, cultural policy was quite tolerant. There were intensive exchanges between Hungarian artists and artists from the West, travel was possible, there was largely free production of films and books in Hungary. We only have to think of the critical and ironic Hungarian films of the time, like those of Gyula Gazdag, Béla Tarr, Pál Sándor, Gábor Bódy, or the experimental films that came out of the Balázs Béla Studio. That was radically different to all the other Communist countries in Europe. We could travel. In the Budapest Kunsthalle, but even more so in the Fészek Gallery, I exhibited artists from Austria, Germany, Italy—regardless of the official cultural policy. I went in Vienna to Lois Weinberger, Franz West, Eva Schlegel, Erwin Wurm, or Hubert Scheibl and said, "We've got this small gallery and want to exhibit your work there." We were all good friends and took care of transporting the works ourselves. The borders were open then, that was important. We put on exhibitions in other countries that presented the progressive, contemporary trends from Hungary, mainly in Germany and Austria. Austria was our base: Vienna and Graz. Dieter Ronte—then the general director of the Museum moderner Kunst in Vienna, which became the Museum moderner Kunst Stiftung Ludwig in 1991—a dear friend and colleague, often came to Hungary. We wrote catalogue texts about Hungarian and Austrian artists together. In Vienna, Ronte had put on a series about Hungarian artists: Dóra Maurer,

Tibor Gáyor, and others. Personally, I was more interested in bringing Austrian or German artists to Hungary.

From the mid-1980s there was, for all intents and purposes, no clear direction in cultural policy. … Chaos, improvisation, and uncertainty were the order of the day—a situation which, in turn, created great latitude for progressive cultural trends.

RW And all that was done before the eyes of the politicians?

LH It was a very exciting albeit contradictory situation. Looking at it objectively, it served to help official politics create the image that Hungary was open to liberalisation and even a pluralisation of culture and politics. But it was also very useful for us. I don't mean that cynically: it was very important that we were able to work in this atmosphere of tolerance, when the party leadership wanted to demonstrate openness and tolerance. We took advantage of that openness. There's something else I would like to say about that: From the mid-1980s there was, for all intents and purposes, no clear direction in cultural policy, as there was no longer clear ideological leadership in the party. Chaos, improvisation, and uncertainty were the order of the day—a situation which, in turn, created great latitude for progressive cultural trends. My first book, *New Sensibility: Change of Paradigm in Contemporary Art* was published by a very good publishing house in 1983 and covered international art from Joseph Beuys up to the New German movement, including the American and Italian Transavantgarde and so on. There were some critical reviews, but the majority were entirely positive: "We've never before had a Hungarian book, in Hungarian, by a Hungarian author, about contemporary art." The exhibitions in the Hungarian pavilion at the Venice Biennale were very important as well, which from 1986 on presented the current state of Hungarian art. Peter Ludwig always visited the Hungarian pavilion and acquired important works for Aachen, such as the large work by Géza Samu, *Etwas geschieht mit dem Gabeldings* (*Something Happens with the Forked Thing*) (1988), and László Fehér's multipart work *Eisenzeichnungen* (*Iron Drawings*) (1990).

[Peter Ludwig] had the reputation in artistic circles of having a vehement and strong personality, while still treating artists with an immensely respectful attitude. That was very likeable—that passion, that emotionality.

RW Good that you mention him! When did you meet Peter Ludwig?

LH If I remember correctly, it was in 1984. The occasion was his visit to an exhibition of new art in the Fészek Gallery that I curated. Ludwig wasn't with his wife on that occasion, but was accompanied by Katalin Néray, director of the Budapest Kunsthalle, who was a passionate, spirited supporter of contemporary art. Beginning in 1986, she curated the exhibitions in the Hungarian pavilion at the Venice Biennale, making a very significant contribution to the promotion of contemporary art in Hungary at the time. She curated the exhibitions and I wrote the catalogue texts. Ludwig didn't just come to Venice for the openings of the Biennale but had also come to Budapest itself much earlier. I visited many contemporary artists with him there and informed him about the current atmosphere in the cultural scene.

RW Can you remember what kind of impression Peter Ludwig made on you?

LH Let me start by saying that he had the reputation in artistic circles of having a vehement and strong personality, while still treating artists with an immensely respectful attitude. That was very likeable—that passion, that emotionality. However, he was always very formal. When he came together with his wife, the two of them looked like typical German bourgeoisie, like those described by Thomas Mann. He was always reserved. It was noticeable that he was always very direct when he spoke to artists or asked them questions. That wasn't typical collector behaviour, nor was it typical curator behaviour. Curators tend to be more friendly, more intimate. He, by contrast, was very formal, but at the same time passionate and curious: "And what do you have there? Could you show it to me?" The artists showed him everything, of course. For instance, in Fehér's studio, he asked, "Why do you always paint this figure? What does it mean?" He asked very specific questions, which made some artists almost nervous, as not all artists can verbalise what they paint. There were also some very good discussions. Actually, many artists were afraid of him, although he was never aggressive or dictatorial. Instead he showed a passionate curiosity, but also expected precisely formulated answers. That was striking.

RW When he purchased works, how was it done? Was it conducted through a state art trading house, or was it handled privately?

LH Of course I don't know about every purchase. When I was present he always spoke directly with the artists. Back then I drove an old Zastava, which were produced in Yugoslavia under licence from Fiat. It was very small, based on a Fiat 600 or something like that. But Ludwig didn't want to take taxis or to use an official car from the Kunsthalle or some other institution. He asked, "Is that your car, Mr. Hegyi?" He got into this tiny car and came with me. He didn't want to show off that he was rich, that he could do whatever he wanted. Instead, he really wanted to see how people lived. We went to see Károly Kelemen, László Fehér, László Mulasics, Ákos Birkás—we visited all the important, leading artists of the time. He often asked: "What does that cost? And what does that one cost?" The prices, of course, were very low. For Hungarian painters, 8,000 deutsche marks was a gigantic sum at that time. He almost always chose one, two, or three paintings and had them sent to Aachen, where the exhibition *Kunst heute in Ungarn* (*Art Today in Hungary*) was being planned. What's more, he always had a small object with him—a telephone I think—which he spoke into.

RW A Dictaphone.

LH Exactly! He always spoke into it: "László Fehér told me that these figures represent family and the past." It was almost cute that he dictated so precisely, repeating exactly what the artists had said. That means that he was really interested in the content, in why they were painting the subjects they paint. It was the same when we visited abstract painters like Imre Bak or István Nádler or György Jovánovics. Referentiality, which was a hot topic at the time, greatly interested him. But he was actually more interested in figurative art, especially in four or five specific artists: Kelemen,

Fehér, Birkás, Mulasics, and Sándor Pinczehelyi. When he chose artworks, he first dictated a couple of sentences and then spoke—almost in secret—with his wife, if she was there. And then, he would suddenly say: "Yes! Look, I want this picture, this picture, this picture! What do you say to that?" The artist would react to that: "Well … I don't know. 6,000 or eight 8,000 marks!?" Those were the prices in those days. Often Ludwig would counter: "Yes, but I'm buying three. Will you give me a discount?" Then he would say how much he was willing to pay. And the artists were, in ninety-nine percent of cases, usually very happy. However, Ludwig didn't purchase all of the works in the exhibition in Aachen in 1989. He made a selection. In the end, around half of the exhibited works stayed in Aachen and formed the core of Ludwig's collection of Hungarian art. This bulk purchase was handled by a company from Budapest called INART. After 1989, Ludwig continued to occasionally buy works, but mostly through private galleries.

Everything was in flux, everything was fluid and unclear. Everything lacked legal clarity, just as it did aesthetically.

RW How were the works brought to Germany?

LH There were two organisations that dealt with art. But the artists whose works Ludwig purchased were sometimes members of neither, not only because they were still too young, but also because their work represented contemporary artistic positions that stood in contrast to those of the official organisations. And this was despite the fact that, by then, there was no longer a clear sense of what so-called officially tolerated art was even supposed to look like! Anything that could be sold, you tried to sell. There were no art foundations or anything like that. One of the organisations was more focussed on social security, health insurance, and providing artist studios. The other organisation, which was more like an art dealership and agency that represented certain artists at their own art fairs, functioned like a gallery managed by state hands. Everything was in flux, everything was fluid and unclear. Everything lacked legal clarity, just as it did aesthetically. There were also two or three new small state companies that acted like private galleries. This is all standard for a transition phase. Today you would call it reform Communism. That is, you sought to devise models in which capitalist economics was practised to an extent under the Communist Party leadership. The majority of works were transported by the artists themselves. If the Kunsthalle put on an exhibition somewhere like Germany or Austria, Katalin Néray would also transport other paintings into the country. There was also no oversight as to whether the forty pictures that left Hungary ever returned. If only twenty came back to Hungary, nobody really took much notice. When we held an exhibition in collaboration with Alexander Tolnay, a Hungarian art historian who lived in Germany, at the Villa Merkel in Esslingen, it was a big transport job, around 120 paintings, some of them large format. That was an official Hungarian art transport job, because it was going to an official exhibition space. Sales were good and nobody asked, "Where are the paintings?" It was, in every sense, a time of transition.

RW And Peter Ludwig?

LH I can recall that Ludwig had seen a beautiful series by Fehér, very melancholic, nostalgic images, park scenes from Budapest in which delicate, ethereal figures appear, as if from the past. Beautiful images. He bought one of them, *Aus Tác* (*From Tác*) (1987). Fehér transported it to Aachen himself. Peter Ludwig was very interested in and had a special affinity for Fehér's paintings. It was because he rightly saw in his pictorial narratives something historical, something communal, such as the life, the history, the fate of the people of Budapest—that is to say a narrative of history or cultural history, in which something universal, something fateful, was embodied. In this sense, one could say that Ludwig was a romantic, that he looked for something empathic and fateful in art, in contemporary painting—and that the paintings he loved touched him very deeply on a personal level.

Of course, this openness also developed into the previously mentioned political objective of promoting cultural tolerance, pluralism, the freedom to demonstrate …

RW Did you follow the negotiations regarding the establishment of a Ludwig museum in Budapest?

LH Officially, I wasn't involved, that was Néray. I often travelled with her though, and we would discuss it then. The Soros Center for Contemporary Art in the Kunsthalle in Budapest, which belonged to the Open Society Foundations, had opened in 1985. They of course had clear political objectives: How can a new *open society* be created using peaceful methods under late Communism or reform Communism? Soros supported art and culture generally, including literature, translation, and more, as well as economic and sociological research. This gave rise in 1991 to what later became the Central European University in Budapest, which Viktor Orbán has since forced out of the country. It has been based in Vienna since 2019. Soros was also active in Hungary when Ludwig came on the scene there. But he wasn't the only visitor that regularly came to Budapest. You could say that, for a time, Budapest was *in*. Curators and art historians like Jan Hoet, Pierre Restany, Harald Szeemann, Achille Bonito Oliva, and Dieter Honisch had visited the country since the end of the 1970s. Michael Kluth made a documentary for German television about the Fészek Gallery and the alternative art scene in Budapest. Similarly, Ronte often visited the artist studios in Budapest and frequently presented Hungarian art in Vienna. Ronte had been the director of the Palais Liechtenstein and the 20er Haus since 1979, where the Ludwig Collection was then on display. His role as a middleman, in both directions, was particularly important because he was in direct contact with Peter Ludwig. He was always involved in any discussion about how a Ludwig museum might be founded in Hungary, in Budapest. There was always a positive response from the official Hungarian cultural politicians. Of course, this openness also developed into the previously mentioned political objective of promoting cultural tolerance, pluralism, the freedom to demonstrate, and friendly dialogue with the West and, above all, with Western social democracy. A Ludwig museum in Budapest was the ideal fulfilment of this policy. I have to stress once more that fundamental change was in the air, even if no one knew how and when it would happen. As early as 1984, Mikhail Gorbachev's so-called perestroika was already in the offing, expectations were high, and the political mood was one of suspense and vibrancy.

RW Which minister was responsible for the Ludwig Múzeum?

LH I can't remember who the minister was; the more glasnost, perestroika, reform Communism, and liberalisation developed, the quicker such governmental positions changed hands. Before long, even the long-time general secretary of the Hungarian Socialist Workers' Party (Magyar Szocialista Munkáspárt), János Kádár, was no longer in office. He was succeeded by Károly Grósz, followed by Miklos Németh as prime minister, who was like Gorbachev, a real dismantler of the system. There were a number of ministers of culture. One was a professor of history, I believe. His name was Glatz, Ferenc Glatz. He was the one from the government side of things who clearly committed himself to the idea of a Ludwig museum and got things going. Of course, Néray did ninety percent of the work, and Ludwig came to Budapest increasingly often. She kept telling me elatedly that things were progressing very well. The discussion of where the museum should be located was, of course, very important. In the end, it was housed on the castle mount, where a part of the National Gallery is located in the Buda Castle. As far as I am aware, there were no major difficulties in determining its legal structure and figuring out questions regarding the selection and number of works.

RW Did Ludwig hold any exhibitions in Budapest with works from his collection during this period?

LH I can't remember. It was only possible to hold large-scale exhibitions from his collection in the Budapest Kunsthalle. But Ludwig often showed Hungarian art in Aachen. I was invited a number of times to give talks as part of such exhibitions. Evelyn Weiss, the deputy director of the Museum Ludwig in Cologne, Wolfgang Becker, the director of the Neue Galerie (New Gallery) in Aachen, and Dieter Ronte all came to Hungary regularly. Weiss also worked very closely with Néray and advised her.

RW One part of the agreement regarding the Ludwig museum and the Hungarian National Gallery that never came to fruition was that the works of contemporary art already belonging to the National Gallery were to go into the Ludwig museum.

LH Yes. As far as I know, the main problem was that the Hungarian National Gallery, which had been founded in 1957, a year after the uprising that was suppressed by the Russians, was organised somewhat haphazardly. Back then, the externally located departments of the Szépművészeti Múzeum, the Museum of Fine Arts, were merged with various public and private collections. Its holdings included Gothic art, art from the Renaissance and the Baroque, as well as art from the nineteenth and twentieth centuries, with a special focus on artists of the Secession movement—who were, by the way, all men. The government of the time wanted to demonstrate that they were creating a museum for *the* Hungarian art, in which contemporary Hungarian artists were also represented. However, it was never really thought out in terms of art history or museology. What period should the National Gallery begin with? What should be done with artists of the 1920s, 30s, and 40s? And what should be done with works that date back to the former monarchy, or that come from the various nations that were part of the former Kingdom of Hungary, like Romania, Yugoslavia, or Czechoslovakia? Similarly, there were artists who were not Hungarian but were active in Hungary prior to 1918, due to the multinational nature of the monarchy. Were they not Hungarian artists? There was a lot of discussion as to whether there was any logic to it. If they had been more courageous—although in the 1950s that wasn't realistically possible—then a museum of contemporary art would have been created without restrictions. That would have been the logical thing to do, a chronological supplement to the Museum of Fine Arts, comparable to the Louvre, the Musée d'Orsay, and the Centre Pompidou in Paris. But that wasn't what happened. Instead the result was a hodgepodge. In spring 1957, there was an exhibition, a political demonstration, which was called *Spring Show*. It only took place once, although it had been initially planned to occur every year. It was a huge exhibition in four sections in the Kunsthalle, one of which included abstract and nonfigurative works. These were, owing to their nature, not officially recognised. The exhibition was intended to demonstrate the liberality of the new government. After the Hungarian Uprising, there was this dreadful retorsion, a retribution: many hundreds of people sat in prison, like the author Tibor Déry, or were even executed, and many people emigrated. The government needed something with which to show its people: We are not Stalinists. We won't continue the things the Stalinist governments did. We are more open. From the end of the 1950s, a relatively open cultural policy developed.

RW And in that period the National Gallery was founded?

LH Yes, with a programme that was unclear and, in my opinion, handicapped from the outset, because they simply didn't know how they should structure the museum and its programme. There were no clear-cut decisions. The Museum of Fine Arts still existed and showed art from antiquity to the end of the nineteenth century. It was paradoxical: Communism was officially pursued in the government's international policies, while in the middle of the twentieth century, it founded the National Gallery in Budapest with a programme of romantic nationalism that belonged more to the beginning of the nineteenth century. Nevertheless, the Museum of Fine Arts continued to acquire modern art. So no conceptual borders were defined. The Ludwig Collection would have picked up where the Museum of Fine Arts left off, as Ludwig collected international and contemporary art. Back then, however, the principal aim of the new National Gallery was to keep contemporary artists who were living and working in Hungary happy by purchasing and showing their works. The so-called modern collection of the National Gallery consisted chiefly of works from the 1940s to the 1980s, when many artworks—which are less valued today—were acquired, mainly former state art or art tolerated or supported by the state, Socialist Realism. That's also when the discussion about Socialist Realism began, which, paradoxically, was never really valued by museums. Museum staff were educated, they weren't like political officers in the army. They knew full well that ninety percent of this laboured governmental propaganda art from the 1950s had no particular artistic value. The art professors at the academy didn't think much of Socialist Realism either. Rather, these professors counted among the prominent figures of late Post-Impressionism. I mean artists like István Szőnyi or Aurél Bernáth, who were in no way Socialist Realists and virtually never painted politically themed works. In the 1970s and 1980s, there were fewer and fewer professors who represented any sort of ideological artistic position. The influence of New Objectivity was very strong, as was that of the Italian *ritorno all'ordine* (return to order), a movement that propagated a form of Neoclassicism. Everything that was bought and shown there actually had very little to do with official Socialist Realism in an ideologically rigorous sense. It was instead a presentation in the spirit of the popular front: we show everything!

When Ludwig came, Néray was, naturally, his contact person when it came to questions of art. She was always present. Everyone in Hungary knew that she was the one who, as director of the Kunsthalle, had radically and without compromise shown contemporary art, both Hungarian and international. There was no alternative other than her becoming the director of a Ludwig museum.

RW The director of the National Gallery back then declined to partake in an interview that included these questions. Do you know why?

LH He was likely not a great supporter of the project, quite probably for personal reasons. Presumably he knew that he didn't have the standing necessary to be a future director of the Ludwig Múzeum. And he also knew that if the National Gallery no longer existed, then he would, of course, no longer be its director. Throughout the entire history of the National Gallery, there were repeatedly serious museological discussions about whether the institution had any sort of functional legitimacy or not. Back then I often said that they should simply continue to collect within the framework of a new, expanded museum of fine arts, or that the existing museum should be divided along chronological and historical lines, let's say from antiquity until the end of the nineteenth century and then from the beginning of modern art through contemporary art, that is 1900 to the present day. Then historical chronology would be the defining factor, instead of the unclear category of national art, which is quite anachronistic for a new museum in this day and age.

RW Did you know the director, Mr. Bereczky?

LH On a personal level, not really, but as a public figure he was well known. He came from a Calvinist family, his father was a priest. His family came from eastern Hungary, a Calvinist region. I believe he had several brothers. He himself was a cultivated individual. I think he was more of a historian then an art historian. In any event, he definitely had no understanding of contemporary art. He was more a director in the business sense, and also a political figure. In that way he seems, from today's perspective, to be a typical figure of the administration's cultural politics sector during late Communism. In a political sense, he tried to be democratic, which doesn't always end up meaning the best for art.

RW That's true.

LH In the 1980s, when Bereczky was the director, the permanent collection of the National Gallery was shown differently, in a broader and more comprehensive manner. For instance, it included Hungarian Constructivists and Expressionists, all the big names from Symbolism, Impressionism, Post-Impressionism, through to the artists of the 1980s. But one thing is certain: he was definitely not a supporter of the Ludwig project. However, he also didn't have the power to stop it. Of course, Ludwig negotiated at a ministerial level, and if the minister wants something … When Ludwig came, Néray was, naturally, his contact person when it came to questions of art. She was always present. Everyone in Hungary knew that she was the one who, as director of the Kunsthalle, had radically and without compromise shown contemporary art, both Hungarian and international. There was no alternative other than her becoming the director of a Ludwig museum.

RW And did she become …?

LH Exactly. She was the first director. She said, "I've been at the Kunsthalle for long enough."

I had a long discussion with Peter Ludwig. … The topic of the Austrian Ludwig museum came up too, as there hadn't been a director there for a number of months.

RW How did it come about that you became the director of the Palais Liechtenstein and the 20er Haus, which later became the Museum moderner Kunst Stiftung Ludwig?

LH Well, that was simply a logical consequence of my being increasingly in Vienna for exhibitions and lectures. In the second half of the 1980s, I published six books, as well as many articles and catalogue texts. In 1986, the sensational Venice Biennale took place, involving four Hungarian artists who were highly significant for the art scene of the time: Imre Bak, Ákos Birkás, István Nádler, and Károly Kelemen. Two generations, all of whom represented a new, eclectic, somewhat provocative, and—in relation to the historical avant-garde—revisionary direction that was present in contemporary Hungarian art at the time. Bak represented an intellectual, theoretically-based postmodern post-geometry, while Kelemen filled his pictorial narratives with references to art history and figurative imagery. Birkás and Nádler represented a more expressive or meditative style. These subversive, critical perspectives were completely new in Hungary at that time and were challenged from all sides. Néray was the curator and I wrote the catalogue texts. Together, we also curated the two subsequent Biennale exhibitions, in 1989 and 1990, in the same roles. In 1990, which was the first Biennale exhibition after the fall of the Iron Curtain and was dedicated to Fehér's works, Peter and Irene Ludwig remained at the Hungarian pavilion long after the opening. They purchased the large-format, multipart sculpture *Eisenzeichnungen* (1990), which was sent to Aachen immediately after the exhibition. At the 1988 Biennale, the Ludwigs had also purchased a large sculptural piece from the Hungarian pavilion, *Etwas geschieht mit dem Gabeldings* (1987–88) by Géza Samu. I had a long discussion with Peter Ludwig, who was very interested in the current changes in cultural policy. The topic of the Austrian Ludwig museum came up too, as there hadn't been a director there for a number of months; the departure of Ronte in 1989 had left a vacuum. Néray never considered going to Vienna as she wanted to establish the Ludwig Múzeum in Budapest. I, on the other hand, was increasingly present in Austria. I taught at the university in Graz, held exhibitions in Vienna—sometimes in collaboration with Viennese galleries—knew and regularly visited many Austrian artists, and, for many years, organised the exhibition series *Positionen Wien-Budapest* (*Positions Vienna-Budapest*). I somehow became a liaison between Vienna and Budapest—and that's how I met Erhard Busek.

RW He was the minister then?

LH He was the minister of science and research until 1994, and then minister of education and cultural affairs until 1995. More important, however, was the fact that he was chairman of the Austrian People's Party. This meant he was the vice-chancellor, because, for many years, Austria was governed by what was known as the grand coalition of the Social Democrats and the People's Party. Busek was a passionate central European who personally knew a multitude of figures from the fields of literature, philosophy, and the then Democratic-opposition political milieu. He also organised conferences about the future of central Europe to which he often invited me. Busek was also friends with the former president of Czechoslovakia Václav Havel, the essayist and author György Konrád, and the Polish civil rights activist and historian Jacek Kuroń.

RW Busek was the successor to Minister Hertha Firnberg, who helped initiate the Österreichische Ludwig-Stiftung für Kunst und Wissenschaft (Austrian Ludwig Foundation for Art and Science). Did Ronte not want to stay in Vienna?

LH He mentioned from time to time that he eventually wanted to return to Germany. It wasn't that he was dissatisfied with the museum or his position. Personally, I never had the aim of permanently staying in Vienna. Instead, I wanted to go to Germany, and I often worked there. For example, I was invited to the Folkwang Museum in Essen. I made documentaries with Michael Kluth about the contemporary art scene in Budapest and, of course, did a series of exhibitions in Mannheim, Dortmund, and Duisburg. I was also friends with Christoph Brockhaus, who was head of the Graphic Arts and Photography Collections at the Museum Ludwig in Cologne from 1970, special commissioner for the new construction of the Wallraf-Richartz-Museum / Museum Ludwig, and head of the Lehmbruck Museum in Duisburg beginning in 1985. And I knew Marc Scheps, the director of the Museum Ludwig in Cologne at the time, and his deputy Evelyn Weiss. So I was known in, and knew my way around, the German "Ludwig world."

The more we worked together on different projects—the Soros foundation, the Ludwig museum, the expo for Vienna and Budapest—the more often I came to be seen as someone who could be a possible successor to Ronte.

RW As far as I remember, there was a call for applications for the position of director of the Palais Liechtenstein and the 20er Haus, which was a federal museum. Who was responsible for the selection?

LH Erhard Busek. I had met Busek a number of times, including at a conference about central Europe. That was my favourite subject—I had always been interested in history. I spoke to him at length about central Europe, about politics, culture, art. As minister of science and research, he was responsible for finding a new director for the Palais Liechtenstein and the 20er Haus. Peter Ludwig knew him too, of course, and they got on very well. There was a third person to whom I am also very grateful, and that was Thomas Messer, who was director of the Guggenheim Museum in New York for twenty-seven years. That was my other connection because Messer knew Soros. Messer came from Bratislava. His mother was Hungarian and his father was Austrian. He spoke five languages and regularly visited Budapest, Vienna, and Bratislava. We met in 1984 in New York at one of the conferences about founding the Soros foundation, to which I'd been invited. From this meeting, there rapidly developed a lifelong friendship and professional collaboration. In his later projects, he often brought me in as a cocurator. We worked together in Barcelona at the Fundación Bancaria la Caixa, as well as in Frankfurt, Vienna, and Belgrade. He was both a friend and a father figure, a great man.

RW Remarkable. Please tell us how things developed back then.

LH In 1988, the idea of organising an expo for Vienna and Budapest came up. This expo was intended to foster closer cooperation and economic and cultural rapprochement between Hungary and Austria, in keeping with the spirit of the later years of Hungarian reform Communism. The idea of a joint expo, with the culture of central Europe proposed as its core theme, corresponded with the conception of a new central Europe in the wake of the Cold War and, as such, with Busek's political ideals, which also held strong support from Hungarian opposition intellectuals. Discussion intensified in 1989, the year the Iron Curtain fell. It was to be a great event between two countries with an open border, rife with symbolism. All of the leading political figures—the Socialists, those who were still Communist, the reform Communists, as well as the liberals and representatives of the People's Party in both countries—agreed: this expo was going to happen! Messer had the idea that the expo should instead represent the cooperation and the cultural structure of the new central Europe. He said: "Commerce and business are coming anyway, but we should get to know each other. We should eliminate our prejudices, we should open up to each other." And so we all came together: Messer, Busek, Ludwig, and Néray. The more we worked together on different projects—the Soros foundation, the Ludwig museum, the expo for Vienna and Budapest—the more often I came to be seen as someone who could be a possible successor to Ronte. Messer said that if one really seriously believed in changing the political situation—not just political openness, the end of the Cold War, and opening the borders—then one had to find a new way of thinking about culture, and that such a change was required in the cultural institutions too. Peter Ludwig was a strong supporter of that, as it was exactly what he had practised through his visits and acquisitions in Russia, Bulgaria, Romania, and Hungary. Slowly but surely, the idea of Ronte's successor coming from Budapest or Prague came to the fore. It was the logical next step. The relationships with Budapest were growing stronger. Ludwig had founded museums in both Vienna and Budapest. Consequently, the idea was sown that somebody from Budapest should be brought to the museum in Vienna.

He said: "I don't want a Ludwig mausoleum or a Ludwig department within the museum. Instead you should work with the art as you and your staff, on the basis of your expertise, see fit." That was, for me, a refreshing sense of freedom.

RW But there *was* a call for applications?

LH Yes, there were actually two calls for applications for the position of director. There was a committee tasked with making a selection, but they couldn't agree on one, so nobody was chosen. I never officially applied for the position. There was a short interim of half a year because Ronte didn't wait for a successor. I started in autumn 1990 and held the position for twelve years. In 2002, Edelbert Köb succeeded me.

RW A problem quickly arose for you: the Republic of Austria had to return the Palais Liechtenstein to the House of Liechtenstein.

LH At that point in time, the conversion of the old Messequartier into the MuseumsQuartier had been planned for years, but had led to long-lasting, heated debate because of the architecture involved. It was only in 2001 that the newly created MuseumsQuartier finally opened. After we left the Palais Liechtenstein in spring 2001, we used the 20er Haus as an exhibition space until we moved to the MuseumsQuartier. We twice held temporary exhibitions in the Vienna Künstlerhaus. For instance, one of the last exhibitions was a presentation of the Ludwig Collection with its new acquisitions: *Zwischenquartier: Das Museum Moderner Kunst Stiftung Ludwig Wien im Künstlerhaus* (*Interim Quarter: The Modern Art Museum Ludwig Foundation Vienna in the Künstlerhaus*). To be honest, I was very happy in the Palais Liechtenstein. It wasn't just me, almost every artist was fascinated by the Baroque building. The tension created between contemporary art and the Baroque architecture inspired them and the public in equal measure. The large installations in the huge Hercules Hall, with its red marble floor, golden stucco, and Andrea Pozzo's ceiling fresco, were unbelievably attractive and unique. On the second floor was the permanent collection, which was more classically modern, ranging from Expressionism to the end of the 1950s and the beginning of the 1960s. The first floor was mostly filled with works from the Ludwig Collection: Pop Art and German painting, along with some new acquisitions that I made with the support of the Österreichische Ludwig-Stiftung für Kunst und Wissenschaft, which had been founded in 1981 as a national foundation. The museum belonged to the state, and the national foundation supports it to this day.

RW And where was the Wolfgang Hahn Collection from Cologne housed, which had come to Vienna in 1978?

LH The Hahn Collection was in the Palais Liechtenstein too, and we regularly exhibited it or presented special exhibitions that included works from the collection. My idea was not to keep the Ludwig and Hahn Collections separate, but to show them combined and grouped according to trends, periods, and a variety of themes. Ludwig supported the idea one hundred percent. He said:

"I don't want a Ludwig mausoleum or a Ludwig department within the museum. Instead you should work with the art as you and your staff, on the basis of your expertise, see fit." That was, for me, a refreshing sense of freedom. Not once in twelve years did he make a critical comment along the lines of: "Why are my paintings not on display?" He also never used the words "*our* paintings" or "*my* paintings." One of the last acquisitions with the assistance of the Board of Trustees of the Österreichische Ludwig-Stiftung für Kunst und Wissenschaft was in 2001. It was a gigantic Jannis Kounellis installation, *Untitled (Boat)*, which he had created in 1991 at the Berlin Wall. It's a poetic metaphor of freedom: an albatross soaring over the border and these cut up fragments of a ship that was named *Albatross*. That was one of the last purchases I coordinated for the museum. It was then integrated into the permanent collection. I always tried to make acquisitions with and in the spirit of the Ludwig Foundation, both to complement the existing collection and to acquire new works by important contemporary artists, such as Roman Opałka. The Opałka purchase prompted extensive discussions with Peter Ludwig, but we ultimately bought three paintings from 1965, along with photographs.

RW Can you tell me what the discussion was about?

LH At the beginning, he wasn't enamoured with Opałka and didn't really want to buy three paintings. I said, "Yes, but if we don't have more photographs, more paintings, his concept won't be understood." By the way, the very first time I ever saw Opałka's work was at the Folkwang Museum. He became a close friend of mine. He was from Poland, I was from Hungary. We spoke German with each other, although he lived in France. I still believe that he's one of the greatest universal artists that central Europe ever produced. We had a discussion about his work with Peter Ludwig that lasted two or three hours. He wasn't convinced about these purchases. The three paintings, plus the photographs, were relatively expensive too. Ludwig said, "Yes, but we don't need three ..." I kept explaining to him how Opałka painted the pictures in a chronological order, day after day, and planned to continue up until his death. Each time, in each painting, he repeats his idea, from darker to incrementally lighter tones, until the paint is gone from his brush. And then he starts over from the beginning. It creates a beautiful rhythm. It resembles the rhythm of life, the way we do the same things every day. Through this monotonously repetitive process of work, an oeuvre emerges. But the oeuvre becomes more and more spiritual, less and less discernible, increasingly disappears. However, we know with certainty: it's there. From materiality to spirituality, from material power to spiritual maturity. And during this working process, life passes—unstoppably. At some point Ludwig said, "You know, Mr. Hegyi, that's really a very beautiful work, a great artist, a message of truth." The works didn't speak to Ludwig in terms of visual pleasure, because he preferred the sensual, the material—not necessarily figurative art, but "real" painting. But he understood Opałka after our talk. And that's why I persist in saying that he was someone who concentrated on the content. He understood that Opałka's art makes a profound, fundamental statement, it sends a message. That excited him, and in the end he supported me. When I showed the works as part of an exhibition of new acquisitions, he said, "That was a good decision!" So not only did he not forget, but he loved the works and remembered that we had spoken at length about them.

RW Do you think that Peter Ludwig exercised any influence on the hiring of the new director? Did he say anything in support of you?

LH Yes, he had a voice. And he was supportive of me. I know that from Messer. As I said, I never applied for the job. When applications were called for the first time, I was unaware that it was even happening. I knew a lot of people who applied, well-known people—as is always the case—from different cliques. Vienna is a clique-based society: one is from this circle, another from that circle. For some reason, I was outside of all of them. I was known in Austria, I was even popular from an artistic perspective, but I was completely neutral, I wasn't part of any circle. Generally speaking, I didn't know the local scene in Vienna very well. I knew some people, artists mostly. I also knew a lot of the gallery owners. When I was offered the position, it was a decision that came after two unsuccessful rounds of applications. Busek made the decision, and that's how I got the job. Of course, in this context, Ludwig's voice was a powerful one.

RW Did you and Ludwig ever come into conflict? Did you ever have differing opinions?

LH No, never in fact. We had relatively few opportunities to do so because the acquisitions committee didn't meet very often. The recommendations for purchases always came from the director. Normally, all the members supported my recommendations, or else they spoke to Ludwig. These were open discussions. Then he would say, "Yes, if that's what you think, then I'm not against it." He was very reserved and stressed that exhibition policy was in the hands of the current director. Ronte's experience was the same, his decisions regarding exhibitions were never disputed either. The Opałka purchase was the only, let's say discussion rather than dispute, that took place during the time we worked together. Surprisingly, Irene Ludwig was in favour of Opałka. That honestly surprised me, because I always took her to be somewhat more conservative than Ludwig. He liked the first exhibition in Vienna, with Jörg Immendorff at the Palais Liechtenstein in 1991, so much that he came back a second time. But after the opening he said, "You know what, I find it somewhat radical that you have taken down the entire collection." I replied, "Yes, that's true, but that will only happen—maybe—every three years, and only when I would take down the collection anyway to do a new hanging. In the meantime, I'm making use of the rooms of the Palais Liechtenstein, but only those on the first floor." In principle, the second floor was always in use. I said, "It's not good for the museum if the same works are on show for too long and, as a result, important works are never accessible to the public." Irene Ludwig agreed with me: "Peter, that's true. The director is right. It has to be changed every now and then." Of course, there were sculptures in the Ludwig Collection that were too heavy for the old palace. They were shown in the 20er Haus instead. There was never, however, an understanding along the lines of "the Palais Liechtenstein is for the Ludwig Collection and the 20er Haus is for everything else."

RW What was your relationship with Irene Ludwig like?

LH She always made me a little nervous because she never expressed her opinion, not in public at least. She was very reserved and somewhat closed off, but always very nice. I was invited to their home in Aachen a number of times, and she was extremely accommodating there. But she came off as being Peter Ludwig's silent companion. I often didn't really know what she was thinking. Once, at an opening, I recall, my parents were there. I introduced them to Peter and Irene Ludwig and she was very friendly. Years later she asked me, “How is your mother?” When my father died, she told me several times: “Yes, I know how terrible that can be. I’m very sorry.” She was very personable. By contrast, we rarely spoke about art.

RW Did you feel at home in Vienna?

A shift toward conservatism occurred in the People’s Party. … As a foreigner I wasn’t thrilled by this, I have to say, and the whole atmosphere in Vienna wasn’t good.

LH Generally speaking yes, for a long time, with the exception of the first few months. At the beginning I was often labelled a foreigner, as someone focussed on Eastern Europe and an Eastern European art historian, as someone from Eastern Europe or as “the Hungarian director,” as the *Kronen Zeitung* newspaper always wrote. That went on for years. Ronte wasn’t described as “the German director,” but that’s the way it was for me at the beginning. To be honest, I found it all very confusing, because I hadn’t expected that. Maybe I was a little naive, as the Communist Bloc was gone and I was now in a free Europe, without borders, without Soviet troops, without the Iron Curtain.

RW You were in Vienna for twelve years. Why did you finally leave?

LH I think twelve years at one museum is enough. Of course, I didn’t know then that I would be in Saint-Étienne, at the Musée d’Art Moderne et Contemporain, for fourteen years. I was concerned about the situation with the MuseumsQuartier, that was the main reason I left. But there was another one: Peter Ludwig died in 1996 and, with the change in government, Erhard Busek was no longer in the government and had been removed from his position within the party. A shift toward conservatism occurred in the People’s Party. The People’s Party entered a coalition with the Freedom Party of Austria, the FPÖ, in 2000—and we know what happened there. As a foreigner I wasn’t thrilled by this, I have to say, and the whole atmosphere in Vienna wasn't good. That was the political side of things.

RW Were there any other reasons for your departure?

LH I also wasn't convinced by the planning for the MuseumsQuartier. I wasn't against the idea of concentrating the important museums in the city centre. Why not? The Louvre, Musée d'Orsay, and Jeu de Paume are all relatively close to each other, and the Centre Pompidou is in the city centre. So why not?

The idea that the MuseumsQuartier should encompass the Leopold Museum, the Vienna Kunsthalle, and the Museum moderner Kunst Stiftung Ludwig, known as mumok since 2001—as well as other smaller institutions, like the Architekturzentrum Wien (Architecture Centre Vienna) and the Tanzzentrum (Dance Centre), close to the Kunsthistorisches Museum (Museum of Art History) and the Naturhistorisches Museum Wien (Natural History Museum Vienna)—suggested a sense of a permanent festival. That was something I didn't like. I was sceptical, and I let that be known. My arguments were of a museological nature. The area planned for the smaller Leopold Museum was larger than that planned for mumok. I couldn't understand that, not least because we, the older federal museum, were growing faster than that collector's museum, which had only been founded in 2001. On top of that, our storage areas were also reduced.

RW I remember that there were fierce protests against the MuseumsQuartier and the construction of the new museums, which was undertaken by the architecture firm Ortner & Ortner BAUKUNST.

LH The conservative Viennese held mass demonstrations. They carried banners through the city which read, "The museum monster," which referred to the new mumok, or "Black monster," "The bunker museum can't be allowed!", and so on. There was aggressive opposition, which I didn't like. I had a good relationship with the architects, partly because my father was also an architect. We saved what could be saved—delivery routes, elevators—but when one thousand square metres of exhibition space and two thousand square metres of storage space are simply taken away for political reasons … Well, I was really at a loss for words.

The final reason was the MuseumsQuartier operating company. I wasn't convinced then, and this hasn't changed, that institutions as different as those sharing the MuseumsQuartier can work together under an umbrella organisation, where they will be permanently beset by compromises. That's not good. I would have had to make too many compromises at the new location. Until then I had been a very independent museum director, with strong support from Ludwig and Busek. Now I was being reproached: "If you don't do this, you will prevent the new museum." There was enormous pressure, so I resigned.

RW Where did you go?

LH To Naples. There I founded the Museum PAN, Palazzo delle Arti Napoli. With the full support of the city, I set up an institution, of course much smaller than in Vienna, in a four thousand square-metre Baroque palace, the Palazzo Carafa di Rocella. The palace reminded me of the Palais Liechtenstein in Vienna, but it was less elegant, had no frescos, no marble columns, no stucco. But it did have an interesting layout of rooms that was ideal for the presentation of contemporary works. I put together exhibitions for three years, because they didn't have the funds to build a collection. In Naples I continued to work with many Austrian artists—my connections to Vienna remain to this day. Later, as I already mentioned, I went to the Musée d'Art Moderne et Contemporain in Saint-Étienne, where I worked for fourteen wonderful years.

RW Mr. Hegyi, thank you very much for taking the time to talk to us.

A conversation with **Iva Haendly** about how the success of the exhibition of the Ludwig Collection in Prague (1987) led to an attempt to found a museum, as well as the deeply personal relationship between herself and Irene Ludwig

The interview took place in Haendly's house in Aachen on November 28, 2020.

DIPL.-ING. IVA HAENDLY-DASSEN (b. 1942, Hradec Králové, former Czechoslovakia) is an architect and urban planner. After studying architecture at the Czech Technical University in Prague (CVUT), she came to the RWTH University in Aachen in 1965, where she studied the newly-established subject of urban planning. During and following her postgraduate urban planning training, she headed the urban planning department of the Faculty of Architecture at the RWTH. Later stages of her career have included positions in the Office of Cultural Heritage of the City of Aachen and in the Aachen branch of the Cologne regional administration. Due to the suppression of the Prague Spring reforms, Iva Haendly decided to remain in Aachen after completing her studies. In 1972, she joined the Freunde der Neuen Galerie (Friends of the New Gallery Society), which became the Freunde des Ludwig Forums für Internationale Kunst e. V (Friends of the Ludwig Forum for International Art Society) in 1991. Since February 2019, she has been chairperson of the society, which supports the museum both financially and nonmaterially, organises events such as lectures and discussions as well as art and architecture tours, and biennially recognises the work of an artist with the Aachen Art Prize.

I often visited the Neue Galerie. … To my recollection, the newspapers ran headlines like, "Hell must be fumigated!" Of course, I found all that highly interesting.

REGINA WYRWOLL Iva, when did you come to Aachen?

IVA HAENDLY Before I came to Aachen in 1965 for my studies, I lived in Prague. During my studies in Aachen, I returned to Prague once more. Alexander Dubček, leader of the Communist Party, came to power at the beginning of 1968; suddenly, a climate of openness and an optimistic spirit dominated the former Czechoslovakia. Everything could be discussed freely and as a result, I didn't really want to return to Germany. But by August of that year, the Russians came and violently crushed these democratic and liberal aspirations. I was in St. Moritz when I heard that things were precarious in Prague. My parents advised against my return. I had an official travel permit for Germany that was valid for several years. In Switzerland I met Bernd Krüger, a well-known athlete. He came from Krefeld and he drove me to Aachen. So I ended up staying in Aachen, although I had originally planned to go to London.

RW What was the atmosphere like in Aachen in those days?

IH There was an exciting atmosphere. It was the end of the 1960s, beginning of the 1970s. It was fascinating to exchange ideas with the architecture students. We had interesting discussions and looked at buildings that had just been constructed in Germany. An exciting time.

RW And when did you meet Peter Ludwig?

IH Everybody here in Aachen knew him. I often visited the Neue Galerie, which had been founded in 1970 and was renamed three years later as the Neue Galerie – Sammlung Ludwig (New Gallery – Ludwig Collection). The exhibitions by Wolfgang Becker, the young director, were well worth seeing, but the city officials didn't always like them. To my recollection, the newspapers ran headlines like, "Hell must be fumigated!" Of course, I found all that highly interesting. I got to know Peter Ludwig better in 1987 when he arranged the exhibition *Zeitgenössische Kunst aus den Sammlungen des Prof. Dr. Peter Ludwig in Aachen* (*Contemporary Art from the Collection of Prof. Dr. Peter Ludwig of Aachen*) in the riding hall of Wallenstein Palace in Prague, which I was visiting at the time. That location was well-known for holding quality exhibitions. The Ludwig exhibition showed Pop Art and American art for the very first time in Czechoslovakia, I believe. It included wonderful works by Andy Warhol, Robert Rauschenberg, Roy Lichtenstein—from all of those icons. It was incredibly well-attended and ran from September 14 to October 18, 1987, just over a month, all too short unfortunately. Long queues formed at the entrance to the palace. A sensation for Prague. Wolfgang Becker arranged for me to translate three reviews in the Prague newspapers for Peter Ludwig. That was my first personal contact with him. He always returned favours very generously—not with money, I didn't want that. But I received cartons full of boxes of pralines. I was able to give them to all of my relatives in Prague. After that we stayed in touch.

RW But isn't it true that prior to that the two of you had been in indirect contact?

IH Yes. Thanks to Peter Ludwig I had a very interesting encounter with Alexander Burganov. He's a Russian sculptor who back then was one of the official state-sanctioned artists in Russia and has been a professor at the state-run Stroganov Moscow State Academy of Arts and Industry in Moscow since 1987. Ludwig had invited him to Aachen to sculpt a portrait of him and his wife, Irene, which would later be cast in bronze. That was, I believe, in 1980, before the exhibition in Prague. Two years later, in 1982, Ludwig purchased a very large sculpture from Burganov in Moscow: *Krieg und Frieden* (*War and Peace*) (1982). It was a monster, it looked like a cage with a group of fighting horses. It was transported to Aachen in 1984, but arrived broken into thousands of pieces, as it was made of plaster. As a result, Burganov had to come to Aachen later that year in order to restore the sculpture. As Peter Ludwig had heard from Wolfgang Becker, the then director of the Neue Galerie, that I could also speak Russian, he asked me to look after the artist. So I took care of him. Burganov saw his sculpture as depicting a battle between life and death. When it had been reconstructed, it was transported to the conference centre near the casino, the Eurogress. It stood there for a number of years at the entrance to the Europa-Saal (Europe Hall), where concerts still take place. I translated the letter Ludwig wrote to the artist when this location had been found. Since then, Burganov has become very successful. In Brussels, he designed a whole park with his surrealist sculptures. There is also a sculpture park by him in Moscow.

Peter Ludwig saw the huge building [of Prague's Trade Fair Palace] with its two inner courtyards and apparently said, "Well, I think I'll have a problem filling it!"

RW Did you serve as a translator for Ludwig again after the exhibition in Prague in 1987?

IH No, he had gotten to know Jiři Švestka in Prague, who helped him. Švestka is a gallerist and art consultant in Prague and Berlin. Ludwig toyed with the idea of founding a Ludwig museum in Prague.

I learned from Švestka that, during a visit by Peter Ludwig in March of 1993, he had given Ludwig a tour of the Trade Fair Palace in Prague. which was being renovated at the time and would serve as the future home of the National Gallery's modern collection. When it was first completed, the Trade Fair Palace was the largest Bauhaus building and the first functionalist building in 1920s Prague. At the end of 1970, the National Gallery in Prague, which is spread across a number of locations to this day, had acquired the building, which had been damaged by fire. In the 1990s, the building was converted into a museum. Peter Ludwig saw the huge building with its two inner courtyards and apparently said, "Well, I think I'll have a problem filling it!" During this visit, the rector of the Academy of Fine Arts in Prague, Milan Knížák, presented Peter Ludwig with the Gold Medal of the academy, an honour that was being awarded for the first time in this form. Indeed, it was probably the main reason for his visit. On the same trip there was a meeting between Peter Ludwig and President Václav Havel in the garden of the latter's residence in the Prague Castle complex. From what I heard from Jiři Švestka, the curator Ivona Raimanová and an interpreter were also present. At the time of the meeting with Václav Havel, Ivona Raimanová was already the curator of exhibitions in the Belvedere within the castle complex.

It's possible that Ludwig also met Jiři Ševčík in Prague, the then head curator at the Galerie hlavního města Prahy, the Prague City Gallery. Ševčík later became head of the Academy of Fine Arts. He was part of my circle of friends and, at my request, accompanied a group from the Freunde des Ludwig Forums on an art tour to Prague. On his recommendation, I gave lectures at the Academy of Fine Arts in Prague after the fall of the Iron Curtain. And Ivona Raimanová visited me in Aachen during that period.

I would speculate that the reason a Ludwig museum in the National Gallery didn't ultimately work out was because the Czechs, for whom their National Gallery is something of a sacred site, were not prepared to see it renamed as the "Ludwig Museum." The talks about it were conducted at the national, rather than city level.

RW Did Ludwig ever talk about this failed attempt to create a museum?

IH Yes, he talked about it. But I also heard about what happened from Irene Ludwig.

RW Was Ludwig upset that it didn't come to fruition?

IH Yes, of course he was disappointed, because he found the building so wonderful. His previous exhibition in Prague had been such a huge success. It got to him, I think.

RW Who organised the exhibition in 1987? Was it the director of the Neue Galerie – Sammlung Ludwig in Aachen, Wolfgang Becker?

IH No, it was organised by the National Gallery in Prague. It's possible that the Prague curator Ivona Raimanová played a role.

RW I have to ask myself why Ludwig started in Prague so late. At that point, he had already founded museums in Vienna and Budapest, as well as St. Petersburg, and the museum in Beijing was about to be completed, opening very shortly after his death in 1996.

IH I ask myself the same question.

I think [Peter Ludwig] enjoyed provoking narrow-minded people. Becker, as the museum director, was an employee of the city. He had to tolerate receiving a number of warnings, but Ludwig always held a protective hand over him.

RW What was your impression of the relationship between the city of Aachen and Ludwig?

IH The relationship was difficult when things became heated in the press—when the people of Aachen said of the Neue Galerie, "Get rid of it! Tear it down!" The exhibition of the work entitled *Hatstand, Table and Chair* (1969) by Allen Jones, which Ludwig acquired at the beginning of the 1970s from Rudolf Zwirner Gallery, particularly aroused anger. In it, one sees realistic, scantily clad female figures: one is on hands and knees and carries a glass tabletop on her back; another is on her back with her legs drawn up to her chest, on top of which is a cushion and chairback that forms a chair; while the third stands posing as a hatstand. Becker was met by strong blowback from the conservatives. The possible closure of the Neue Galerie was a very real danger and couldn't be quickly assuaged. But he found allies among the RWTH's professors, who supported the new institution. The professors Kurt Lücke, Walter Biemel, and Hugo Jung, well-known figures in Aachen, founded the booster club Freunde der Neuen Galerie (Friends of the New Gallery) in 1971, which I joined a year after it was founded. After the museum moved to the former Brauer umbrella factory building in 1991, the group was renamed the Freunde des Ludwig Forums für Internationale Kunst, an incorporated society of which I am the current chairperson.

RW As members of the Freunde der Neuen Galerie, did you have direct contact with Peter Ludwig?

IH Not necessarily direct, as we never discussed things with each other. Ludwig made his decisions, we made ours. We didn't coordinate.

RW Can you imagine what prompted Ludwig to buy works like the Jones sculptures?

IH I think he enjoyed provoking narrow-minded people. Becker, as the museum director, was an employee of the city. He had to tolerate receiving a number of warnings, but Ludwig always held a protective hand over him.

RW I've heard that Ludwig was a brilliant speaker. Is that true?

IH Yes, he could speak captivatingly about art. I can remember his speech about Andy Warhol's *Portrait of Peter Ludwig* from 1980, which was being shown at the time. It was always fascinating to listen to him, and his anecdotes were very inspiring. That's why his tutorials, which essentially consisted of talks given in front of original works in the Museum Ludwig in Cologne, were particularly popular among art history students. I can personally vouch for that.

RW Did he speak more like an art historian or a collector?

IH He combined both styles of speaking. He had studied art history, so his lectures weren't purely visceral, but it was very personal. He also knew many individuals from the art world well, like Leo Castelli, Mary Boone, and so on. He often talked about his encounters with them.

RW Even after all the anger he inspired among the residents of Aachen, did people still enjoy his talks?

IH Yes, most enjoyed them a lot.

[Irene Ludwig] was clever, down-to-earth, forthright, and had a sense of humour—and she was tolerant, too!

RW What role did Irene Ludwig play?

IH At the very least he always consulted with her, and if she wasn't there with him he would do so by phone. I recall a story from the 44th Venice Biennale in 1990, where the Jeff Koons sculpture *Jeff and Ilona (Made in Heaven)* (1990) was being shown at the Arsenale. Peter Ludwig was determined to acquire that scandalous, large wooden piece, depicting Koons lying atop his wife, the well-known Hungarian-Italian porn actress and parliamentarian Cicciolina (Elena Anna Staller), while making love. I happened to be standing by and heard Irene say, “Peter, let’s sleep on it.” But he didn’t do it, the sculpture was already bought.

RW But she wasn’t explicitly against it?

IH No, but Irene Ludwig was never as spontaneous as her husband was when it came to acquiring art.

RW There were other people in Aachen who collected. Did they ever feel overshadowed by the Ludwigs?

IH The largest collection besides the Ludwigs’ was the collection of Ingrid and Hugo Jung. Hugo Jung had cofounded the Freunde der Neuen Galerie in 1971. The Jungs had a fantastic collection. Part of their collection was donated to the Hamburger Kunsthalle with the rest later going to their children. Today, the collection of Gaby and Wilhelm Schürmann is the largest in Aachen apart from the Ludwig Collection. The couple have been immersed in the world of contemporary art for forty-five years and have been collectors from the outset.

RW It was a dreadful shock for Irene Ludwig when her husband died so suddenly and unexpectedly. How did she comport herself afterwards?

IH She was very tough, in my opinion. And she began to visit all of the Ludwig museums. I believe she first went to Cologne. Then she said, “If something needs to be discussed, please contact me.” She then systematically looked after all the Ludwig museums.

RW Did you spend more time with her privately during that period?

IH I was often at her home, and we sat either in the cosy kitchen or in the library. My husband and I were invited to her birthdays, which were always very nice.

RW Did the Ludwigs also have parties in their house?

IH Yes, there were invitations to parties at the villa, but also to some in the Ludwig Forum. One lasting memory is the lovely party at their villa in 2007, following the opening of the exhibition *Chuck Close. Erwiderte Blicke. Die Porträts 1969–2006* (*Chuck Close: Returned Glances. The Portraits 1969–2006*), at which the famous artist himself was present.

After Peter Ludwig's death, I often went with Irene to the picturesque village of Sankt Aldegund where Peter was buried, and where she was also laid to rest after her death in 2010. We drove there together for every anniversary, whether it be of his death or his birthday. It was a ritual. We always began by visiting the mayor, that was obligatory. There we had coffee or tea and there was always a huge torte. Everyone was given a large slice, it was delicious. That has stuck with me. Afterwards, we went to the beautiful little medieval church, beneath which his tomb is located. There was usually a concert or a memorial service held in what is referred to as the Alte Kirche (Old Church). After that we would visit the mayor's brother, who was a vintner. The atmosphere at his place was classic, you could say. In any case, it wasn't as chic as the tasting rooms of the younger generation. It was very down-to-earth and always very nice. And, of course, we had to try the wines, because Irene liked to drink Moselle wines! That's how it always was for Peter Ludwig's birthday and the anniversary of his death. There was no celebration, but he was remembered.

RW For the first two years after his death, Irene Ludwig lived reclusively and established the new foundation, the Peter and Irene Ludwig Foundation. Is that right?

IH Yes. The Ludwig Stiftung für Kunst und Internationale Verständigung (Ludwig Foundation for Art and International Understanding) was a nonprofit limited company founded in 1982. After Peter Ludwig's death, Irene Ludwig set up a proper foundation. She ran it with great warmth. We admired her greatly. Irene Ludwig has to be given credit for continuing to acquire art after her husband's death, such as Neo Rauch for the Ludwig Forum in Aachen. She would always buy one or another of the exhibited works after almost every opening in Aachen, especially of exhibitions curated by Harald Kunde, the director of the Ludwig Forum from 2002 to 2008. She got on very well with him, she really liked him. Kunde came to Aachen from Dresden. He and his wife, Anne, once took a trip to Leipzig and Dresden with Irene Ludwig, during which Kunde happily took the lead. He also came to Sankt Aldegund on several occasions.

RW Does anything else come to mind about Irene Ludwig?

IH She was clever, down-to-earth, forthright, and had a sense of humour—and she was tolerant, too! When I visited her at her villa I could talk to her about anything that was on my mind. She was a good listener. There were occasional problems, either in the society or with the city. Irene Ludwig always had good advice, I valued that in particular. Later I missed her a great deal, of course. Oh, I've just remembered something: my husband Ulf and I sometimes went to Cologne, to the Museum Ludwig, with her. On March 17, 2006, the Salvador Dalí painting *La Gare de Perpignan* (*The Railway Station at Perpignan*) (1965) was being shown at an event there. Irene Ludwig said, "I'm not going to stay long." I kept an eye on her, until she gave me a nod to tell me she was ready to leave. It was relatively late. On the way back to Aachen, we were driving along Aachener Straße. I asked her if we could drop in briefly at Figge von Rosen, which was open that day—today it's known as the Philipp von Rosen Galerie. "I'll come with you," she said. She chatted spiritedly with the young audience of gallery visitors, which included many students. There was soon a crowd gathered around her. She drank wine, her cheeks became red, and she was very merry. The students hung on her every word. It was a lovely evening. I was always watching to see if she wanted to go home, as we were already feeling tired, but she wasn't. She was open to everything. A brilliant, wonderful woman.

RW My dear Iva, thanks so much for taking the time to talk to us.

A conversation with **Radu Dobre-Sima** about the failed attempt to found a museum in Bucharest and his travels with Peter Ludwig through Romania

The interview was conducted at his house in Aachen on June 16, 2020.

DIPL.-ING. RADU DOBRE-SIMA (b. 1940, Bucharest) holds a graduate degree in engineering and studied architecture in Bucharest. In 1975, he left Romania to work on a project at the Rostock Convention Centre in the former GDR. In 1978, he fled from there via West Berlin to West Germany by taking advantage of a day visa. After spending time in Oldenburg and Bad Zwischenahn, Dobre-Sima moved to Aachen in 1982, where he has lived and worked ever since. There he met Wolfgang Becker, the then director of the Neue Galerie – Sammlung Ludwig (New Gallery – Ludwig Collection), and Peter Ludwig. Beginning in 1988, he inspired an interest in Romanian art in Becker through a number of trips to Romania that they took together. In 1994, Dobre-Sima also travelled to Romania with Peter Ludwig, later accompanying him again in 1995 when Ludwig was awarded an honorary doctorate in Bucharest. Ludwig commissioned Dobre-Sima to acquire Romanian art and to lead negotiations for the founding of a Ludwig museum in Bucharest. The negotiations were terminated after Peter Ludwig's death in 1996.

REGINA WYRWOLL Mr. Dobre-Sima, you settled in Aachen in 1982. When did you meet Peter Ludwig?

RADU DOBRE-SIMA I believe it was in 1983, but I'm not sure.

RW Can you recall the occasion when you first met him?

RDS Yes. In those days the Neue Galerie – Sammlung Ludwig was here. I met Wolfgang Becker, the then director, and Peter Ludwig there. We only got to know each other better later on, though.

RW You're an architect. Were you interested in the visual arts back then?

RDS Yes, I had begun to curate exhibitions of Romanian art as early as 1984. I mainly worked together with a couple of galleries here in Aachen, but sometimes also in Belgium and France. In 1988, I travelled to Romania with Becker for the first time—just the two of us. We visited fifty artist studios on that trip. Then there was a second trip, in 1989 I think, when Becker stayed in Romania for two weeks and travelled around the country.

[In 1994,] Peter Ludwig had already been planning for two years, together with Becker, to set up a Ludwig museum in Bucharest.

RW When did you really get to know Peter Ludwig?

RDS That was during our first trip to Romania together, from October 30 to November 3, 1994. At that time, Peter Ludwig had already been planning for two years, together with Becker, to set up a Ludwig museum in Bucharest. We talked to various people in the Romanian government, and a couple of locations were suggested. Mr. Ludwig favoured the site where the National Museum of Contemporary Art (MNAC) has since been built.

RW Do you mean the People's House—the enormous building that was still unfinished when you were there in 1994 and had been begun in 1971 by Romania's former president, Nicolae Ceaușescu, who was sentenced and executed in 1989?

RDS Yes, that's the building, known as the Casa Poporului or People's House, as well as the Palatul Parlamentului, which means Palace of the Parliament. If I remember correctly, Peter Ludwig was offered twenty thousand square metres of floorspace in which to set up his museum. That was in the northwestern section of the building, where only reinforced concrete had been used in the construction—a huge space. Ludwig was excited by the size. I suggested something else, but he wanted that location and only that one. Unfortunately, he died two years later, and the project was abandoned.

RW How did the MNAC, which was opened there in 2004, come about? What role did you play in that?

RDS Adrian Năstase was at the National Assembly when I was negotiating for the Ludwig museum in 1994. He was responsible for facilities and art at the People's House at the time. He promised me that as soon as his party, the Partidul Social Democrat (PSD), the social democratic party in Romania, won an election, they would create a museum for contemporary art in the People's House. They won the election in 2000 and Năstase was named prime minister. In the spring of 2001, I spoke with him again and reminded him of his promise. In October, the art academy held a celebration at which Năstase received an award. There he announced that the construction of building extensions and renovation work would be carried out for the museum, and that the funds were available. So I officially submitted my plans for the museum project and presented them to him. The conversion of a wing of the People's House for use as a museum began in spring 2003.

RW How did it proceed?

RDS I was to build the museum and be its director. I was made an offer, however, which I couldn't accept. It was like this: 84 million dollars had been approved, and during internal discussions it was suggested to me that I should transfer thirty percent of the money on to the PSD. At first I was stunned, I couldn't believe it! Then I said: "Firstly, I'm a German, which means if this comes out everyone will say, 'The German came and swindled us.' Secondly, I no longer have any connections in Romania, I left Romania in 1975. And thirdly, I don't know how to do something like that, and I don't want to learn." And then they said, "Fine, we'll find someone else then."

RW Let's get back to Ludwig and, with him, the events that preceded the creation of the MNAC.

RDS Until 1993, only two Romanian artists were included in the collection of Peter and Irene Ludwig. One of them was Horia Damian, who lived in Paris. Peter Ludwig had met him there at the beginning of the 1970s and invited him to create an installation for the ballroom of the Neue Galerie – Sammlung Ludwig. The work, titled *Galaxy (Voie Lactée)* was made and shown in 1974, but not acquired. In 1993, I went to Becker and said: "Listen, I'm going to set up a stipend. I'll cover the upkeep of artists who come here from Romania, and the museum will make an apartment available, as well as a studio where they can work." The Ludwig Forum made a couple of apartments available. In 1993, I brought Paula Ribariu to Aachen. She was the first recipient of the stipend. She subsequently had an exhibition in her studio with the works she had created in Aachen and gifted one of her pieces to the museum. In 1994, when I was in Romania with Becker and Ludwig, Peter Ludwig bought one of her works, among pieces by other Romanian artists. We saw a triptych she had made. He told me he wanted to buy it. I replied that I wanted to buy it myself. He immediately changed his mind and decided on a much larger and more imposing multipart installation—*Altar* (1987/1988). After some delay, it was acquired in 1995/1996. In 1997, after Ludwig's death, Becker and I organised a large exhibition at the Ludwig Forum called *Bukarest nach '89. Kunst in Rumänien heute* (*Bucharest After '89: Art in Romania Today*), with over three hundred works from sixteen Romanian artists, many of which came from the Peter and Irene Ludwig Collection.

RW What was the trip to Romania with Peter Ludwig like?

RDS Did you know Ludwig?

RW I did.

RDS He was a little bit … stubborn, wouldn't you say?

RW You could put it like that.

RDS He took me and Becker from Aachen to Frankfurt in his luxury car driven by a chauffeur. He had all these VIP passes and we went to the airport lounge. It surprised me that he was interested in the chocolates and sweets there. We didn't talk about art much during the flight to Bucharest. He really wanted to see a specific work by Constantin Brâncuși. There is a large group of sculptures by him in his home village of Târgu Jui, a good three hundred kilometres from Bucharest. I organised a helicopter and we flew to Târgu Jui. Ludwig was very excited: "That was my first time flying in a helicopter." He was thrilled to bits, like a child—it was fantastic. Brâncuși's large piece in the park in Târgu Jui from 1937/1938 is a three-part memorial to those lost during the First World War. It made a great impression on Ludwig. The three parts of the sculpture ensemble are called *Colonne sans fin* (*The Endless Column*), *La Table du silence* (*The Table of Silence*), and *La Porte du baiser* (*The Gate of the Kiss*). From there we flew to a convent. It was absolutely enchanting. It was autumn and we landed in a forest. The ground was covered in leaves and the helicopter stirred them up into a huge cloud. In the convent was a school that taught stained glass making. Ludwig made a donation to the convent. He liked it a lot.

We were in Bucharest for five days. Ludwig got up every morning at seven and went to bed every evening at nine. I had organised everything very carefully so that we were always on time for our appointments. He visited a lot of studios as well as a large exhibition. We also met with two collectors. He even insisted on visiting shops to see if his products were being sold.

RW His chocolate?

RDS Exactly.

RW And? Was it?

RDS Yes, he was pleased.

RW Did he have business contacts in Romania?

RDS No, not as far as I know.

RW Then where could you buy his chocolate in Romania?

RDS All of the big companies already had a presence in Romania then—Lidl, Metro, Kaufland, and so on. You could buy his products there.

Ludwig himself had no direct contact, I was the contact person. I had to speak to people and do the negotiating.

RW Which artists did he particularly admire or was especially interested in?

RDS Paula Ribariu, Ioana Bătrânu—a work of hers hangs in the Ludwig Múzeum in Budapest—Mihai Sârbulescu, Aurel Vlad, Dan Perjovschi, Mihai Buculei, Marian Zidaru, and others too. But other than that, he didn't reveal too much. Of course you're aware that he was always speaking into his voice recorder. We couldn't listen to what he recorded because he mandated that the recordings can only be made public thirty years after the death of him or his wife.

RW He died in 1996, and his wife, Irene, in 2010. That means they won't be released until 2040.

RDS Exactly. He didn't want to discuss it, and he never stated whether this or that was of special interest to him. Wolfgang Becker was important to Peter Ludwig. He was the director in Aachen, but he was also a confidant. Ludwig encouraged him to travel all over the world to discover art and organise exhibitions. For instance, Becker had been in Moscow and encountered a group who exhibited their art in a forest because they weren't allowed to do so in a gallery. Becker said to Ludwig, "Look, here are some artists who exhibit in a forest." Ludwig bought all the works—a whole train car full of them. At least that's how the story goes. Their works are part of the collection.

RW Did Peter Ludwig return to Romania?

RDS He was in Romania twice. The second time was when he was awarded an honorary doctorate by the Universitatea Națională de Arte București, the Bucharest National University of Arts. We were all there, as was his wife Irene. Ludwig was well-known in artistic circles, and the German ambassador at the time was very taken with him. He organised a meeting when Ludwig came to Bucharest and invited a lot of well-known people. That was in 1995. The minister responsible for the arts was not in Romania at the time, he was travelling, but the speaker of the parliament and other politicians were in attendance. Ludwig himself had no direct contact, I was the contact person. I had to speak to people and do the negotiating.

RW In 1994, Peter Ludwig wrote you a letter that reads like a power of attorney.

RDS That's right, and I flew to Bucharest with it and said, "Here, I will negotiate with you on behalf of the Ludwig Foundation."

RW In the letter it says: "The Ludwig Stiftung für Kunst und Internationale Verständigung (Ludwig Foundation for Art and international Understanding) in Aachen, Prof. Dr. h. c. mult. Irene Ludwig and Prof. Dr. Dr. h. c. mult. Peter Ludwig hereby personally commission Mr. Radu Dobre-Sima to attend to the interests of Romanian art and Romanian artists in the framework of their international activities. In the fulfilment of this task, Mr. Dobre-Sima will make recommendations for exhibitions and handle the technicalities of acquisitions for the foundation. Mr. Dobre-Sima may suggest acquisitions himself."

RDS Ludwig wanted to buy the works that I had recommended and made an offer for them. I didn't agree with it at all. I said: "These are all young artists. They haven't made any money so far. You have to increase your offer." Then he said, "OK, fine, we'll pay double." That was the first deal made on his first visit.

RW How many works did he intend to donate to the planned Ludwig museum in Bucharest? Did he discuss his ideas about this?

RDS Yes, we spoke about that. He said: "The museum is a Romanian museum, but it's a Romanian museum that bears my name. Therefore, forty percent of the works in the museum's permanent exhibition will be donations from my collection." And he wanted to support the museum with an annual financial fund that would cover various exhibitions, artistic exchanges, and things like that. We never discussed the exact amount.

RW Forty percent of the museum's collection is a very large amount.

RDS Yes, he wanted to donate forty percent of the museum collection, of the collection held by the museum in Bucharest. The museum had nothing at the time. So if, for example, the museum wanted to have a collection of two hundred works, eighty of them would have come from Ludwig. That was what he meant.

RW Does that mean, for example, that he would have bought eighty works of Romanian art?

RDS No, he wanted to provide works of international art from his collection, rather than Romanian art. The Romanian art was to come from the museum's side. All over the world, that was his concept for the foundation of each museum. A portion of the works exhibited would either loaned or donated by the foundation, and the remainder would be works that already belonged to the museum. He insisted that the museums exhibit national and international works together, so that there was always a dialogue between the two, both for the benefit of the public as well as for the artists themselves.

RW Were the negotiations difficult?

RDS Personally, I faced no problems in Romania. But it was difficult because the government at the time wasn't really interested in the proposal. They were mainly interested in the financial side of things. Everyone wanted to stick the money in their own pockets; it was terrible. The idea of a museum for modern and contemporary art, as I described earlier, only arose again with the election in 2000.

RW So with the death of Ludwig, the idea for a Ludwig museum was over?

RDS After Peter's death, I went to Irene Ludwig and said: "What shall we do with the museum there? Are we going to pursue it?" She told me: "No, for me the subject is closed. That was my husband's project, and I don't want to carry on with it." In the end, the project came to nothing.

RW Mr. Dobre-Sima, thank you for taking the time to talk to me.

Dieter Ronte wählte Kunst nach 1960 für Gastschau in Ungarn

Kurzlehrgang in Westkunst

Das „Selbstporträt mit blauer Guitarre" (1977) ist eines der schönsten Bilder des britischen Künstlers David Hockney. Das Bild gehört dem berühmtesten deutschen Sammler Peter Ludwig.

Eines der schönsten Bilder von Oswald Oberhuber heißt „Biographie" (1973). Es gehört der Oesterreichischen Nationalbank. Es ist wohl auch eines der größten Bilder der Gegenwartskunst: fast 15 Meter lang und 5 Meter hoch. Es ist mit Oberhuber-Köpfen locker bedeckt.

Um diese schönen Bilder zusammen zu sehen, muß man nach Budapest fahren. Wegen Platznot in der sonst geräumigen Kunsthalle Müscarnok mußte allerdings das Kolossalgemälde Oberhubers auf beiden Seiten ein wenig zusammengerollt bleiben.

Die Ausstellung „Museum moderner Kunst, Wien, mit Stiftung Ludwig" in Budapest (bis 14. August) könnte als ein „Kurzer Lehrgang der Westkunst nach 1960" bezeichnet werden. Überwiegend aus dem Stiftungsbestand in Wien hat Direktor Dieter Ronte 58 Werke ausgewählt, und so liegt der Schwerpunkt bei der Pop-art, dem Neuen Realismus und dem Fotorealismus, einstigen Vorlieben Ludwigs.

Glücklicherweise befinden sich unter den 40 Künstlern auch neun Österreicher: Adolf Frohner mit einem Sessel-Objekt von 1962; Josef Mikl, Markus Prachensky und Gotfried Mairwöger mit abstrakten Farbkompositionen; Hermann Nitsch mit einem tachistisch-aktionistischen Gemälde (1960); Walter Pichler mit architekturhaften Zeichnungen; Arnulf Rainer mit Übermalungen von Totenmasken und Hubert Schmalix als Vertreter der Neuen Wilden. Wie Dieter Ronte sagte, hätte es seitens der Ungarn keine Beschränkungswünsche gegeben.

Die Ausstellung findet im Rahmen des österreichisch-ungarischen Kulturabkommens statt. Auf – bei ähnlichen Ausstellungen sonst übliche Dokumentation des Wiener Aktionismus – hat Ronte leider verzichtet. Sonst aber ist die Auswahl durch einen hohen Informationswert gekennzeichnet. Ereignis wird sie aber kaum werden: Die ungarische Kulturpolitik zeichnet sich traditionell durch weitgehende Offenheit der Moderne gegenüber aus, das ungarische Publikum ist gewöhnlich sehr gut informiert. Davon, daß ungarische Künstler keine Hinterwäldler der Weltkunst sind, kann man sich in den überaus sehenswerten Sammlungen der Ungarischen Nationalgalerie überzeugen.

Dennoch schienen die ungarischen Partner Zurückhaltung geübt zu haben: Statt des verhinderten Kulturministers nahm die Eröffnung ein Staatssekretär vor. Aus Wien waren immerhin der Bundesminister Heinz Fischer und die Vorsitzende der Ludwig-Stiftung, Hertha Firnberg, angereist.

Als Gegenleistung der Gastgeber wurde eine Ausstellung alter Gobelins vereinbart. Eine Retrospektive ungarischer Gegenwartskunst sollte man trotzdem im Auge behalten. Sie könnte in Wien zu einem Ereignis werden – das österreichische Publikum ist diesbezüglich besonders schlecht informiert.

JAN TABOR

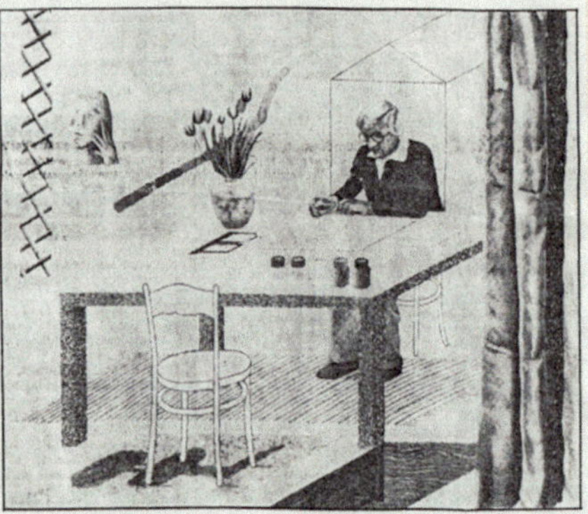

Museum moderner Kunst, Wien, mit Stiftung Ludwig: „Selfportrait with Blue Guitar"

Pages from Peter and Irene Ludwig's private press archives, with reports on the exhibition *Kunst seit 1960. Ausstellung des Museums Moderner Kunst, Wien, mit Stiftung Ludwig* at the Kunsthalle in Budapest, 1983.

Newspaper article about the exhibition *Kunst seit 1960. Ausstellung des Museums Moderner Kunst, Wien, mit Stiftung Ludwig* (*International Art Since 1960: Exhibition of the Modern Art Museum, Vienna, with the Ludwig Foundation*) at the Kunsthalle in Budapest.
"Crash Course in Western Art," Kurier, 18.6.1983

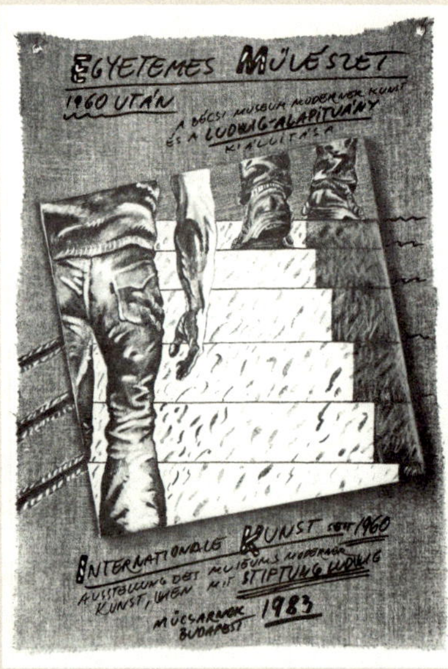

Exhibition catalogue, *Kunst seit 1960. Ausstellung des Museums Moderner Kunst, Wien, mit Stiftung Ludwig*, Kunsthalle Budapest, 1983.

Wahrheit

Graz

16. [illegible]

Museum Moderner Kunst/Stiftung Ludwig:

Ausstellung in Budapest

Wissenschaftsminister Heinz Fischer eröffnete kürzlich im Beisein der Präsidentin der Ludwig-Stiftung, Dr. Hertha Firnberg, und des ungarischen Statssekretärs Dr. Andras Korcsok in der Budapester Kunsthalle eine Ausstellung aus Beständen des österreichischen Museums für Moderne Kunst und der Sammlung Ludwig. Diese Ausstellung wurde vom Museum für Moderne Kunst gemeinsam mit der österreichischen Ludwig-Stiftung im Rahmen des österreichisch-ungarischen Kulturabkommens gestaltet.

Dr. Heinz Fischer unterstrich bei dieser Gelegenheit die zwischenstaatliche Bedeutung dieser Ausstellung und des damit verbundenen kulturellen Dialogs zwischen den guten Nachbarn Ungarn und Österreich. Die intensiven politischen und wirtschaftlichen Beziehungen zwischen zwei in einer sehr langen Tradition miteinander verbundenen Völker bekäme durch die Ludwig-Ausstellung einen wichtigen kulturellen Impuls. Dr. Fischer lud bei dieser Gelegenheit die ungarischen Gastgeber zu einer gleichartigen Präsentation in Österreich ein.

Die Ausstellung steht unter dem Motto „Kunst nach 1960" und wird bis 13. August geöffnet sein. Präsentiert werden 58 Werke von 40 Künstlern, darunter die Österreicher Rainer, Prachensky und Nietsch und die Amerikaner Warhol, Liechtenstein und Rauschenberg.

…ner Zeitung

Datum:

29. Juni 1983

Kulturnotizen

MODERNE KUNST — Wissenschaftsminister Dr. Heinz Fischer und Bundesminister a. D. Dr. Hertha Firnberg als Vorsitzende der österreichischen Ludwig-Stiftung werden am 8. Juli in der Kunsthalle Mücsarnok in Budapest die Ausstellung „Museum moderner Kunst, Wien, mit Stiftung Ludwig" eröffnen. Diese bis 14. August gezeigte Präsentation im Rahmen des österreichisch-ungarischen Kulturabkommens, von Museumsdirektor Dr. Dieter Ronte zusammengestellt, zeigt 58 Werke seit 1960 von 40 Künstlern.

Ausschnitt aus:

Die Presse

Wien

29. Juni 1983

IN BUDAPEST stellt sich vom 8. Juli bis 14. August in der Kunsthalle Mücsarnok das Wiener Museum moderner Kunst und die Sammlung Ludwig mit einer von Direktor Ronte zusammengestellten Auswahl von 58 Werken vor, die seit 1960 entstanden sind und von 40 Künstlern stammen.

Ausstellung in Budapest

Stiftungspräsidentin Hertha Firnberg und Wissenschaftsminister Heinz Fischer waren eigens angereist, um in Budapest eine Ausstellung „Kunst nach 1960" zu eröffnen: In der Budapester Kunsthalle werden Werke aus dem Österreichischen Museum für moderne Kunst und der Sammlung Ludwig gezeigt – zur Überraschung der ungarischen Kunstfreunde keineswegs nur Österreicher oder westliche Künstler, sondern auch Beispiele für die Sammlertätigkeit Peter Ludwigs in der Sowjetunion.

Ausschnitt aus:

A.Z. Tagblatt für Österreich

Wien

Datum:

9. Juli 1983

Wiener Sammlung Ludwig in Budapest

Wissenschaftsminister Doktor Heinz Fischer eröffnete gestern in der Budapester Kunsthalle eine Ausstellung aus Be[…] österreichischen Mu[…] Moderne Kunst und […]lung Ludwig. Diese […] wurde vom Museum f[…] Kunst gemeinsam mit […]reichischen Ludwig-S[…] Rahmen des österreich[…]rischen Kulturabkomm[…]tet.

[…] 1437 Neuzugängen der letzten beiden Jahre — Ankäufe der Stadt, Leihgaben des Sammlerehepaares Peter und Irene Ludwig sowie Schenkungen — wird aus Platzgründen nur ein kleiner Teil präsentiert. Einen Schwerpunkt bildet dabei die russische Avantgarde mit Arbeiten von Larionow, Exter, Ender und Rodtschenko. Einen weiteren Akzent setzen die Ankäufe der Klassischen Moderne in Italien mit mehreren bedeutenden Gemälden von de Chirico, Campigli und Morandi sowie mit Plastiken von Medardo Rosso, Fabri und Fontana. Die zeitgenössische Abteilung wurde durch die phantastische „documenta"-Installation „Die Pfauenmaschine" aus dem Rebecca-Horn-Film „La Ferdinanda" verstärkt. (AP)

Ausschnitt aus:

Salzburger Nachrich[…]

Salzburg

4. Juni 1983

Ludwigs DDR-Sammlung

OBERHAUSEN (dpa). Die Städtische Schloß-Galerie in Oberhausen soll zu einem Zentrum für Kunst der DDR in der Bundesrepublik Deutschland werden. Als Grundstock erhält die Galerie als Dauerleihgabe für zunächst zehn Jahre etwa 150 Werke von DDR-Künstlern, die der Aachener Fabrikant und Sammler Peter Ludwig seit Mitte der siebziger Jahre erworben hat. Außerdem wird in dem Museum ein „Ludwig-Institut für Kunst der DDR" errichtet, das Ausstellungen organisieren, Kataloge herausgeben und wissenschaftlich tätig sei[…]

1983

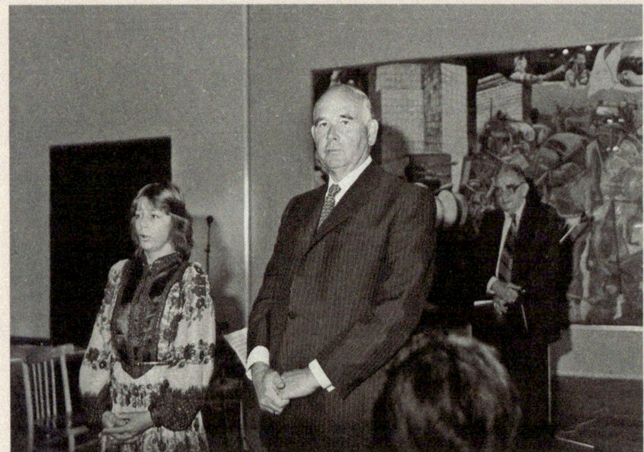

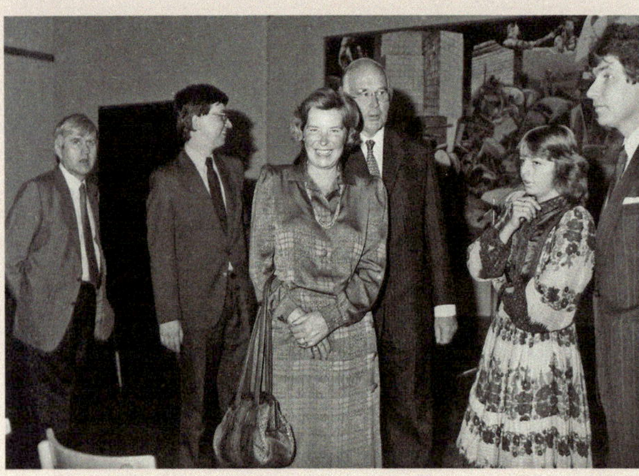

Opening of the exhibition *Zeitgenössische Kunst aus den Sammlungen des Prof. Dr. Peter Ludwig in Aachen* (*Contemporary Art From the Collection of Prof. Dr. Peter Ludwig in Aachen*) at the Wallenstein Palace in Prague, 1987. *Photos: private*

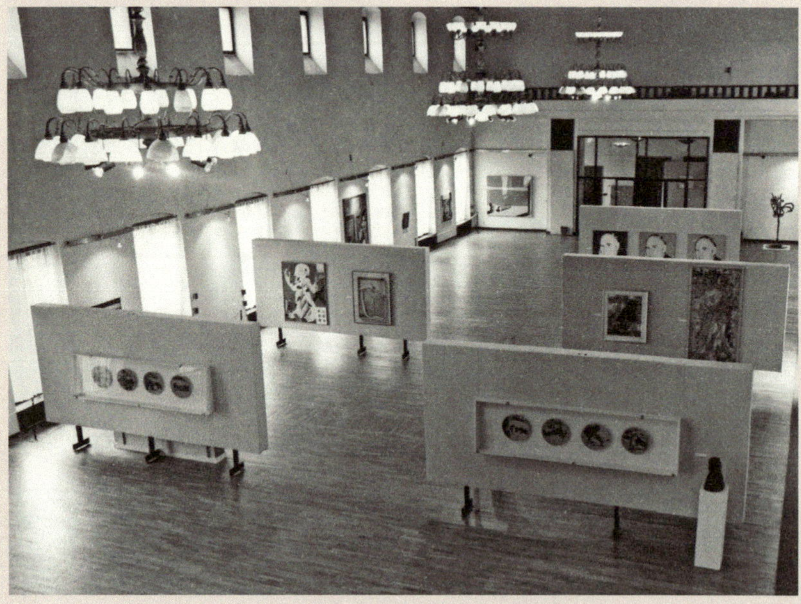

View of the exhibition *Zeitgenössische Kunst aus den Sammlungen des Prof. Dr. Peter Ludwig in Aachen* at the Wallenstein Palace in Prague, 1987. *Photo: unknown*

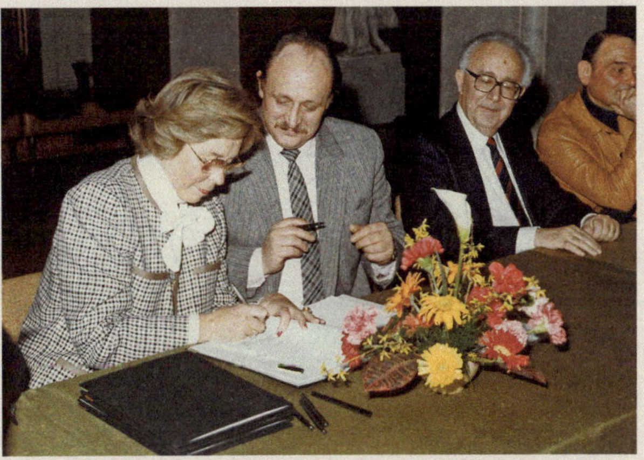

Signing of the contract establishing the Ludwig Foundation in Hungary, Budapest, 1988. From left to right: Irene Ludwig and the foundation board members Lóránd Bereczky, Miklós Mojzer, Zsuzsa Lovag.
Photo: unknown

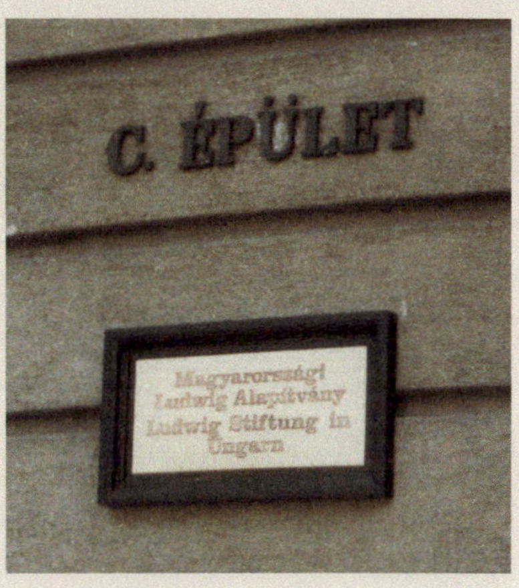

Ludwig Foundation in Hungary sign at the entrance to the National Gallery in Budapest, 1988.
Photo: private

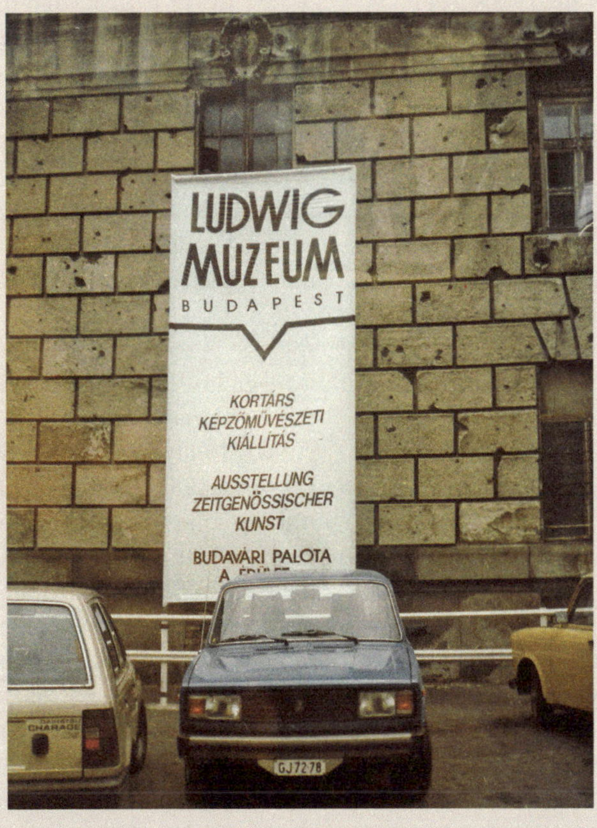

The Ludwig Múzeum in Budapest on the day of its opening, 1991.
Photo: private

SOVIET UNION RUSSIA

When, at the end of the 1960s, Peter and Irene Ludwig began to increasingly focus their collecting on international contemporary art, their collection already included numerous works by the 1920s Russian avant-garde. Their focus was on, among other things, movements and styles that until then had been poorly represented in Western European museum collections, such as French contemporary art and both American and English Pop Art. From the 1980s onwards, this also included art from what was then the Soviet Union (USSR), a state that was largely cut off both politically and culturally from Western Europe by the so-called Iron Curtain. In 1979, the Ludwigs met the Soviet ambassador to Bonn, Vladimir Semyonov. An art collector himself, he was able to provide the Ludwigs with the necessary permit to purchase artworks in the Soviet Union. The opportunity now presented itself for them to expand their collection of Russian art with contemporary works and, beyond that, to strive toward greater cultural understanding and cooperation. In April 1980, Irene and Peter Ludwig travelled, for the first time, to Moscow and Leningrad (now St. Petersburg). On this trip, they visited artist studios and museums and met with high-ranking representatives from the Ministry of Culture.

The first purchase of Soviet contemporary art—eighty-four paintings, 143 works on paper, and ten sculptures—for the Ludwig Collection was acquired in February 1982 through the international trading company Mezhdunarodnaya Kniga, which organised art exports for the state in Moscow with the assistance of the Soviet art export salon. Four months later, an exhibition of these works, titled *Aspekte sowjetischer Kunst der Gegenwart. Sammlung Ludwig* (*Aspects of Contemporary Soviet Art: Ludwig Collection*), opened at two locations: the Kölnisches Stadtmuseum (Cologne

City Museum) and the Neue Galerie – Sammlung Ludwig (New Gallery – Ludwig Collection) in Aachen. The show triggered a furore, in part because it included works by artists such as Ivan Lubennikov, Tatyana Nazarenko, and Natalya Nesterova, whose work did not follow the guidelines of official Soviet state art—Socialist Realism. The Soviet art collection continued to grow in the ensuing years. At the end of the 1980s, Mikhail Gorbachev incrementally opened up the Soviet Union and adopted freer cultural policies under the slogans of glasnost and perestroika. Important works from the Moscow Conceptualism and Sots Art movements—by the likes of Erik Bulatov, Ilya Kabakov, Komar & Melamid, and Sergey Mironenko—could now be incorporated into the Ludwig Collection.

In 1988, the Ludwigs officially made a proposal to Mikhail Gorbachev and Vasily Zakharov, the Soviet minister of culture, for the creation of a museum of international contemporary art in Moscow, a project that had already been discussed for some years with the director of the Pushkin State Museum of Fine Arts, Irina Antonova. Given the course of Gorbachev's policy of détente, the political climate seemed favourable for implementing the project. However, the negotiations, which saw Thomas Krings-Ernst travel to Moscow a number of times as the Ludwigs' representative, proved to be long and drawn out. Above all, the planning for a new building to house the Ludwig Museum within the Pushkin Museum was continually delayed. Although a final draft agreement was formulated in October 1994, it ultimately came to nothing.

Since the beginning of 1994, the Ludwigs had also been in close contact with the director of the Russian Museum in St. Petersburg, **Yevgenia Petrova**. The Ludwigs were now offered an impressive building for the permanent presentation of their collection: the Marble Palace, which the German-born tsarina Catherine the Great had built for her lover Prince Orlov. During a visit in April 1994, they were so taken with the lavish building, which was planned to be renovated, that less than five months later they signed a contract for the founding of the Ludwig Museum at the Russian Museum. As part of the museum's founding, over one hundred works of international contemporary art from the Ludwig Collection were donated and sent to St. Petersburg. Transport of the works was carried out by the art transport company headed by **Hans Ewald Schneider** and his father. For the museum's ceremonial opening on March 10, 1995, an exhibition of works by Pablo Picasso from the Ludwig Collection was shown alongside a selection of the works donated to the museum.

A conversation with **Hans Ewald Schneider** about international transport and his work with the art collectors Peter and Irene Ludwig

The interview was conducted in his office in Frechen on December 30, 2020.

HANS EWALD SCHNEIDER (b. 1950, Cologne) studied economics in Cologne. His career includes working for the Galeria Kaufhof department store chain in Germany and for Container Transport International in the US. In 1981 he joined hasenkamp, the family business. The transport and logistics company was founded in 1903. Directly after the Second World War, it turned its attention to the transport of artworks, and was met with increasing success. Schneider's father, Ewald, won the trust of the art collectors Peter and Irene Ludwig at the beginning of the 1960s. From then on, the company transported artworks from the Ludwigs' collection to museums and exhibitions throughout the world, a process that Hans Ewald Schneider helped oversee. In 1991, Schneider became a managing partner in the family business. In 2018, his son, Dr. Thomas Schneider, joined the company's management—the fifth generation of the family to do so. Hans Ewald Schneider has been a member of the Board of Trustees of the Peter and Irene Ludwig Foundation since 2012.

In my opinion, Peter Ludwig was a businessman first and a collector second.

REGINA WYRWOLL Hans Ewald, when did you first meet Peter Ludwig?

HANS EWALD SCHNEIDER It must have been in 1964 or 1965, on the occasion of the exhibition *Sumer, Assur, Babylon* in Cologne. It took place in the Rautenstrauch-Joest-Museum. My father's company did the transport for the exhibition.

In my opinion, Peter Ludwig was a businessman first and a collector second. Some might see it differently, but it was his business activities that afforded him the opportunity to collect. During that period he took an interest in young businesspeople, like my father, Ewald. Peter Ludwig found it strange that my father had allowed me, at my young age, to travel to Baghdad in a Deutsche Bundesbahn (German Federal Railway) baggage car. I was fifteen or sixteen years old and was joined by one of his colleagues, and we accompanied the works from the exhibition as they were transported back to their original location. In Vienna, our goods carriage was attached to the Orient Express, and then it was off to Istanbul, where there wasn't a railway bridge across the Bosporus yet, on to Ankara and, finally, Baghdad. Ludwig had a weakness for archaeological matters, and he found it fascinating that one of our relatives was an archaeologist working on the excavation of the Tower of Babel, south of Baghdad. After the transport job was finished, I was able to visit the excavation sites, which I later told Ludwig about. This led to discussions between my father and Ludwig. I often just stood there and listened to everything. Ludwig was always interested in learning more about transport solutions. He was thrifty; it was his opinion, for example, that a Picasso didn't necessarily have to be packed in a crate, but could be transported in the boot of a car. My father explained to him that that wouldn't necessarily be pragmatic. That was how I met him and, a short time later, his wife Irene too.

RW You met Irene Ludwig back then?

HES Ludwig was often together with his wife. She was actively involved in the collection herself.

RW How did you become interested in art?

HES I often worked at my father's company during the school holidays, and later during my semester breaks at university. I had the wonderful opportunity to become acquainted with the entire world both with and through art. I met Wulf Herzogenrath, who was director of the Kölnischer Kunstverein from 1973 to 1989. In 1968, he had published the catalogue for the first large Bauhaus exhibition at the Württembergischer Kunstverein in Stuttgart and organised an exhibition tour to a further eight locations in Europe, the US, South America, and Asia. We organised the transport of the works. As a school and later university student, I accompanied the artworks to all the exhibition locations around the world, sometimes even together with Herbert Bayer, one of the last living representatives of the Bauhaus.

RW When did hasenkamp start transporting art?

HES The Hasenkamps were a family of counts and large-scale farmers from Westphalia. Between the world wars, they transported art on a small scale. After the Second World War, when a multitude of artworks that had been stored elsewhere were being returned to museums, reliable shippers were needed. Kurt Hackenberg, councillor for cultural affairs in Cologne from 1955 to 1979, stood in opposition to the other councillors: "Do you want to bring Stefan Lochner's *Madonna im Rosenhag* (*Madonna of the Rose Bower*) (ca. 1450) back in one of the city's garbage trucks, or do you want to use a professional?" That professional was my father.

RW What proportion of your business consists of artwork transport?

HES It's always less than fifty percent. But it is, of course, a very important aspect of the business. Our company is the largest transport and logistics firm specialising in art in Europe.

RW Your father, Ewald, is famous for constructing climate-controlled crates for artworks. When did he begin doing that?

HES That story goes back more than fifty years ago. It was 1965. Our climate-controlled crate was ahead of its time because it was reusable. A new crate didn't need to be built for every transport of the artwork, which, by the way, is what still happens in the US today. My father designed a variety of sizes which could be used again and again. That was, and still is, an ecological and economical triumph.

RW Was the company involved with the transport of Pop Art works from New York to Aachen in the mid-1960s?

HES Yes, we carried out a number of shipments during that time, quite a lot of them. That wasn't, however, due to the size of the exhibition. The insurance companies had insisted on breaking up the shipments owing to the enormous amount for which the works were insured. Splitting the works up into numerous shipments was a requirement they set in order to reduce risk.

RW Am I correct in saying that when hasenkamp undertook a transport job, the shipment was often accompanied—right up to the opening—by the transport team and, when appropriate, by the boss as well?

HES That's right, we provided a comprehensive logistical plan that covered packing, transport, customs clearance, unpacking, installation, and hanging, as well as insurance. One example is the exhibition *Parler und der schöne Stil* (*The Parlers and the Beautiful Style*), at the Museum Schnütgen in Cologne in 1978.

RW Did that include any works on loan from the Ludwigs?

HES Possibly. I remember that he considered it one of most outstanding exhibitions in Cologne!

RW It undoubtedly was, but the exhibition has since been all but forgotten. The full title was *Die Parler und der schöne Stil 1350–1400. Europäische Kunst unter den Luxemburgern* (*The Parlers and the Beautiful Style 1350–1400: European Art under the Luxembourgs*).

Peter and Irene Ludwig knew exactly what they wanted. Both were always very clear that their artworks should be transferred permanently to the general public.

HES Ludwig was very generous when it came to loans from his collection. He wanted the works to be seen. Pieces from his collection were also included in the exhibition *Westkunst. Zeitgenössische Kunst seit 1939* (*Western Art: Contemporary Art Since 1939*), cocurated by László Glozer, Marcel Baumgartner, and Kasper König, held in 1981 in the Rheinhallen—now the Messehallen—in Cologne. I had the impression that Ludwig always strove to support museum curators or directors in their decisions. He wasn't the type to dictate conditions.

RW How did transport and insurance costs relate to each other and how have they changed? I presume that these kinds of exhibition costs were lower back then.

HES No, relatively speaking it is cheaper today than thirty or forty years ago. If anything, there has been a disproportionately low price increase across the range of services we offer. Our company has accepted the challenge of remaining at the forefront of a competitive field. We've achieved this through training, innovation, economising, investing in buildings and IT, and much more.

RW Your company has successfully built and rented storage facilities. Was this something you did in the past?

HES Yes, we've always operated storage facilities on a small scale, but since 2000—that is to say in the last twenty years—we've significantly expanded in this area.

RW There were a number of large art transport companies in the Rhineland. Was it difficult to withstand the competition?

HES What can I say, we submitted tenders and were awarded—with any luck—the contracts. That's how the free-market economy works. Back then, it was also the case that decisions were based more on quality than on price. In my opinion, it would be good if quality was still the focus but, unfortunately, that's no longer the case due to the mandates of the public tender system.

RW What do you consider "quality" to mean when it comes to transport?

HES Moving art from point A to point B undamaged! Quality comes down to staff, packing, service, transport, dealing with customs … Everything plays a part. Today, the lowest price usually wins in a public tender, even if it doesn't actually comply with the legal guidelines. That's changing a little at the moment, thank God!

RW Peter Ludwig once said that there should be a kind of permanent documenta in Aachen: new works of art should regularly come to the city to be presented in exhibitions, before touring other locations.

HES I believe that Peter and Irene Ludwig knew exactly what they wanted. Both were always very clear that their artworks should be transferred permanently to the general public. It was not: "The public sector creates a museum and then we make long-term loans to it for ten or twenty years." This practice of permanent transfer speaks volumes about their extreme generosity. It's also why Peter Ludwig always left decisions regarding purchases or exhibitions to the museum directors. His role was always more of the patron in the background.

RW Wolfgang Becker, the former director in Aachen, has said that he always honoured the many requests he received to exhibit the collection in other cities, some of them off the beaten track. Aachen became the hub of these activities.

HES That was also an aspect of his patronage, I think. Ludwig didn't finance those exhibitions, but he did make the artworks for them available. And that meant that these works of art could be seen by a broader public throughout the country, not just in Aachen or Cologne. I found that remarkable. Ludwig showed his collection all over the world, even in Tehran. Exhibiting in Russia was also important for him.

As a cultured people, the Russians understood very well exactly who was coming to them. That's why they respected him.

RW Speaking of Russia, were you involved in the negotiations with Moscow and, later, St. Petersburg?

HES Not really. Evelyn Weiss, the deputy director of the Museum Ludwig in Cologne, was chiefly involved. Peter Ludwig and she were friends. Weiss and I had travelled to Moscow once, in 1969 or 1970, and visited the collector George Costakis. We had the opportunity to view his collection in his apartment, which he had assembled in Russia over several decades. He had to leave more than half of it behind when he left for Athens in 1977. Our company transported the remainder. During his travels, Peter Ludwig had interacted with Irina Antonova, the director of the Pushkin Museum. One could say that Antonova was the "cultural queen" of Russia for more than sixty years, from Stalin to Putin. She was involved in everything that happened in the art world during that long period. She was a very shrewd and highly intelligent woman. She died only recently, on November 30, 2020, at the age of ninety-eight. She and Peter Ludwig immediately respected and understood each other upon meeting in 1988. I can only presume that Ludwig knew full well that art looted by the Soviets—such as "Priam's Treasure"—was secretly held in the basement of the museum, a fact long denied for political reasons. It was a young Antonova who had unloaded the crates containing it in Moscow in 1945. It only became publicly known in the mid-2000s that the objects taken from Berlin at the end of the Second World War were all in her museum. Peter Ludwig was an independent figure, he neither needed nor was bound to any state institution. As a cultured people, the Russians understood very well exactly who was coming to them. That's why they respected him.

RW Ludwig had collected a lot of Russian art, but around 1983/1984 there was a period when he was suddenly unable to do so. For several months, his letters to Russia went unanswered.

HES Yes. The process has to be viewed from a long-term perspective rather than a short one; you can't give such machinations and practices too much credence. If you are aware of them and expect them, then you know how to deal with the Russians. I believe that Ludwig knew exactly what was going on.

RW It was agreed that an exhibition made up of pieces from the Ludwig Collection would be shown at the Pushkin State Museum of Fine Arts, with the works to be included set out in writing. Antonova had even offered to build an extension to the museum to house the Ludwig Collection, but then there was a sudden shift in focus to St. Petersburg.

HES It's possible that the project was no longer the highest priority. Gorbachev had come to power; it was the time of perestroika and there was a lot of uncertainty.

RW There was ultimately no exhibition of works from the Ludwig Collection in Moscow. Instead, Ludwig chose to found his museum at the Marble Palace of the State Russian Museum in Leningrad, now St. Petersburg. Do you know why?

HES There has always been a rivalry between St. Petersburg and Moscow. St. Petersburg's importance had grown and the Hermitage Museum, headed by Boris Piotrovsky, came to the fore. That was still the elder Piotrovsky—his son, Michael, has been the director of the Hermitage Museum since 1992. A shift had taken place in Russia. I believe Peter Ludwig had realised that Antonova was no longer enthusiastic about the project, and that St. Petersburg was cosmopolitan and increasingly cognizant of its historical importance. The fact that the current Russian president, Vladimir Putin, comes from St. Petersburg has given it a status similar to that of Moscow. Peter Ludwig had perhaps—with the help of Yevgenia Petrova, the deputy director of the State Russian Museum—realised early on that it wouldn't be a terrible idea to go there. The Marble Palace is a wonderful building. It was built between 1768 and 1785 by Empress Catherine the Great for her lover, Prince Grigory Orlov.

RW Is it true that, when the decision was made to house the Ludwig Museum in the Marble Palace, your father had an office set up on the top floor in the apartments that had been intended for Prince Orlov?

HES Yes, that's right—but when it was finished our company wasn't allowed to move in, unfortunately.

Peter Ludwig was both bourgeois and avant-garde. He was a middle-class entrepreneur type, conservative in the best sense of the word and, at the same time, open to and interested in new things. I would describe him as a highly dynamic individual.

RW What was an average working day with Peter Ludwig like?

HES Peter Ludwig was a very detail-oriented man. I can remember clearly how he toured me around the in-progress structural shell of the Museum Ludwig in Cologne. He described to me where his private toilet and shower would be—both still there today. There is one thing that the people who work there today probably don't know: in the loading dock area, a wall was originally planned to be built between the Museum Ludwig and the Philharmonie, spatially separating the loading docks of the two institutions. I told Ludwig, "That makes no sense," and explained to him that a wall would only get in the way; coming to an arrangement between the two organisations would allow one large space to be better utilised than two small ones. He agreed with me: "Complete nonsense." Of course, I had no power when it came to the City of Cologne, but he did and declared, when the concrete wall was already half-finished: "That has to go. It's in the way." Because it was Peter Ludwig who demanded it, jackhammers were brought in to remove the wall. That's how obsessed with detail he was. I liked it. He was the same when it came to packing: he would look everything over carefully and always wanted to know where his money was going. He didn't automatically trust the Cologne City Council. He liked to say, "A donation will only be made when the museum is completed."

RW That's Ludwig the businessman.

HES That's the businessman who said: "I know what I have, and I know what it's worth, and I want to give it to the general public. But I don't trust politicians." In this regard, he was hard as nails.

RW Was hasenkamp also involved in transporting the medieval manuscripts that Ludwig sold to the J. Paul Getty Museum in Los Angeles in 1983?

HES We handled the export of the manuscripts and I personally accompanied them. Ludwig took it extremely hard. He was devastated that he was forced to sell them for financial reasons. He was deeply aware of their intangible value. But financial pressures forced him to sell; he had no choice.

RW Was it a loss for your company when Ludwig died in 1996? Has anything changed as a result?

HES On a personal level, it was obviously a terrible loss for my family. On a business level, our working relationship with Ludwig wasn't an exclusive arrangement. Ludwig accepted and valued our service as being of high quality, something that was important to him. When it came to his private residence in Aachen, he wanted to always use the same people because he wanted as few people as possible coming around his home. There were artworks hanging in the bedroom too, and that required a special degree of discretion. There were four specially chosen, experienced employees of ours who worked with the Ludwigs. Naturally, they were not only good, but also discreet.

RW What works of art hung in the bedroom?

HES A Lichtenstein hung there, *Still Life with Pitcher and Apple* from 1972.

[The Ludwigs] were both collectors and she always supported him in public. I believe, however, that in their private relationship she was a strong woman who also guided him.

RW Were your parents, or later you, ever invited to the Ludwigs' home?

HES Yes, I was invited for dinner three or four times, as were my mother and father.

RW Can you remember who else was present?

HES There was Evelyn Weiss or Marc Scheps, for instance, who was the director of the Museum Ludwig in Cologne from 1991 to 1997. There were also guests from America, people who had lent or borrowed works of art. There was never anyone from the world of politics, if that's what you want to know.

RW What was served?

HES Relatively simple home cooking, nothing fancy. Completely ordinary.

RW And how late did you stay when you were invited for the evening?

HES We went home between ten and quarter past, that's when the evening was over.

RW What was Irene Ludwig's relationship with her husband like?

HES She counterbalanced him; I think she was a very good steadying hand. They were both collectors and she always supported him in public. I believe, however, that in their private relationship she was a strong woman who also guided him.

RW When you knew the Ludwigs, did they continue to collect works other than contemporary art? Or had they stopped collecting from their other areas of interest, such as East Asian or medieval art?

HES No, there was a bit of everything. Ludwig was interested in very old art as much as in contemporary art. You could talk to him about a Madonna on a medieval reliquary from the Museum Schnütgen as easily as you could about the former porn actress Cicciolina in the work *Jeff and Ilona (Made in Heaven)* by Jeff Koons, from 1990.

After he had saved his company by selling the medieval manuscripts, he used part of the US$40 million proceeds to found the Ludwig Stiftung für Kunst und Internationale Verständigung (Peter and Irene Ludwig Foundation for Art and International Understanding) in 1983. After his death, Irene Ludwig transferred it to the Peter and Irene Ludwig Foundation. All the museums that Peter Ludwig worked with could submit applications for support. For instance, the Museum Schnütgen in Cologne, or the Suermondt-Ludwig-Museum in Aachen. The spectrum ranged from medieval to East Asian art. Pop Art was always the focus, but Peter Ludwig's interests were very broad. I wouldn't say that any category was excluded.

RW How did you find him as a person?

HES Peter Ludwig was both bourgeois and avant-garde. He was a middle-class entrepreneur type, conservative in the best sense of the word and, at the same time, open to and interested in new things. I would describe him as a highly dynamic individual.

RW What was his communication style?

HES He always stated clearly what he wanted. Communication generally took place through his secretary, Elke Beyer. She would call and inform us of his wishes. In our company his wishes were, naturally, always graciously received, and we sought to fulfil them as quickly as possible.

RW What was his relationship to politics?

HES Whenever possible, he steered clear of it. Peter Ludwig was a shrewd man. He knew what he wanted and he sometimes used people. But he never allowed himself to be instrumentalised by others. He worked on a basis of trust—that was very important to him—and he took note when someone went off course. He took note, too, when someone helped him. Here's one example: According to customs regulations, when his Picasso collection was to be transported from Switzerland to Germany, Ludwig would normally have had to pay import sales tax. Given the circumstances he didn't understand why: "They are crazy! I'm doing this for the country and then I am supposed to pay a tax on it? That can't be right." I went to the Ministry of Finance in Düsseldorf to talk to someone about it, as the customs department is part of the Ministry of Finance. The officials understood our problem. There was a specific procedure and paperwork that applied to our particular case, but not many people knew about it. As the Picassos were to be immediately transferred to the City of Cologne, the shipment could be officially imported duty-free from Switzerland to Germany through this procedure. Peter Ludwig never forgot what I had done for him.

RW In 1977, did you transport the works for display in a permanent exhibition at the Altes Museum in East Berlin? There were frequent changes of the works in East Berlin, as well as exhibitions that toured throughout the GDR, such as Picasso's *Vollard Suite* (1930–1937).

HES Back then in the GDR there was the company DEUTRANS, which had been Derutra (Deutsch-Russische Transport-Aktiengesellschaft, or German-Russian Transport PLC) and also transported art. Sometimes, when it was paid for by the West, we did the transport. When the West wasn't paying, then the company from the GDR did it.

RW What was the most spectacular trip that you went on with Peter Ludwig?

HES The most spectacular trip was not with him, but with his wife, Irene, to Beijing, on the occasion of the opening of the Ludwig Museum for International Art in the National Art Museum of China in 1996. Ludwig had signed the contract, but unexpectedly died afterwards. The trip made a great impression on me because I realised just how greatly appreciated Peter and Irene Ludwig were in China. At that time, there was no first-rate contemporary Western art anywhere in China. They made it abundantly clear that they understood what a great gift was being given.

RW How did Irene Ludwig react to that?

HES She was a highly sophisticated woman and she was very sensitive to their feelings. We travelled from Germany with a large group that included Scheps. We sat together that evening at the hotel and spoke about the opening, which had been carried out by the German president, Roman Herzog, and the Chinese president, Jiang Zemin. Irene Ludwig displayed incredible poise. She had just lost her husband and she loved the works of art she had just given to the Chinese people very much. In spite of her pain, she carried out the wishes of her dead husband. Her demeanour greatly moved all of us who were with her in Beijing.

RW Hans Ewald, thank you very much for taking the time to talk to us.

A conversation with **Yevgenia Petrova** about her encounters with Peter Ludwig and the founding of the Ludwig Museum at the Russian Museum in St. Petersburg

The conversation with Yevgenia Petrova took place online on May 25, 2021. The interview was consecutively translated by the head of the translation department of the Russian Museum, Dr. Tatjana Kalugina.

DR. YEVGENIA PETROVA (b. 1946, St. Petersburg, formerly Leningrad until 1991) began studying art history and theory at Leningrad State University in 1971, where she later received her doctorate in 1979. Since 1966, she has worked at the Russian Museum in present-day St. Petersburg, where she was named deputy director for academic research in 1986. She is a member of the St. Petersburg Union of Artists (Art History Section) and the International Council of Museums (ICOM).

We were thinking about what we could use this palace for. Then the idea arose to acquaint Mr. Ludwig with the building.

REGINA WYRWOLL Ms. Petrova, many years before your discussions with him, the German chocolate manufacturer and art collector Peter Ludwig had first tried to arrange for a Ludwig museum to be set up in the Pushkin State Museum of Fine Arts in Moscow. When did you first learn of him?

YEVGENIA PETROVA I had heard of Peter Ludwig many years before we met each other. I knew that he had tried to set up a new museum housing part of his collection within the Pushkin Museum. That was a lengthy and complicated affair. One day, at the beginning of the 1990s, we met for breakfast in Vienna. The gallery owner Krystyna Gmurzynska had introduced us. Our colleague, Joseph Kiblitsky, was there too. I was already certain that we should support Mr. Ludwig in founding a museum in St. Petersburg. During the Soviet era, very little Western art was on display in Russia, and the major works of the Russian avant-garde remained hidden in storage.

RW In your first meetings, did you already discuss the possibility of forming a Ludwig museum at the Russian Museum?

YP There were no concrete discussions about it. However, we already knew that the city was going to transfer the Marble Palace to us, a building which Empress Catherine the Great had built for her lover, Prince Grigory Orlov. By the beginning of the 1990s, that time had come. It so happened that we were thinking about what we could use the palace for. Then the idea arose to acquaint Mr. Ludwig with the building and discuss with him the possibility of exhibiting part of his collection there, since the idea of doing so in Moscow had petered out. We immediately suggested a concept for the exhibition of his donation: "Russian Art in the Context of World Art."

RW How was the Marble Palace used in prior years?

YP For many years, the Marble Palace housed a branch of the Moscow-based Lenin Museum. The interior of the palace was severely damaged and needed to be restored. We realised straight away that if we were going to pursue a collaboration with Peter Ludwig, the palace would need to be renovated differently than if we were only going to exhibit part of our collection there—whether as a permanent exhibition or through temporary exhibitions.

RW Did you tell Peter Ludwig about these plans during your first meeting in Vienna?

YP We told him about it in vague terms at our first meeting and invited him to St. Petersburg. He was very interested. We told him that we had a beautiful palace available that could house his museum, and we showed him a photo. There's a funny story connected to that, which we believe played an important role in the founding of the Ludwig Museum at the Russian Museum. Kiblitsky had written at the top of the photo, in big letters, "Ludwig Museum." Naturally, Mr. Ludwig was very excited and pleased by this. Shortly afterwards, within a month, he came to St. Petersburg for the first time, and the talks took concrete shape. We showed him the Marble Palace, gave him a tour of the building, and broadly explained to him what we had already planned.

RW Peter Ludwig had previously negotiated with Irina Antonova about a museum within the Pushkin Museum for almost ten years.

YP That project fell through because Moscow offered him the former Marx-Engels Museum building, in a park near the Kremlin, as the location for a Ludwig museum. That museum had previously been part of the Marx-Engels-Lenin Institute. If I remember correctly, it was a very small space, perhaps one hundred square metres. He remarked to me that this space didn't suit him. I think he would have preferred to be closer to the Pushkin Museum, or to have seen his donation housed within the Pushkin Museum itself. Nothing came of it and he later told us that the endless waiting wore him down. That's why he was immediately interested when we suggested the Marble Palace as a location for his museum. But, of course, it wasn't quite that easy. He was very pleased with both the Marble Palace and our concept of "Russian Art in the Context of World Art," but he wanted to test us first—he informed us all about this after the fact. The test went like this: To begin with, he offered us around thirty works which we could select ourselves.

He paid very close attention to how we decided on our selection and which works we settled on. Then we said to him: "Thirty works is not enough for our concept. We need at least thirty-three." And he agreed to that.

RW So that was the first step?

YP The first stage was the donation of these thirty-three works. Mr. Ludwig asked us to put together a booklet or small catalogue about them. We agreed to that and scheduled a very short period in which do it, less than six months. Six months later, Mr. Ludwig came to see us in the Marble Palace for the second time. At that point, the selected rooms had been restored and the small catalogue, entitled *Peter and Irene Ludwig's Gift to the Russian Museum*, was completed. Then he invited us to Aachen, where we selected further works for a second, larger donation. Of course we chose them ourselves, but he observed the process very closely and offered his advice.

RW Did you then exhibit the thirty-three works in the Marble Palace?

YP Yes, in 1995. He was very impressed with our selection: "You've chosen the best!"

RW Did the selection include works of contemporary Russian art?

YP You see, at the time the Russian Museum had a fine collection of official Soviet art, a category which was also represented in Mr. Ludwig's collection. But we had absolutely no artworks from our dissident compatriots—from the Nonconformists for example. They couldn't work in the Soviet Union and only gained public recognition in 1988, with the Sotheby's auction in Moscow, *Russian Avant-garde and Contemporary Soviet Art*. That's what was so interesting: when it came to the Russian part of the donation, Mr. Ludwig personally decided which works from his collection of Soviet underground art would be included.

RW Do you mean, for example, artists like Grisha Bruskin, Ilya Kabakov, or Vladimir Yankilevsky? From that generation?

YP Yes, he offered us works such as those, and we gladly accepted his offer.

Naturally, during the preparations for our exhibition, we also showed him our storage. He was deeply impressed; many works by Kazimir Malevich, Wassily Kandinsky, Marc Chagall, and others … had never left storage.

RW What happened next?

YP Step by step, we finalised the selection for the next donation. But we had also agreed with Mr. Ludwig that the Russian Museum would make further acquisitions and could accept artworks as donations, which would then be obligatorily included in the holdings of the Ludwig Museum at the Russian Museum. This included Russian art, as well as European works or world art from the second half of the twentieth century. However, we couldn't just choose arbitrarily, but had to make our selections in connection to planned exhibitions we wanted to include them in. That was the basic framework of our cooperation. Subsequently, we took Mr. Ludwig to meet our then mayor, Anatoly Sobchak. Sobchak was very well-known nationally and internationally because he was the first democratically elected mayor of St. Petersburg from 1991 to 1996. The talks in Sobchak's office were very congenial and constructive, and shortly thereafter we began refurbishing additional rooms in the Marble Palace for the next, larger exhibition of works to be donated from the Ludwig Collection.

RW Was Peter Ludwig satisfied with the way things were moving?

YP Every time he came to the Marble Palace he could observe the developing renovations. I don't know of any other person who has so excitedly followed the progress of renovations. Naturally, during the preparations for our exhibition, we also showed him our storage. He was deeply impressed; many works by Kazimir Malevich, Wassily Kandinsky, Marc Chagall, and others from our extensive collection had never been internationally exhibited. There were many works that had never left storage. He saw a lot of works there for the first time.

RW How did you come up with the concept of "Russian Art in the Context of World Art"?

YP Because it was such an important topic for the enormous collection of the Russian Museum, as Russian art has always developed in dialogue with global artistic movements. The Pushkin Museum in Moscow had proposed a completely different exhibition concept. There, his collection would have been exhibited alone, as a discrete unit in the city, without context and without being integrated into the museum's collection.

In the course of our preparations for the Ludwig Museum at the Russian Museum, we organised a large exhibition in the Marble Palace of works by Pablo Picasso from the Ludwig Collection. Mr. Ludwig himself said that the contrast was very surprising to him. He had never imagined that works by Picasso could look so beautiful and impressive in a palace's interior.

RW In the archives of the Peter and Irene Ludwig Foundation in Aachen, I found a letter from Ludwig to Krystyna Gmurzynska from August 1995, in which he complains bitterly: "What have you done? You convinced me to go to St. Petersburg! And now nothing is working …" It's an astonishing letter. This must have been some time after the opening, when progress on the building restoration had stopped, and misunderstandings subsequently accumulated.

YP That's right. In the summer of 1995 there were delays. But you have to remember that it was a time of great upheaval in both Russia and Germany! Peter Ludwig always wanted everything done yesterday, something I'm sure you know from experience. But the restoration of a palace, after all, takes time.

RW The Marble Palace is a prestigious and beautiful building, a gift from an empress with German roots to her lover. Its history would certainly have made it an appealing site to Ludwig. However, not only to him, but also to Ewald Schneider—the then head of the transport company hasenkamp, which worked with Ludwig on the majority of his exhibitions. Is it true that Schneider tried to have an office built for his company on the top floor of the Marble Palace, in what were once Prince Orlov's rooms?

YP That's right.

RW Why was he unable to do so?

YP It is not suitable—in my opinion—for transport company offices to be housed in a palace. It wouldn't have been appropriate. Schneider's company already had rooms in the Benois wing of the Mikhailovsky Palace, one of the other buildings belonging to the Russian Museum. Those rooms weren't bad. The Marble Palace would really have been a bit too much.

As a surprise for Peter Ludwig, we installed a sign at the entrance to the Marble Palace, even though not all of the contracts had been signed.

RW The Ludwig Museum opened on March 10, 1995. How did you celebrate the opening?

YP The opening took place in the Marble Hall. This hall is one of the palace's highlights, with thirty-two kinds of marble in various colours, inlays in the parquetry floor, beautiful chandeliers—in short, a unique interior! A number of the city's functionaries took part, including Mayor Sobchak. It was a festive atmosphere. The German consul-general was also there, of course. It was highly ceremonial. As a surprise for Peter Ludwig, we installed a sign at the entrance to the Marble Palace, even though not all of the contracts had been signed. On it was written, in both Russian and English, "Ludwig's Collection in the Russian Museum." He didn't know that, from the Russian side, the institution was as good as formed, and that his name would already be written at the entrance.

RW Did Peter Ludwig receive an Order of Merit from the City of St. Petersburg? Such honours were important to him.

YP We had initially sent all the relevant paperwork to the Ministry of Culture in Moscow. A medal from the state would have been a bit more meaningful than one from the city. But the Ministry of Culture put it on the back burner. Nothing was going to happen, at least not in the near future. We then organised everything here in the city, and he was awarded an Order of Merit from St. Petersburg.

RW Did Irene Ludwig often accompany him to St. Petersburg?

YP She was always with him when he came to St. Petersburg. She would never have let him meet with Russian women alone.

RW When he was in St. Petersburg, did Peter Ludwig buy artworks directly from artist studios in the city?

YP Yes. There are artists from St. Petersburg represented in his collection; for instance, Vitaly Tyulenev, Andrei Mylnikov, German Egoshin, Yuri Dyshlenko, and Zaven Arshakuni—but he didn't buy these works through us, nor at the time of the museum's founding. That was earlier, before we began to work together.

RW After the death of her husband, how did your working relationship with Irene Ludwig develop?

YP Up until her death in 2010, she was—if I remember correctly—only once here in the Marble Palace. I don't think there were any other big events, but the relationship continued. The then CEO of the Peter and Irene Ludwig Foundation, Walter Queins, was a regular visitor.

The Ludwig Museum at the Russian Museum continues to be a collection unique in the entire country.

RW What is the relevance of the Ludwig Collection for the Russian Museum today?

YP The Ludwig Museum at the Russian Museum continues to be a collection unique in the entire country. First of all, greatly differing artistic positions from the second half of the twentieth century are represented here. As you know, Russian—Soviet at the time—museums were not allowed to purchase that kind of art. There was no money for acquisitions of that kind. Therefore, the Ludwig Museum was, and remains, the only opportunity for people who don't have the money to visit foreign museums to become familiar with these works of art.

Moreover, it conveys that these various international artistic movements also have certain parallels with and connections to the trends seen in Russian art from the first half of the twentieth century. For example, the abstraction of the Russian avant-garde has a great deal in common with abstract movements in Western European art.

The Ludwig Collection at the Russian Museum is not particularly large, but it complements our permanent collection and fills gaps in our holdings of national and international art—such as with Russian (previously Soviet) underground art. This is almost exclusively represented in the Ludwig Museum at the Russian Museum because state museums were not permitted to collect it. There are no collections that include such works in Moscow or St. Petersburg. So only the Ludwig Museum at the Russian Museum fills this gap.

And, lastly, it is very important to us that, through contemporary exhibitions, the Ludwig Museum at the Russian Museum gives us the opportunity to present current global art in the Marble Palace. By doing so, we continue to fulfil the mission that was agreed upon with Mr. Ludwig.

RW Do I understand correctly that the Ludwig Collection in Russia is the only collection in a state museum in which dissident or Nonconformist works of art are represented? Conversely, does that mean that such works are to be found almost exclusively in the West?

YP Today, things are different. In recent times, the Tretyakov Gallery, the Russian Museum, and, of course, private collectors have acquired some works from this category. But during the 1990s, these artworks were neither collected nor purchased.

RW Do any other anecdotes about Peter Ludwig spring to mind?

YP There are many, many stories connected with the Ludwig Museum. Perhaps I should mention that, whenever we picked him up from the airport by car, Mr. Ludwig had the car stop at all the supermarkets so he could check if his Schogetten was in stock.

RW Did he ever combine his business endeavours in the then USSR with his artistic projects?

YP He kept them strictly separated. I have a story about that too. Peter Ludwig brought two small suitcases full of blocks of chocolate with him to his talks with Mayor Sobchak, but the conversation revolved solely around art. The suitcases were unused, so to speak. Sobchak additionally mentioned that his daughter is allergic to chocolate; in the end, Ludwig had to take both the suitcases with him.

RW I could see from the files that Peter Ludwig would have liked to set up a chocolate production facility in the St. Petersburg area.

YP Yes, that's right.

RW But it didn't work out. Do you know why?

YP That had nothing to do with us, so I can't really say. But as I said before, those years were ones of upheaval. After the opening of the Ludwig Museum, the position of mayor constantly changed hands. For whatever reason, the factory just never came about.

RW Ms. Petrova, when you think about Peter Ludwig now, how would you characterise him?

It was not for nothing that [Peter Ludwig] pursued an interest in very different forms of art. ... I would say that art was a kind of cornerstone of his life.

YP I've seldom met an individual like him. I'm referring primarily to his relationship to art, to all art, regardless of the national or historical context from which it came. He was interested in everything, in every form of art. He possessed a rare trait: he was enthusiastic. That's actually very rare, especially among people who are active in the art world. It was a genuine pleasure to visit exhibitions with him. Otherwise, he was a humorous person. We laughed a lot together and told lots of jokes. He was also a very democratic individual. You never felt unimportant or overlooked in his presence. It was particularly important for him that whoever he was with was genuinely interested in art—then the conversation flowed effortlessly. He might begin the conversation a bit loftily or a little too formally, but as soon as he noticed that his companion was genuinely interested in art and had something to say, he became more human, approachable, and open. He was an exceptional, extraordinary person. It was not for nothing that he pursued an interest in very different forms of art and collected a variety of objects.

RW From your personal experience, can you define what art meant to Peter Ludwig?

YP I would say that art was a kind of cornerstone of his life. He could occupy himself with other things, but beneath the surface he was always thinking about art and his interest in it. I say that based on how much and how intensively we talked about art when we were together.

RW Ms. Petrova, thank you for taking the time to talk to us.

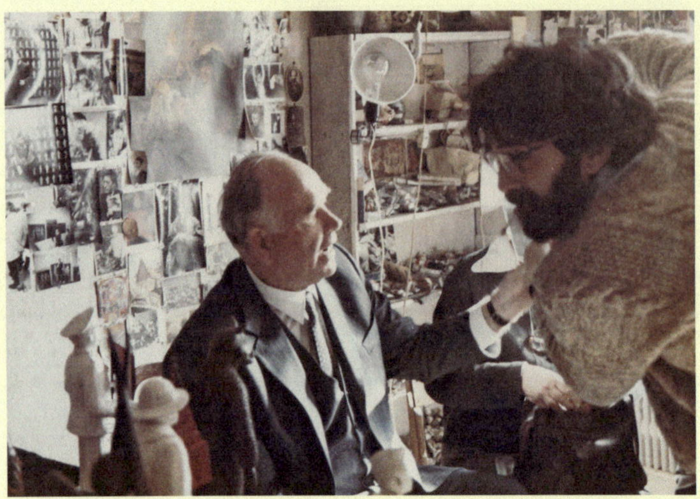

Peter Ludwig in Grisha Bruskin's studio in Moscow, 1988.
Photo: private

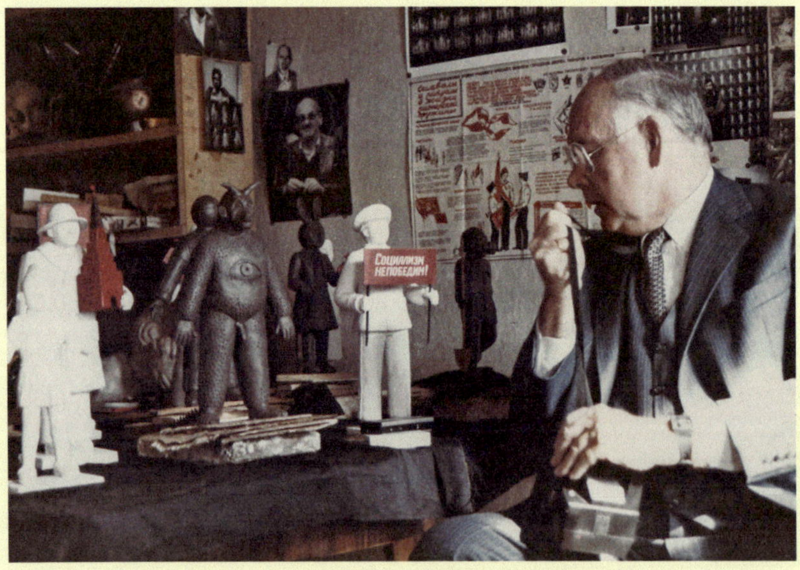

Peter Ludwig in Grisha Bruskin's studio in Moscow, 1988.
Photo: private

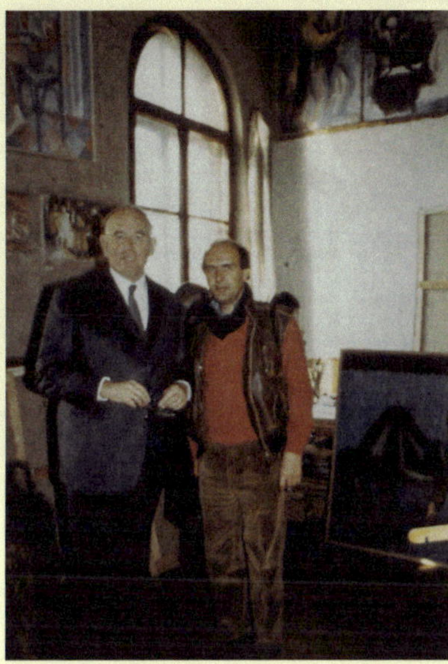

Peter Ludwig and Thomas Krings-Ernst visiting a studio in Moscow, 1988.
Photo: private

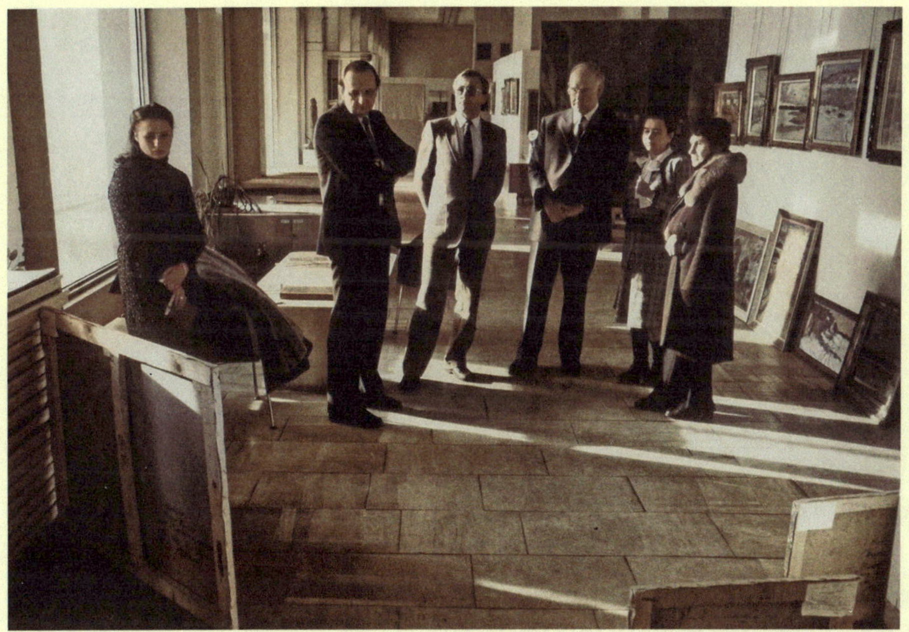

Peter Ludwig in an unknown art institution during one of his trips to Russia. On the trip, he was accompanied by the editor in chief of the journal *art*, Axel Hecht, and the journal's photographer Dirk Reinartz. The journal published an article in April 1982 about Peter Ludwig's art acquisition activities in Russia.
Photo: Dirk Reinartz

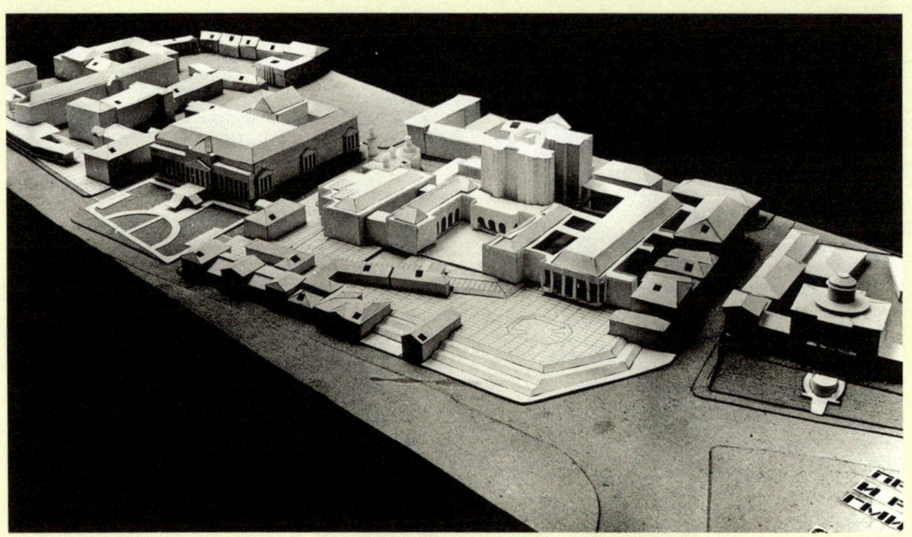

A design model made during the Ludwig Museum in Moscow's planning phase—between 1988 and 1994—which was never built.
Photo: unkown

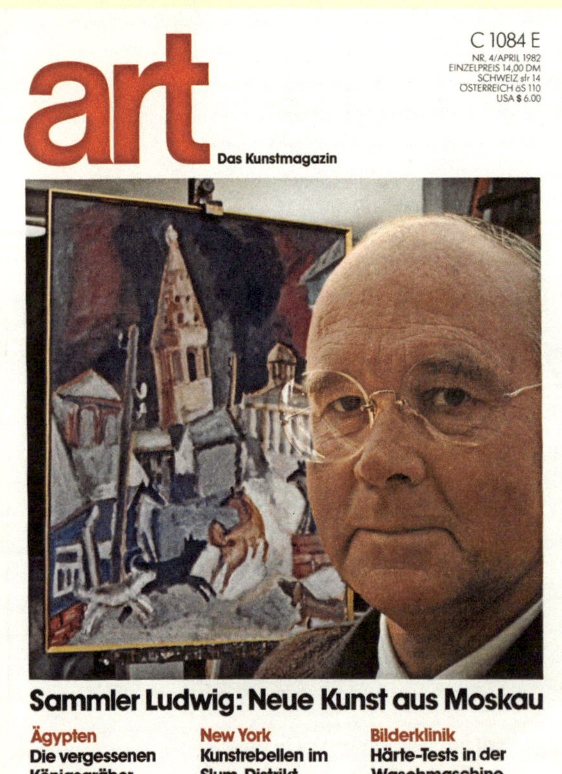

Cover of *art*, April 1982, titled "Collector Ludwig: New Art from Moscow."

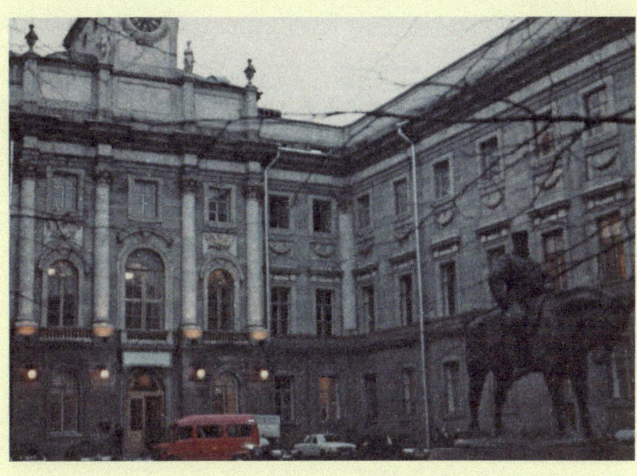

Entrance to the Ludwig Museum
at the Russian Museum, St. Petersburg, 1995.
Photo: private

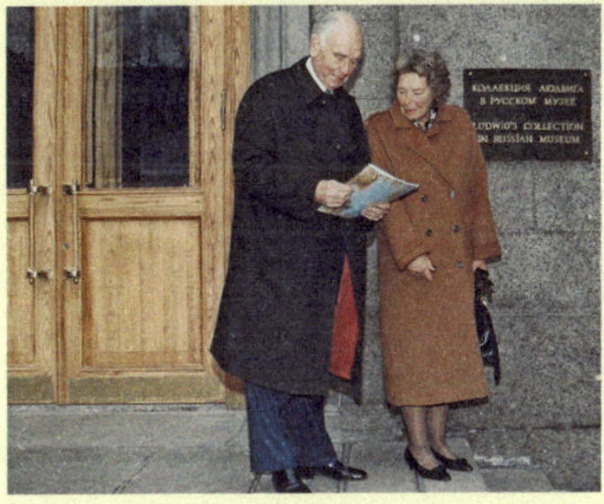

Peter and Irene Ludwig in front of the entrance sign at the opening of the Ludwig Museum at the Russian Museum in St. Petersburg, 1995.
Photo: private

Das schönste Museum Ludwig wurde eröffnet

Im St. Petersburger Marmorpalais – Zwei Ausstellungen

Von Eckhard Hoog 584.17

Aachen. Von allen Museen der Welt, die den Namen des Aachener Kunstmäzens Peter Ludwig tragen, dürfte das jüngste zugleich auch das schönste sein: das „Museum Ludwig im Russischen Museum St. Petersburg", so der offizielle Name. Untergebracht im wahrhaft ersten Haus am Platze: im Marmorpalais an der Newa, ein paar Schritte entfernt von der Eremitage, erbaut auf Veranlassung von Katharina der Großen. 67 Jahre lang, bis 1991, war der Palast das Lenin-Museum. Seit der Vertragsunterzeichnung zwischen den Ludwigs und dem russischen Museum im vergangenen Jahr wurde der Bau, eines der prächtigsten und wichtigstens Architekturdenkmäler Petersburgs, in Rekordzeit in den historischen Zustand zurückversetzt. 4000 Quadratmeter Ausstellungsfläche stehen zur Zeit bereit, am Ende soll es mindestens das Doppelte sein. Am Wochenende nun wurde das Museum feierlich eröffnet.

Peter Ludwig zeigte sich nach seiner Rückkehr gestern im Gespräch mit unserer Zeitung noch tief beeindruckt von dem außerordentlichen Publikumsandrang und vor allem der in jeder Hinsicht freundschaftlichen Aufnahme. „Es war schon ein sehr bewegender Moment, als der Oberbürgermeister von Petersburg, Anatolij Sobtschak, seine Rede mit den Worten begann: ‚Ein großer Tag für unsere Stadt. Wir bekommen zu den herrlichen Museen, die wir haben, nun ein wichtiges neues hinzu, das uns die deutschen Sammler Irene und Peter Ludwig ermöglicht haben ...'"

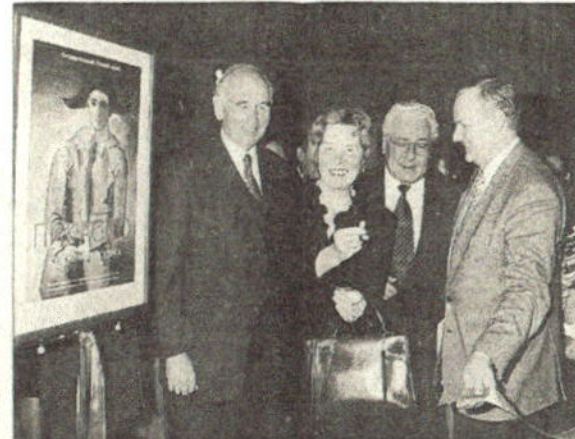

Die feierliche Eröffnung: (von links) Peter und Irene Ludwig, Kölns Oberbürgermeister Norbert Burger und der Petersburger Oberbürgermeister Anatolij Sobtschak.

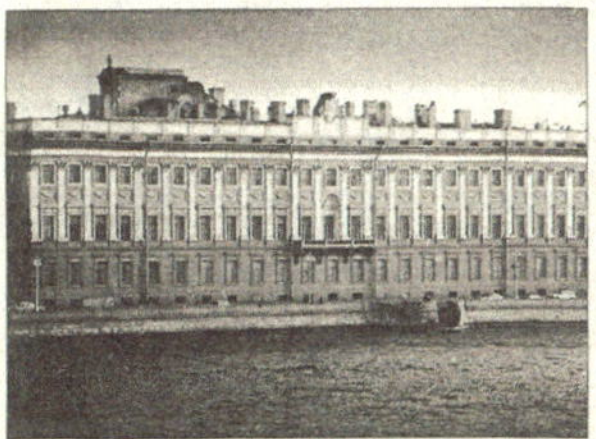

Das neue Museum Ludwig hat in St. Petersburg ein eigenes Gebäude: das Marmorpalais. Einer von drei Palästen des Russischen Museums.

Kölns Oberbürgermeister Norbert Burger war mit einer ganzen Reisegruppe der Gesellschaft der Freunde am Museum Ludwig ebenso angereist wie der Vorsitzende des Aachener Museumsvereins, Hans-Josef Thouet, um der Eröffnung der ersten beiden Ausstellungen beizuwohnen. Zum einen jene 33 Werke westlicher und russischer Künstler wie Andy Warhol und Ilya Kabakov, die das Ehepaar Ludwig dem Russischen Museum geschenkt hat. Zum anderen eine Picasso-Schau mit 140 Werken aus allen Schaffensperioden. Ludwig: „Das ist die erste Picasso-Ausstellung, die jemals in Rußland stattgefunden hat." Der Andrang dürfte gewaltig werden.

Diese Präsentation ist das Resultat eines Kooperationsvertrages zwischen dem Museum Ludwig in Köln und dem Russischen Museum St. Petersburg. Im Gegenzug kann das Museum Ludwig im Herbst aus den Petersburger Beständen die größte Malewitsch-Ausstellung veranstalten, die der Westen je gesehen hat. Und Aachen soll in irgendeiner Form aus dieser Kooperation ebenfalls profitieren, verspricht Ludwig.

Das Thema „Beutekunst" im übrigen – völlig unabhängig von der Museumseröffnung – hat in allen Gesprächen Ludwigs in Petersburg eine große Rolle gespielt. Ludwig: „Ich habe immer für die Rückgabe plädiert." Gleichwohl sei besondere Sensibilität gefragt. Dabei verweist Ludwig auf das Beispiel des Quedlinburger Domschatzes: „Da wurden den Erben eines überführten Diebes Millionen für die Rückgabe gezahlt. Rußland will die deutsche Kunst nicht verkaufen. Aber verhandeln muß man in irgendeiner Form schon ..."

Newspaper article about the opening of the Ludwig Museum at the Russian Museum in St. Petersburg.
"The Most Beautiful Museum Ludwig Opened," Stolberger Volkszeitung, 14.3.1995

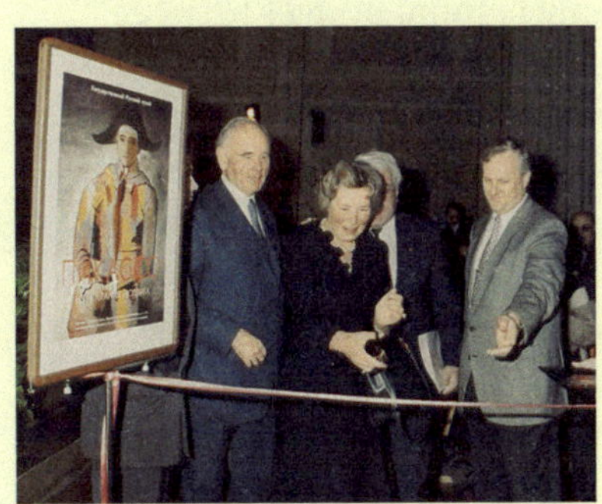

Opening of the Ludwig Museum at the Russian Museum in St. Petersburg, 1995. From left to right: Peter Ludwig, Irene Ludwig, Norbert Burger (mayor of Cologne), Anatoly Sobchak (mayor of St. Petersburg).
Photo: unkown

CUBA

At the beginning of the 1990s, Socialist-ruled, post-revolutionary Cuba was still a hotly debated political subject. However, its cultural scene remained largely unknown. With the collapse of the Soviet Union and the Communist Bloc, upon which Cuba was economically dependent, the island state faced immense economic turmoil. When the exhibition *Kuba o.k.* was shown at the Kunsthalle Düsseldorf in 1990, Peter and Irene Ludwig were able to encounter the country's contemporary art, which represented new artistic territory for them both. The exhibition grew out of a visit to Cuba by the Kunsthalle's director, **Jürgen Harten**. In collaboration with Cuba's Centro de Desarrollo de Artes Visuales (Centre for the Development of the Visual Arts), he presented the work of nineteen young Cuban artists. When the exhibition closed, gallerist Thomas Krings-Ernst procured a number of contemporary Cuban artworks and sold them to the Ludwigs—including the majority of the works shown in Düsseldorf. The acquisition—around forty-five works—marked the beginning of a focus on Cuban art within the Ludwig Collection.

In December 1991, Peter Ludwig travelled to Havana for the first time, with his intentions extending beyond merely acquiring more Cuban art. With the idea of building cultural bridges between Cuba and Europe, he strived to foster a long-term cooperation with the local art scene. One of the most important players in Cuba was **Helmo Hernández**. At the National Council for Fine Arts, the curator and professor was responsible for international relations and opened doors for the Ludwigs, both to Cuban artist studios and to cultural institutions.
An important public institution for the promotion of contemporary art in Havana already existed: the Centro de Arte Contemporáneo Wifredo Lam (Wifredo Lam Centre of Contemporary

Art). Its director, Llilian Llanes, had started the Bienal de La Habana (the Havana Biennial) in 1984, together with the minister of culture, Armando Hart Dávalos. This exhibition focussed on contemporary art from Latin America; from the second biennial on, it additionally focussed on works from African and Asian countries.

During Ludwig's first trip, and on two subsequent meetings—in March 1992 in Aachen and in November 1993 in Cuba—negotiations were conducted with the Cuban deputy minister of culture, Omar González Hernández, which produced concrete results. From 1992, an annual scholarship programme made it possible for two Cuban artists to work at Aachen's Ludwig Forum für Internationale Kunst (Ludwig Forum for International Art). Beginning in 1993, two German artists also received scholarships to spend time in Havana. Initially, the founding of a modern art museum in Havana was also discussed, for which the Ludwigs had earmarked up to one hundred works from their collection to serve as either donations or permanent loans. In the course of negotiations, however, the founding of a museum was abandoned in favour of the establishment of a Cuban Ludwig foundation, due to Cuba's economic problems.

On August 18, 1994, the Fundación Ludwig de Cuba, or FLC, was created with the aim of supporting young Cuban artists. Helmo Hernández was appointed as its president. The Fundación was the third international Ludwig foundation, following those in Vienna and Budapest. As an additional outcome of the negotiations, the fifth Havana Biennial in 1994 was not only financially supported by the German Ludwig Foundation, but a part of the exhibition was also shown at Aachen's Ludwig Forum on the initiative of Wolfgang Becker, the museum's director. Just weeks after the Fundación Ludwig de Cuba was set up, the exhibition *Die 5. Biennale von Havanna. Eine Auswahl* (*The 5th Havana Biennial: A Selection*) opened in Aachen. It was the first time that an offshoot of the biennial was officially shown in Europe.

As with all of their work, the Ludwigs viewed their cooperation with Cuba as engaging in cultural politics. In the final point of a memorandum from March 1992, the signatories, Peter Ludwig and Omar González Hernández, wrote: "These activities serve the improvement of relations between Germany and Cuba and the development of friendship between their two peoples."

Today, the Ludwig Collection's Cuban holdings number around 150 works, including pieces by Belkis Ayón, Carlos Cárdenas, Glexis Novoa, and José Toirac.

A conversation with **Jürgen Harten** about the 1990 exhibition *Kuba o.k. – Aktuelle Kunst aus Kuba* at the Kunsthalle Düsseldorf, which led to Peter and Irene Ludwig's first acquisitions of contemporary Cuban art

The interview was conducted in Harten's apartment in Berlin on October 18, 2019.

JÜRGEN HARTEN (b. 1933, Hamburg) studied education, anthropology, and art history from 1953 to 1960. From 1961 to 1967, he was a primary and secondary school teacher. In 1967, under Arnold Bode, he was secretary of the fourth documenta in Kassel. From 1969 to 1972, he was a research assistant and deputy director of the Kunsthalle Düsseldorf; he subsequently became its director, a position he held until 1998. As its founding director, Harten was involved in the planning for the museum kunstpalast—today known as the KUNSTPALAST—in Düsseldorf. He has lived in Berlin since 2002.

I don't think there was any specific feeling regarding Cuba. … The time when people were discussing Cuba was twenty years earlier to then. … I flew there because I was interested to find out what had changed culturally following Fidel Castro's revolution.

REGINA WYRWOLL Mr. Harten, you were the director of the Kunsthalle Düsseldorf from 1972 to 1998. Did you visit the Havana Biennial in that role?

JÜRGEN HARTEN Yes, I travelled to Cuba for the third biennial in winter 1989. My coworker at the time, the curator Ulrich Krempel, had been to the previous biennial in Havana in 1986. He had been invited due to his connections with local leftist groups. I was not involved with that, but I signed off on his trip of course. When he returned he was very enthusiastic and said that it had been well worth it. Then I didn't hear anything for a while. When the next biennial took place, I received an invitation.

RW That means you were invited by the organisers in Cuba? Was that owing to Krempel's involvement?

JH No, Krempel had nothing to do with it. He had just been there before me. Maybe he had given them a good impression of Düsseldorf, who knows. But he wasn't the director, that was me. I was also a member of the board of CİMAM, the International Committee for Museums and Collections of Modern Art, a part of the of the worldwide umbrella organisation for museums ICOM, the International Council of Museums—something they were probably aware of in Havana.

RW The Havana Biennial was, at that time, something out of the ordinary due to its focus on art from Latin America and, more generally, from countries in the Global South. What was the general feeling in Germany in regard to Cuba at that time?

JH I don't think there was any specific feeling regarding Cuba, certainly not in Düsseldorf. The time when people were discussing Cuba was twenty years before then. Today, people would know the value of such an opportunity. Back then, few knew and fewer cared. I flew there because I was interested in finding out what had changed culturally following Fidel Castro's revolution. I had no explicit goals and my invitation came without conditions, demands, or expectations. I was simply invited as someone who wanted to look at everything—and that's exactly what occurred.

RW How did it play out?

JH Everything turned out differently to how I had imagined. I was supposed to be picked up at the airport but there was no one waiting for me, so I had to find a taxi. Thank God I knew which hotel I was staying at. It was a typical Intourist hotel. A young woman who spoke fluent English approached me and asked me a few questions. Over the course of our conversation, I realized that she had the right connections. Maybe she was employed by the hotel specifically for people like me, I don't know for certain. In any case, I introduced myself first! This start to my visit did nothing to put me at ease. Since the ICOM Congress in 1977, I had often travelled to the Soviet Union to prepare exhibitions, where I was always met with exceptional treatment. The kind of "wait and see" situation I found myself in at first in Cuba was a bit strange, although it didn't upset me. I told myself, "Okay, that's just how it is in Cuba." Llilian Llanes was the one who had invited me. At the time, she was the head of the Centro de Arte Contemporáneo Wifredo Lam (Wifredo Lam Centre of Contemporary Art), which was responsible for the biennial.

RW Was your travel covered by the Cubans?

JH I paid for my own travel while the Cubans covered my accommodation—a standard arrangement.

RW Was the biennial held at a single location or spread across several?

JH There were a number of exhibition spaces throughout Havana. This included one or two galleries and the Centro de Arte Contemporáneo Wifredo Lam, which continues to organise the biennial today. The exhibitions were excellent. Among them was the Museo Nacional de Bellas Artes (National Museum of Fine Arts), which had rehung its collection for the occasion. I approached all of it with an open mind. If anything, I had a positive bias, because one or two years earlier a work by the Cuban artist Flavio Garciandía at the São Paulo Biennial had caught my eye. Prior to my visit, that was the only example of Cuban art that I had seen in person. I saw Flavio again in Havana. He was the teacher, so to speak, of a number of young artists at a time when the minister of culture, Armando Hart Dávalos, had spurred a turn away from Socialist Realism—the official style of the Soviet Union—something quite evident in the exhibitions. At this biennial there was, for example, a fresh take on the hammer and sickle using tropical vegetation—very bright and vivid. There were also individual object-like paintings that incorporated plants. What really impressed me were the large installations by Glexis Novoa and Ciro Quintana, not to mention works by the sculptor Alejandro Aguilera. I found the biennial refreshing. It was completely different to my expectations of the art from a Socialist country. It was eclectic, with very different styles represented. There was no conformism as far as I could see.

I'm reminded of another episode that I just have to tell you about: The woman at the hotel had told me about Trinidad, a city in the centre of Cuba with many magnificent buildings in the Colonial style, which are World Heritage listed and had been laboriously restored with support from UNESCO. I wanted to see them and was even willing to hitchhike there if I couldn't find another means of transport. My hosts were appalled at that idea and wanted to provide me with a car, but then came up with all manner of excuses for why that couldn't happen: the car had broken down, there wasn't a driver available, the usual problems under Socialism. But in the end it worked out anyway. On the drive, which took several hours, we stopped for a break at the house of some of the driver's relatives, who served me some delicious coffee they had harvested themselves. During the return trip, one of the employees of the Centro de Arte Contemporáneo Wifredo Lam tried to pump me for information. I flew home again with these vivid impressions—both of the art and the people. I had come with no intentions and no plans.

RW Was Peter Ludwig also in Havana at that time?

JH No, Ludwig didn't travel to Havana until after me. I never met him in person, by the way. When I was leaving Havana, I was approached by Beatriz Aulen, the then director of the Centro de

Desarrollo de Artes Visuales (Centre for the Development of the Visual Arts). The centre is a central contact point for contemporary art in Cuba, organising exhibitions, supporting artists, and promoting international cooperation. She asked if I couldn't do something for Cuban art; she was clearly interested in money but didn't understand how things worked in Germany. She thought I could promote Cuban art and help foster sales. My reaction was: "That's not my job at all. I am interested in exhibitions. I don't do the kind of promotion that has to do with the commercial domain." And then I flew out.

RW What a story …

JH I'm just getting started! Some months later I was planning an exhibition of the early works of the Italian painter Giacomo Balla, the Futurist who lived in Düsseldorf for several months between 1912 and 1914. I was already in contact with his daughters, who both lived in Rome and had the beautiful names of Luce and Elica—meaning Light and Propeller, truly Futurist names. They were constantly interrupting each other, and visiting them was always highly entertaining. They were both very helpful until it came out that they had already promised all of their artworks to a planned foundation for Balla. This dragged on and on, and nobody knew what would become of it. As all of the important works—Balla's drawings—belonged to the daughters, I ultimately had to abandon the exhibition.

I came up with a daring idea: asking the Cubans if it would be possible to put together an exhibition in Düsseldorf of works I had seen during my time in Havana.

RW So you had a vacant spot in your programme?

JH Yes, what should I do with it? I came up with a daring idea: asking the Cubans if it would be possible to put together an exhibition in Düsseldorf of works I had seen during my time in Havana. That would mean returning to Cuba to look for works. The Cubans, of course, would have to assist me. I made enquiries with Llilian Llanes, who had amicable relationships with other representatives of the Cuban cultural administration. In Cuba, they were very enthusiastic about my proposal, and I was invited to Cuba to prepare the exhibition. At the start, Tonel, a Cuban artist and critic whose real name is Antonio Eligio Fernández, was assigned to help me. We got along wonderfully and we're still friends today. I was there for fourteen days altogether. Each day, often until midnight, we visited artist studios in Havana, having discussions and searching for works. I made a lot of notes for the exhibition catalogue and, in the process, developed an idea of what would be included in it, what it would look like, and who should write it. I came back to Düsseldorf well prepared with a virtually finished exhibition.

I had the impression that the criteria the Cuban artists adhered to in their work were exactly the same as the ones I followed in my curatorial work. There were no local criteria or ideological reservations.

RW Did you concentrate on people whose work you had seen at the biennial, or did Tonel suggest other artists to consider?

JH Most of them were ones I had already seen. Tonel and I always agreed with each other. However, there was one suggestion that I rejected and he acquiesced to me, and another where I respected his decision. We decided cooperatively and always in deep consensus. I had the impression that the criteria the Cuban artists adhered to in their work were exactly the same as the ones I followed in my curatorial work. There were no local criteria or ideological reservations.

RW There was no censorship?

JH There were borderline cases where the state exercised censorship. One example was an exhibition of Hans Haacke where prints based on the famous portrait of Che Guevara were to be on sale. It wasn't allowed to open. Nor was I able to meet the artists Eduardo Ponjuán and René Francisco, who, if I remember correctly, were included in the third biennial. I only learned later that an exhibition of their works, which included slightly manipulated portraits of Fidel Castro, had been closed.

In this context, two things must be taken into consideration. First, free artistic representations of Fidel Castro were frowned upon. And second, the same went for direct criticism of the Socialist system or how it had been implemented. My being there represented the freedom of art, because in Cuba everyone worked in a system of—more or less—ideological subordination. But nobody expected me to conform. I was treated as a prominent European guest, who they hoped would understand the Cuban system. Even though he had long been retired, Llilian Llanes' husband Regino still served as one of Castro's close advisers, and he had personally driven me around in his car and described their achievements in agriculture, education, and medical advancements. I also visited the art university in Havana, the Instituto Superior de Arte (ISA). I saw a work there that been created by Blinky Palermo, Beuys's student from Düsseldorf. That was very impressive. The local scene was completely up-to-date in terms of the latest developments in the international art scene. Appropriation art was big in America at the time. Two artist couples, José Toirac and Tanya Angulo on the one hand, and Juan Ballester and Ileana Villazón on the other, made clear through Tonel that they didn't want to take part in the Düsseldorf exhibition because they didn't think it was right for a German curator to come and select Cuban art. In response I said: "That's great. I'm not the only one doing this sort of thing, but I can understand their point of view. Let's do something different then. Let's invite them to be part of a critical exhibition, which will comment on this exhibition." That's what we did. In their exhibition, the four of them imitated the works of others in the style of appropriation art, thereby commenting on our exhibition concept. They also included works by an artist who we had not chosen for our exhibition and whose name was not to be mentioned. This was all announced and presented in the catalogue.

RW Were any of Tonel's own works included in the exhibition?

JH He chose not to take part so that there wouldn't be a conflict of interest between Tonel the artist and Tonel the critic. Instead, he later had a small solo exhibition in the Kunsthalle Düsseldorf. Everything went well, but there was disagreement about the catalogue texts. We had agreed that the catalogue would be put together by both sides: Düsseldorf would pay for it, but it would be a joint production. It was important to me that the Cubans support the entire project. I had suggested two main authors. One of them, Gerardo Mosquera, wrote all the texts about Cuba and South America. He wrote professionally, critiqued the art, and never strayed into the realm of party propaganda. It was informative and easy to read. Then I suggested a second author, Osvaldo Sánchez, who was better known as a writer. The Cuban Ministry of Culture wouldn't agree to him. In the end we came to a compromise. I said: "Good. If it can't be printed in our joint catalogue, then I will print it in Düsseldorf as a supplementary text that can be enclosed in the Düsseldorf edition of the catalogue." And that's what we did. His text explicitly referred to the actions of the two artist couples. It also contained images of Hans Haacke's censored exhibition.

RW How was the exhibition organised?

JH We had agreed that I would invite a number of the artists to Germany so they could set up their installations in Düsseldorf. Some of this was done on-site, partially because some required materials were unavailable in Havana, such as neon tubes. I can no longer say who exactly was part of that. I remember that there were five or six of them. They flew to Frankfurt am Main with Cubana Airlines, paid for by the Cubans. Upon their arrival, they were our guests. They returned to Cuba the same way.

RW You drew up the list of works which were to be exhibited. How were they brought to Düsseldorf?

JH There was a central point of contact responsible for international affairs in the Ministry of Culture. Helmo Hernández held that position and he was very helpful. I met him briefly, if I remember correctly. By the way, he later became the president of the Fundación Ludwig de Cuba. In any case, the Ministry of Culture decided that the works which Tonel and I had selected would be flown to Frankfurt am Main by Cubana Airlines. From there, we would have to arrange for their transport to Düsseldorf out of our own pocket.

RW The exhibition *Kuba o.k. – Aktuelle Kunst aus Kuba* (*Cuba OK: Current Art From Cuba*) took place from April 1 to May 30, 1990. How was it received in Düsseldorf?

Of course, there were always the big exhibitions for the general public. I made sure of that. But things like the Cuba show, that was a purely experimental affair.

JH To be honest, I don't know for certain. Our most important audience back then was the Düsseldorf artistic community. I won't pretend otherwise. Of course, there were always the big exhibitions for the general public. I made sure of that. But things like the Cuba show, that was a purely experimental affair. At the opening, something surprising happened: a group of young people suddenly appeared, playing Cuban music with instruments and dancing. Where they came from, who arranged for them to be there, and how they even knew about it, I don't have the faintest idea. Nor did I ask any questions. That's how it was in Düsseldorf—if something like that happened, then it happened. I welcomed it because it created a great atmosphere.

RW Who spoke at the opening? Were there any Cuban officials there, for example from the embassy? It must have been a huge event for Cuba, after all.

JH I can't recall seeing any official Cuban representatives at the opening and, as a general rule, we didn't have speeches at such events. On rare occasions, for diplomatic reasons, the mayor said a few words, which I would write for him.

RW Was that the case at the Cuba exhibition?

JH I really can't remember. It didn't really interest me either.

RW Were there a lot of visitors to the exhibition?

JH Not a huge number.

RW Can you remember any of the newspaper articles or reviews?

JH No. You have to remember that the Kunsthalle only had a very small team. I held a press conference for every exhibition, but there was no one who kept an eye on the results. To get to the point: I had no idea about Peter Ludwig's interest in Cuban art. What followed transpired without me.

RW Ludwig had his scouts. Wolfgang Becker, for example, the director of the Neue Galerie (New Gallery) in Aachen, and Thomas Krings-Ernst, the gallerist from Cologne. They saw the exhibition.

JH I knew of Becker and I had met Krings-Ernst once, because I had connections to some young, emerging artists from Moscow who he had first exhibited. It's possible that they both visited the exhibition, but they didn't let me know of their visit and I never had personal contact with them.

RW That's interesting! Helmo Hernández mentioned that it was through Becker and Krings-Ernst that Ludwig's interest in Cuban art was stirred.

JH That may be the case, but I don't know anything about it. But that works from the exhibition in Düsseldorf should go directly to the Ludwig Collection, that I knew.

RW How did you learn of it?

JH Someone had told me that Peter Ludwig wanted to buy the works in the exhibition. I naturally thought that was wonderful. But then at the same time, I was informed that the works would have to be returned to Cuba regardless. That didn't make sense to me, but it wasn't in my power to change it. I thought it was only right to stick to the agreements as they had been made.

RW And why did the works have to go back?

JH I was told that the Cubans insisted that all the works first be returned to Cuba for customs reasons before being sold to buyers in Germany. So the entire exhibition went back to Havana on the Socialist route. That is, on a Cuban ship from Rostock. Instead of taking them to Frankfurt, we took them to the harbour in Rostock, where a Cuban ship took them back to Havana.

By the way, Ludwig had previously bought a work from one of my Düsseldorf exhibitions: *The Portable War Memorial* by Edward Kienholz from 1970, which is now in the Museum Ludwig in Cologne. However, I never met Peter Ludwig personally.

RW Mr. Harten, thank you very much for talking to us.

A conversation with **Helmo Hernández** about Peter and Irene Ludwig's activities in Cuba and the founding of the Fundación Ludwig de Cuba in Havana

This interview was conducted on January 24 and 26, 2015, at the office of the Fundación Ludwig de Cuba in Havana.

HELMO HERNÁNDEZ (b. 1947, Havana) is an art historian and expert in the fields of visual arts, theatre, cultural policy, and community development. He was a key advisor to Peter and Irene Ludwig on building their collection of Cuban art and in the subsequent establishment of the Fundación Ludwig de Cuba, where he has served as president since 1994.

He finished his studies in art history in 1970, receiving a master's degree in cultural studies at the University of Havana. Currently, he serves as an advisor in several institutions and organisations, including the Cuban Ministries of Culture and of Education and the Instituto Superior de Arte (University of Arts of Cuba) in Havana. He is a faculty member at several universities in Havana and has lectured extensively in Cuba, the US, and other countries.

The Fundación Ludwig de Cuba, established in 1994 under the sponsorship of Peter and Irene Ludwig, is an autonomous, non-governmental, and nonprofit institution based in Havana whose aim is to support and promote contemporary Cuban art.

In Cuba, the strongest critical expressions came from the arts.

REGINA WYRWOLL Helmo, we are conducting this interview on January 24, 2015 in Havana. You just celebrated the twentieth anniversary of the Fundación Ludwig de Cuba, which is the occasion for this conversation. My first question: In our European understanding, the Havana Biennial, founded in 1984, has been the most important event for the visual arts in Latin America. In 1990, the first exhibition of young Cuban artists in Germany, *Kuba o.k*, came to Düsseldorf. Did the latter create a special or new situation for the artistic scene here in Cuba? Were there other important exhibitions of Cuban art abroad?

HELMO HERNÁNDEZ I am sorry that my voice is not strong today, and I have to discuss these complexities in English, which is not my mother language. Although belonging to the international Socialist system, the cultural policies that applied in Cuba were different from those in Eastern European Socialist countries. In his 1961 speech to Cuban intellectuals, Fidel Castro meant—according to my understanding—that we would always remain inserted within the Western world tradition, in which artists are a part of the critical consciousness of society.

Anyhow, nothing has remained the same over time, nothing was ever really homogeneous. It always depended on the political trends that prevailed in a given moment, on the influences that were the strongest at the time. I mean that you cannot approach Cuba as a homogeneous place. You will always find different trends, even if you look at the people who have supported the revolution through all these years. In order to make things easier to understand, let's divide the latter people into two main groups: those who—in a dogmatic way—wanted Cuba to follow the path of the former international Communist movement; and those who did want a revolution in Cuba, but searched for its own unique way of doing it, keeping in mind that our own identity and postcolonial status—placing us within the so-called Third World—needs its own standards. We should also keep in mind the economic, political, and diplomatic harassment fostered by dominant forces in the US, which created a defensive mentality within Cuba in which the more dogmatic groups grew stronger in periods when this harassment has been more intense. In short, Cuban cultural policy has navigated through these troubled waters.

Progressive and liberal ideas prevailed in the cultural field. The only exception was the first five years of the 1970s, when strategic positions within this field were held by pro-Soviet officials. After that, the creation of the Ministry of Culture and the nomination of Armando Hart (a well-respected intellectual) as minister in 1976 was a clear message that cultural policy would evolve in a positive way, aiming to reverse all the mistakes that the bureaucracy and dogmatic influences had caused during the previous years. It paved the way for the changes in the cultural policy of the 1980s. In 1976, the ministry founded the Instituto Superior de Arte (ISA, or University of Arts of Cuba), a university where young people from every background and social status in the island could be admitted to study art as well as music, theater, dance, et cetera. In their classrooms, as well as through catalogs or magazines, these students were in contact with what had been produced in the rest of the world at that time. The school faculty—artists who fostered avant-garde ideas—clearly had a crucial role in these dynamics. The 1981 exhibition *Volumen 1*, which can be considered a turning point in the history of Cuban art, could never have happened without this newly created environment. Coming back to what I said earlier, there was also opposition to such progressive cultural policies; it came from the organization of young Communists—the Unión de Jóvenes Comunistas (UJC)—or even from some officials within the Communist party. The revolutionary process has always been a field for ideological and political conflicts.

The 1984 creation of the Havana Biennial was an initiative that emerged from a conversation between Fidel Castro and Wifredo Lam, where Armando Hart and other people were present. They discussed the state of promotion of the arts in the world at the beginning of the eighties. They realized that there were important artists living in African, Asian, and Latin American countries—in the so-called Third World—who didn't receive visibility in those centers where contemporary art was promoted. With this in mind, the Ministry of Culture founded the Havana Biennial as a platform where Cuban artists could exhibit and exchange ideas, both with each other and with artists from the rest of the world. Of course, this event was very important and interesting for European and North American curators, especially for the best among them.

The Biennial was a unique event. For example: *Magiciens de la Terre* (*Magicians of the Earth*) (this well-known exhibition in Paris) was curated with a European point of view. The curators of the Havana Biennial looked for artists and works that could establish the presence, uniqueness, and special characteristics of the art that was being produced in the areas of the world that I mentioned before. They were searching for new standards of quality, for different senses of beauty, that could enable fair dialogues in artistic terms with their counterparts from the North. The uniqueness of the event, plus the international network of the Centro de Arte Contemporáneo Wifredo Lam (Wifredo Lam Center of Contemporary Art) and its director Llilian Llanes, attracted increasing numbers of artists, curators, and intellectuals from Europe and North America to come to Havana. While these foreign individuals came and participated, the most prominent individuals came from our own countries. At that time, the world needed this new point of view. I am basically talking about curatorial issues. Among many others, Jürgen Harten came to Cuba in 1989 to participate in the third edition of the event, and subsequently paid attention to the local art scene. This led to the *Kuba o.k.* show you mentioned in your question.

Anyhow, the international interest for Cuban art grew steadily in the 1980s, owing to a boost of local artistic creativity and the promotionial efforts of the Havana Biennial and other cultural institutions, as well as political circumstances. Several international exhibitions of works by artists emerging from the ISA took place during the same period when *Kuba o.k.* was staged. For example, from a larger group of international exhibitions with young Cuban art and artists promoted in collaboration with Cuban institutions, I recall *The Nearest Edge of the World: Art and Cuba Now*, which toured the US; *No man is an Island*, at the Pori Art Museum, Finland, which was also shown in Hungary and Austria; and another exhibition in Venezuela and Colombia in 1991, titled *Los hijos de Guillermo Tell* (*The Sons of William Tell*).

Did I answer your question, or was it not enough? This was only the beginning of a process, because these artists had a lot of people opposing them within Cuba. The dogmatic people disagreed with the artists' aesthetic and political positions, and obviously also with the cultural institutions that promoted their work. The eighties were a very critical decade all over the Western world. In Cuba, the strongest critical expressions came from the arts.

In any case, *Kuba o.k.* was a very important exhibition, and a great opportunity for the young Cuban artists that took part in it to gain visibility in Europe. It luckily initiated our relationship with Peter and Irene Ludwig.

In general, philanthropy was an activity neither accepted nor fostered by the Cuban government.

RW Could you help improve our European understanding in outlining the legal or political circumstances in Cuba at that time? As far as I know there were not many external initiatives to create foundations in Cuba then—but maybe I am wrong?

HH As you know, the Cuban Revolution happened and developed on the stage of the Cold War. And in my opinion, the US government started a wrong policy toward that new process. That's why—at that time—the situation here was so complicated. I mean, when I was young in the 1960s we already knew about Socialism and that European Socialism had not succeeded. We never wanted to be like them. But of course, due to military and economic concerns, Cuba fell into a dependency on the Soviet Union and the other so-called Socialist countries. Anyhow, in Cuba, it was mainly the artists and intellectuals who developed a strong criticism of the ideas that came from the East. The later collapse of European Socialism didn't surprise us much.

The big question was: What is going to happen to this country? We lost our market for a second time. We were still suffering under the restrictions of the US embargo. I can tell you that that was the most difficult time in our history as far as I can remember. Due to a lack of almost everything—I mean living without anything—and also a lack of hope, not knowing where we were going to. At that point, very few people came to this country looking to invest in our economy, although the government was trying to attract them. Only step by step did we start to receive foreign investors and the first tourists later in the nineties, but not in the cultural field. In general, philanthropy was an activity neither accepted nor fostered by the Cuban government. Before the revolution, we did have philanthropic associations but not foundations, which are not really part of our legal tradition. After the revolution, the importance of these associations declined and the new ones that appeared were not really of the same type. Philanthropy was not part of our civic society, and the support to arts and culture was regarded to be a governmental effort, a public responsibility.

In the nineties, Armando Hart, the same minister of culture, conceived a new kind of philanthropy for the future development of this country. He fostered the creation of a small group of cultural foundations. Anyway, it is important to stress that foreign investments were not allowed in the cultural field. Therefore, the answer to your question is: no, we didn't receive any offers at this time to create foundations or other philanthropic bodies connected with the cultural field because, simply, this was not the official policy of the government. Is this a sufficient answer, or do you need more?

RW No, it is perfect. Let us start to talk about how the Ludwig Foundation, the Fundación Ludwig de Cuba, emerged. What led to the first contact with Peter Ludwig?

HH As I told you, Jürgen Harten learnt a lot about the current Cuban art scene during his trip to the Havana Biennial in 1989. He immediately thought it would be a great idea to organize an exhibition at the Kunsthalle Düsseldorf, which he ran at the time. It finally happened in partnership with the Centro de Desarrollo de las Artes Visuales (Center for the Development of the Visual Arts, an institution that supported local emerging artists). That is the origin of *Kuba o.k.*, which was ultimately organized by him and the Cuban curator Antonio "Tonel" Eligio Fernández, as well as other collaborators from the Centro de Desarrollo. So Cuban experts organized and proposed the entire project to him: the concept of the exhibition, the artists to be included, and the authors to write texts for the catalog. The title of the exhibition came from a work by Carlos Rodriguez Cárdenas, one of the artists in the exhibition (and who now lives in the US): Cuba, ok. It worked very well, and I do not have to explain why: The exhibition happened in 1990, right after the collapse of the Eastern Bloc. That apparently simple title embodied both the complexities and ironies of the situation. *Kuba o.k.* was the outcome of, I would say, an exemplary intellectual collaboration between Germans and Cubans, where both learnt from the other. The result was excellent.

I wanted to show to Cuba that a collector as prestigious as Peter Ludwig was interested in these artists.

RW How did Ludwig come into the picture?

HH As an art historian, I worked as a curator and a professor. I had professional relations with the Cuban curators, and of course, I knew the artists very well. I was also in charge of foreign relations at the National Council of Visual Arts. In some ways, the exhibition in Düsseldorf was my personal responsibility. When the exhibition took place at the Kunsthalle Düsseldorf, it was a very difficult moment for these artists in Cuba and for us exhibition organisers as well. As a rule, conservative individuals are always very powerful when the economic situation gets bad. I don't know why. At this point, and for a few years, the circumstances had placed them in a powerful position. Of course, we wanted to continue promoting artists whose work addressed poignant issues with a very contemporary language.

Then I received good news from Düsseldorf: Tonel, the main Cuban curator, called me from Germany and said that the very important collector Peter Ludwig was interested in possibly buying all the works in *Kuba o.k.* I hadn't met him yet at that time. Due to his reputation, I tried hard to sell the whole exhibition. I wanted to show to Cuba that a collector as prestigious as Peter Ludwig was interested in these artists. Unfortunately, the export permit of the works was only a temporary one, so they had to go back to Cuba. I had to inform them about that problem. Thomas Krings-Ernst and Wolfgang Becker, who later on became friends of mine, advised me to invite Professor Ludwig to Cuba.

So, in 1991, Thomas Krings-Ernst and Wolfgang Becker came to familiarize themselves with the Cuban art scene and to prepare for Ludwig's visit. It was a challenging time for young local artists to be able to show their work in official institutions. The economic and political conditions were tense, and the more dogmatic groups, who held more power at that moment, were reluctant to showcase criticism. Thomas and Wolfgang played a very important role in the preparation for Ludwig's visit. Wilfredo Benitez, Luisa Marisy, and I, just the three of us, worked very hard to put together a program for Thomas and Wolfgang. They didn't come exactly to purchase works but to prepare their next visit with Professor

Peter Ludwig himself. He arrived not much afterwards. In a series of trips, together with Thomas, Wolfgang, and sometimes other collaborators, Ludwig visited both private artist studios and local institutions in order to familiarize himself with Cuban art—a process that eventually culminated in the Ludwig collection of Cuban art that we know today, comprising 132 works by thirty-five different artists. We, the Cubans, were obviously very much involved in this process of acquisitions as we were the ones who knew the artists and their work, as well as all the Cuban bureaucratic limitations.

Now comes a very important point: You can follow the list of the works in the *Kuba o.k.* exhibition and the list of works that Mr. Ludwig acquired. The works that compose the Ludwig Cuban art collection were all selected on site—I mean at the artist studios—and purchased in Cuba. Some pieces that had been exhibited in *Kuba o.k.* were obviously selected, while some others were not. Some others belonging to that show were selected but couldn't be bought because the National Museum of Cuba always has the right to buy local art pieces before anyone else. That's why you can find pieces from the *Kuba o.k.* show in the collection of our National Museum.

We didn't have something like an art market in Cuba at this time: nobody knew about that, not even me.

Almost all of these young artists were selling their work for the first time. The collection steadily grew, while Peter learnt about Cuban art by meeting the artists and discovering their work together with them. At that time, he couldn't buy directly. He had to do it through a cultural institution that gave the artists the equivalent in Cuban pesos (the local currency with low value), although he always paid in deutsche marks. We didn't have something like an art market in Cuba at this time: nobody knew about that, not even me. I have to be honest: for me, at that time, the art market was evil. Anyhow, I learnt a lot from him.

However, it is important to say that the discussions about prices were always directly between Ludwig and the artists. I normally translated these discussions with Ludwig, Thomas, and Wolfgang, because at that time not many of the Cuban artists could speak English. Now most of them do. My ongoing dialogues with them, and directly with Professor Ludwig, introduced me to the means and procedures of the art market. He was always very generous in that sense. I mean that he increasingly shared his ideas and comments during our working sessions.

RW Irene Ludwig did not come to Cuba this first time?

HH Not during the first trip. Peter Ludwig came first in 1991; she only came in 1993, in order to receive the Doctor Honoris Causa from the University of Havana. On that occasion, Fidel met them in the house where they were hosted, and they decided many things together—Irene, Peter, and Fidel.

RW Only the three of them?

HH I was not part of that lunch, Armando Hart was. The Ludwigs were accompanied by Wolfgang Schreiner and his wife. So, the four of them had lunch together with their Cuban partners.

RW Coming back to the first visit: What was your impression of the personality of Peter Ludwig? How did he behave, how did he feel in your country?

HH There were a lot of changes in Cuba during the 1990s. We developed new ways of receiving visitors, a new way of cooperating with them. Earlier, I had had the chance to travel all over the world because of my position at the International Theater Institute (ITI). For example, in the 1980s I used to organize the International Theater Festival of Havana. While I had gained some experience with international celebrities, I had never met anybody who was both a collector and an entrepreneur like Ludwig. I became very curious.

Since the very beginning, my personal relationships with Thomas and Wolfgang were very good. I felt very comfortable with them. We used to talk very openly about Cuban society, political issues, artistic issues—about everything. I was very sincere with them, sort of like an accomplice. We prepared everything together and they made me a little afraid of Peter Ludwig. They said to me: Everything has to work in the proper order and at the right time. He doesn't wait for one minute, everything has to be ready, the decisions have to be made. If people are not there on time, he will leave, and you will lose him. Therefore, we had to prepare for his visit properly. However, you cannot imagine our conditions at the time—everything was so difficult!

Ludwig was living in a government house and had an assigned Mercedes Benz. I could use a Soviet Lada belonging to the Council of Visual Arts. It would have been very challenging to transport the artworks to a specific place for Ludwig. Due to the lack of gasoline and car parts, bicycles had become the main means of transportation. Indeed, the visit happened at a very difficult moment. Ludwig, Thomas and Wolfgang were transported in the Mercedes from the government house; I came along in the other car of the council, and Wilfredo went in advance riding on a bicycle, like the famous cat in Perrault's story, to prepare the artists, prepare the artwork, prepare the set. That was the role of Wilfredo, preparing everything on time. When we arrived, everything was in perfect shape. So little by little, day after day, I was speaking more often and more directly with Peter Ludwig, discussing the works of art, learning more about his preferences and the way he developed his conversations with the artists. Step by step, we built our relationship that turned into a friendship. At the very start, it was only a professional relationship, of course. I can tell you: he always knew and noticed everything. For example, he learned about how someone on a bicycle was always riding ahead of us, and he liked that; it seems that he enjoyed our way of doing things. He liked to push the envelope, so Cubans could learn to do things properly under the changing circumstances. This whole trip was the start of a wonderful friendship—not only with Peter Ludwig, but also with Wolfgang Becker, who is a person I admire and who played, together with Thomas Krings-Ernst, an important role, both in Cuba and in other areas where Peter Ludwig was involved.

Since the very beginning it was clear to me that Peter Ludwig thought Cuban art was interesting, mainly because it was very different from what he had seen in the former Socialist countries.

RW I would like to dive a little deeper into your discussions about the art: What were Peter Ludwig's personal preferences?

HH Since the very beginning it was clear to me that Peter Ludwig thought Cuban art was interesting, mainly because it was very different from what he had seen in the former Socialist countries, even compared to dissident artists like Kabakov and others. The Cuban artists were very close to some German artists—I am talking about names like Joseph Beuys, Gerhard Richter, as well as some others. He was very curious why Cuban artists were so similar to such foreign artists. However, I do not think that he bought Cuban works because he thought that those products were necessarily really great art. It seems that he was interested in the Cuban art phenomenon as a whole. He was also trying to identify the individuals that were the most important ones within this milieu. When he conceived of his collection, it was not so much about this particular artist, then that artist, and again another artist. He understood them less as individuals and more as part of a set of artistic productions in a country with specific conditions. Mainly through the biennial, and secondly through the process of buying Cuban art, Ludwig discovered a new contradiction in the world that was not yet visible in his collection. He had documented very well the contradictions between capitalism and Socialism, the differences between art of the United States and that of Europe. What had been missing was the confrontation of North versus South. That was new. He discovered this through his emerging knowledge of art in Cuba, and he was interested in documenting it. His preferences focused on those artists who best succeeded in trying to stress what it meant to be a Cuban while also being interested in the development of the most contemporary trends in Western art. I cannot say that he was interested in this type of art, or this specific trend, or in another one. Later, of course, he developed preferences based on what he liked best and on his personal sympathies.

He then understood that the Havana Biennial, the Centro Wifredo Lam, and its staff could be important sources of knowledge and networking with the arts scene of Third World countries. In 1994, the Ludwig Stiftung für Kunst und Internationale Verständigung (Ludwig Foundation for Art and International Understanding) had granted a donation to the fifth edition of the biennial. It also had sponsored an initiative that brought together experts from both the Centro Wifredo Lam and the Ludwig Forum für Internationale Kunst (Ludwig Forum for International Art) to bring a selection of that biennial to the Aachen institution. Unfortunately, he passed away in 1996, and his visionary plan couldn't go beyond those initial initiatives.

RW Because he wrote his doctorate dissertation on Picasso, with a focus on the human figure in his paintings, many in Europe are under the impression that Ludwig preferred realistic artworks over conceptual or abstract ones. According to your experience with him: Did he act like this in Cuba?

HH No, no, because in Cuba the strongest trend at that time was a particular version of conceptualism. And Ludwig understood that. How do I know? Because he discussed it directly with the artists. He talked—perhaps with Wolfgang and Thomas, and he was always talking, asking, or explaining to me—about what he saw. For example: why a work may be important in Cuba, why an idea could be subversive in this country, why it may be very important for a young audience … I never had the idea that he was really interested in realism, until I learned that an artist like Lev Kerbel was interesting to him. Not because he matched his aesthetic preference, but because Kerbel meant something in the artistic field in the former Soviet Union and in the rest of Eastern Europe. He wanted his collection to preserve the different ways of developing images in the present times in the world that we live in, with all of its contradictions. As you can easily notice, he was very interested in the language the artists were using, but his interest always went far beyond art itself. Through art, he wanted to understand the different ways that people approach real life—as well as their dreams, illusions, desires, et cetera—in a very synthetic way. He wanted to understand the contemporary world through a dialogue between the different types of expression of artists from very different latitudes.

RW Would you say that—under your guidance and that of Thomas and Wolfgang—he was trying to buy masterpieces? You described very well what was his interest in Cuban art, but when it came to the details, the choice between the one or the other artwork, what was the discussion then?

HH He always tried to buy the ones he considered the best. Were these masterpieces? I am not so sure about that, but he bought the best. Did he pay attention to Wolfgang Becker's point of view? Yes. Did he pay attention to Thomas? Yes. Did he pay attention to my point of view? Yes. It was not that I told him: "Buy this and that." No, because in the end it was always he who decided. But we had discussions; after some years had passed by, we had discussions more and more about culture, about paintings, about politics, the means of democracy, about everything ... the future of Cuba, whatever.

RW You told us already a lot about the important roles of Thomas Krings-Ernst and Wolfgang Becker. Of these two, had there been one who initiated the acquisition process?

HH This is the point: when you are buying art, there needs to be someone in between who has to write the order for the art, who has to organize the transportation or has to protect the art between the artist and you as a buyer. That was mainly the role of Thomas. He was always the dealer involved in the process. He handled the payment, he was doing that job. And he was very good in public relations. Wolfgang Becker, on the other side, developed the idea with Ludwig to create the Ludwig Forum, which I believe is a very useful and refined concept of what a contemporary museum should be. It is not exactly a museum in the traditional way, but a forum, a place to have a dialogue about artists' cultures, to bring artists from all over the world to work there and to spread their ideas. Not only in the visual arts, but also in performing arts, in films, and in all media. That was how they used to work in this place. In my opinion, Wolfgang had been an intellectual aide to Peter Ludwig, a very responsible person in conceptual terms, not only regarding the collection itself, but also how this collection could function in different social realities. Did I explain myself? I think that was more or less the division of roles. However, you couldn't lock Thomas or Wolfgang into fixed roles, no. They were a team. I am very grateful to them, as they were very helpful to me.

His idea about these Ludwig museums was to put together all that diversity ... so as to start dialogues over their differences.

RW I read that Ludwig wanted to create a museum of contemporary art in Havana. What was this process and how did it end?

HH Ludwig was always talking with the officials: the vice minister, the minister of culture, even Fidel. In Havana, like everywhere else, he wanted to have a base where he could show part of his collection, not necessarily just Cuban art. His idea about these Ludwig museums was to put together all that diversity he had acquired in Western European countries, US, Russia, Czechoslovakia, Hungary, even China—everywhere—to put all the art, the most different pieces, together so as to start dialogues over their differences. That was his way of understanding the world. And when I asked him why he was interested in this mission, he explained it from his point of view, starting with how the Second World War ended, how he felt then, and how art helped him to survive as a human being and as an intellectual. That's why he wanted to do the same in Cuba. He came and said: "You know, I will give you as a present a lot of artworks. On this side of the world, there is not yet a Ludwig museum, so it would be the first and the only one." But believe me, Cuba didn't have the money to spend on a new museum. Our own museum was facing difficulties at that time. So, he was thinking and thinking what to do in this situation …

In those years, many people—including artists—left the country and established themselves in Mexico, in Miami, or in other places. After they had left Cuba, some of them tried to establish direct contact with Ludwig in order to continue selling art to him. But Ludwig didn't seem interested at that point, perhaps because their art was no longer created in Cuba.

The end of the museum issue was this: We wished to have such a museum, we even received a list of pieces that would come to Cuba, but Cuba did not have the money to build the venue. Ludwig was realistic enough to understand that it was not the right moment for the plan. At that time, we were close enough to conspire together, and we knew that we were creating a kind of staircase, step by step. He then proposed the creation of the foundation to the Cuban government. He proposed to do for young Cuban artists what the Cuban government had done before but now could no longer do. It wasn't certain then, but now we know it was the truth that the government would no longer be able to support artists. He proposed a foundation in 1993 and the foundation was approved in 1994. It was the only foreign cultural investment in the cultural field in this country. Why was it approved? I believe that Ludwig was very important for Cuba. The Cuban government greatly appreciated the friendly hand of Peter and Irene Ludwig. I think the Cuban government really trusted him. But to tell you the truth, I even think that neither Wolfgang Becker, nor Peter Ludwig, nor Wolfgang Schreiner (who came with him on later trips), nor the rest of the officials, nor me could think that we were going to achieve something like we did with the foundation. At the beginning we didn't know what to do, how to handle the planning, or how to manage a foundation.

RW How did it happen that you became president of the foundation?

In his second trip, he brought me a pair of Birkenstocks, … so we were wearing the same shoes all the time, in meetings, everywhere—the most important collector of the world was wearing Birkenstocks!

HH I was present when Professor Ludwig proposed the creation of the foundation to the Cuban government through the Cuban minister of culture Amando Hart, and that was one of the conditions he posed. When Ludwig was asked why, he answered: because I know him, and I know he is an honest person.

RW How was your day-to-day relationship with Ludwig?

HH Ludwig noticed that I was very informal during his first trip in Cuba: I never wear jackets, I am always wearing sandals and things like that. In his second trip, he brought me a pair of Birkenstocks, the same color for me and for him, blue ones, so we were wearing the same shoes all the time, in meetings, everywhere—the most important collector of the world was wearing Birkenstocks! Now he wore jackets only for very special occasions. In public he always wore a shirt just like me; he supported me all the time. In the Cuban context, these insignificant issues could easily become political issues with an important meaning. In the end we were talking about cultural signs. He was sensitive enough to understand them and supported me.

Let me tell you another example of his sensitivity toward me. In one of his trips, he decided to enter through Santiago de Cuba (a city on the east of the island) where he wanted to spend some days. The officials in charge of attending to us should have arranged a car to transport us to Havana. However, they didn't, and at the last minute I had to do it myself to avoid getting stranded. I had to do that alone, without any local support. The same officials had scheduled a final dinner with Mr. Ludwig in the same guest house where we were staying (we were supposed to leave the city very early the next morning). They arrived and sat around the dining table, but he didn't leave his room. He sent a message to them that he would wait for me to arrive with the news of the arranged car so that I could have dinner together with them. I arrived in the house while they were receiving that message, so I couldn't avoid overhearing it. Then I told him privately: "You are getting me into big problems. Now they are going to hate me." He was so sensitive. He said, "These people only came to have dinner, to eat, and you were outside doing what they should have done for us."

In my opinion, in his personal relationships Ludwig was not at all arrogant. Perhaps at the very beginning, I perceived a kind of arrogance, but not by the end. We became very, very close. I could never have the same kind of relationship with Irene, as we didn't work that closely together.

RW Can you tell us something about the print behind you on the wall?

HH Sandra Ramos belonged to a group of artists that emerged from the art schools in the nineties. When Peter Ludwig visited us, she was exhibiting abroad more than in Cuba. Her second solo show was actually the one we organized in 1995. But, nevertheless, Ludwig visited her many times, and her work is well represented in his collection. He liked her work. This particular one has been in my office since the day the foundation opened. It is a print. She is a marvelous printmaker. Later, she decided to also work in other media: painting on canvas, installations, objects, et cetera. But as a printmaker, I think she is really very good, especially from a technical point of view. This particular work appropriates the first verse of an important Cuban poem from the forties—in Spanish: "La isla en peso;" in English maybe: "The island in its own weight."

What the verse says in Spanish is, "La maldita circunstancia del agua por todas partes." In English, it is more or less, "The damned circumstance of water surrounding everything." As you see, she is posing in the center of the print in a kind of self-portrait that she typically used during those years. The face that you see there is a face that she found in an old Cuban print from the nineteenth century that looks like her, so it functions as a self-portrait. She made it appear as if she were Cuba, because through her body pose she creates the shape of Cuba in a map. You can see the palm trees on her in red coloring. I perceive her as a kind of female Saint Sebastian, as the palm trees look to me like arrows. The yellow frame around the whole print suggests the Malecón wall—I would say it in English as the "seaside wall." Actually, the Malecón wall is our northern border. Ninety miles north from that wall there's Florida. The Cubans at that time used a lot of this type of iconography: First, the representation of the shape of the island and the relationship between themselves, their portraits, and the shape of the country. Second, they frequently invoked the seaside wall as our border, our limit. Finally, they often wrote things directly onto their work—this combination between images and words comes directly from the conceptual art tradition.

RW Does this continue to exist?

HH No, not anymore. But it was very important in those days. Let me say something more about this piece: At that time, we were all losing friends who were leaving the country, which is a very difficult journey as Cuba is surrounded by water. On a deeper level, she is also talking about the sense of sacrifice which was instilled in her generation through their education, as if sacrifice was an inevitable fact for everybody. She clearly thought that this wasn't necessary and addressed it in an ironic way.

RW When you talked with Ludwig about such art, did he also develop his vision of world art with you? And how did you as a Cuban feel hearing about world art from a German collector?

HH If we pay attention to the global art trends today and see this new concept of globalized art that we experience in all of the art fairs, it seems that there has been a kind of homogenization of values in art: what we are doing in Cuba, they are doing in China, in Germany, and everywhere. I think that is exactly the opposite of what Ludwig wanted and what he had explained to me. He discovered at that time that in every cultural, political, social place —in every country—you will find different expressions of the arts. I think if we would carefully look, we would discover the same even now, beneath the surface of the large corporations that have spread over the world. So, what he was trying to do was to put together all these different expressions of art, starting from European art and then confronting European art with American Pop artists and then with artists from the former Soviet Union or Eastern European countries—not only the officially sanctioned artists, but also those who were considered dissidents at that time. What he loved was the idea of putting together in one museum all of this diversity of expression. Once he told me, "Helmo, would you like the Cuban collection to come back to Cuba?" And I said to him, "No, as you told me, I believe it is better to spread it all over the world in different museums, together with the rest of the art in your collection." So that was his dream, and it became my dream too. This is an idea of world art that we also maintain here in this foundation. And this idea is far away from what you could call "corporate art" today.

The government had never accepted a foreign investment in the cultural field before. I think they mostly accepted this idea because of the importance of the figure of Peter Ludwig.

RW We were already speaking the other day about how Cuba did not have the money to fulfill Ludwig's idea for a museum. Following this, he came up with the idea to create a foundation. What were the essential points you discussed with Ludwig about creating such a foundation?

HH Ludwig noticed that the economic situation was very bad at that time, incredibly bad. This worst moment had been labelled "The Special Period" by the government. Following our cultural policy, the Cuban government initially used to do a lot for artists, both in the art schools and later in the development of their careers. Outside of market purposes, the government did a very satisfactory job of promoting work.

Year after year, more artists were leaving the country to try and develop their careers outside of Cuba. As I told you, Ludwig was disappointed about that, and proposed to the Cuban government to create a foundation that would do for the young artists what the state used to do but no longer could due to lack of resources. The government had never accepted a foreign investment in the cultural field before. I think they mostly accepted this idea because of the importance of the figure of Peter Ludwig. They also liked it because Mr. Ludwig was creating a kind of small-scale experiment with this project, which would only amount to a kind of donation every year that he agreed to in a contract with the authorities. Later he said, "Okay, I want Ludwig to be the name of this Cuban foundation, and I want to have the right to check annually how the grant will be used." This was an idea that Ludwig and I had discussed privately before, because it was a way to protect the work and the money of the foundation. And he asked the government that I, Helmo, should be named the president of the foundation. Privately, we had discussed the ways to create a foundation that would be capable of becoming a real institution, of building a sense of citizenship among the artists, among the audiences, and always through cultural politics. At that time, institutions and their reputations had been damaged in Cuba. If you ask me about this period, I think we didn't have problems with human rights, but we did have problems with civil rights. That's why it was very important to us to create an institution in which people could trust and which could be an umbrella for artists to live properly, to live as citizens with rights and duties, to recognize that they are citizens and to recognize that the others are citizens too. The second point was to create relationships and bridges with the rest of the world; even though Cuba is an island, it is an island with ports, and Cuban culture was built through dialogues with the rest of the world. Isolation would be the worst enemy for the future of our young people and our young intellectuals. We assumed the responsibility of building bridges.

And Ludwig did that even before the foundation existed, because he started to give grants to Cuban artists every year so that they could come to Germany to work there. He brought to Germany, for the first and only time in history, the essential parts of the Havana Biennial. So, when the Havana Biennial first went to the Ludwig Forum and then on to Berlin, it was one of the very first times in Europe that there was an exhibition of works of art from artists of the Third World that was curated by curators who were also people living in Third World countries. That was the importance of his selection of the Havana Biennial. He was expressing his ideas through these ways.

To be more concrete: The foundation was created to promote young Cuban artists and to protect their rights when they didn't have the chance to show their work because of censorship. We also wanted to create a very strong institution in which people could trust. Finally, we wanted to create bridges with the rest of the world. But most important was that we wanted to create something absolutely legal. We knew since the first day that we were always walking on very thin ice, because we were going to work with the same artists who had previously faced censorship. We wanted to prove to society that these artists were good and important and that all of them were a result of their revolutionary education in the art schools. Although they were critical of society, this was always in the spirit of the new Cuban social values: we had made the next generation better than us. That was our dream when we were young. But it had to be a legal institution, absolutely legal, because I didn't want the bureaucrats to come to me tomorrow saying, "Oh, I am sorry, you know what, you are not very legal, there is something wrong with the foundation, we have to close it, not because I don't like the art but because there is something wrong in the way that your institution is functioning." If such people wanted to do something like that, they would have to fight with me and admit that they did not like the art we support. This was very clear to us since the very beginning. It is not the same in other countries, but these kind of debates are an issue in Cuban Socialism.

RW Coming back to Ludwig: In other Socialist countries where he collected, he invested in economic projects. Did he ever try to do the same in Cuba?

HH I wished he would have. I couldn't convince him to do it. Believe me, I tried hard, but he immediately noticed that was not possible. He didn't want to do it. He was interested in seeing how the country's politics were changing little by little, year after year, and how Cuban artists could change and could help society to change. But believe me, I couldn't convince him to invest a cent in Cuba.

RW When we create a foundation in our country, this is normally intended to last for eternity. It is very difficult to dissolve a foundation. The spirit is that it is for a very long term. Was it the same here?

HH There wasn't a culture of philanthropy in this country. The creation of this foundation, contemporaneous with five other foundations, was the beginning of a culture of philanthropy in Cuba. Of course, I personally understand the concept of a foundation and of how important it can be for the future of this society. But since the foundation's conception, we have faced a lack of understanding. I am talking about politicians, bureaucrats, the public at large, and even artists, who all wonder what philanthropy is and how philanthropy could benefit the entire society. I think that perhaps we have now partially succeeded in responding to such doubts, but not yet completely. There is still a long way in front of us in order to properly address that lack of a philanthropic culture.

Later, a lot of people started offering grants to Cuban artists. But at first, this was only offered by the Fundación Ludwig.

RW From the very beginning, you found partners besides Ludwig, other partners who were mainly from the US. For example, did Ludwig know Alex and Carole Rosenberg, the New York art dealers and appraisers who have until now continued to run the American Friends of the Ludwig Foundation in Cuba? How did this partnership happen?

HH Ludwig survived the foundation by less than two years. Yes, I think he met the Rosenbergs, but they did not then play the same role that they were going to play later on for this foundation. Fifteen years ago, I proposed to them and other friends in the States that they should create a nonprofit entity. I had learned enough about the philanthropic world in the US, so I understood the importance of having a tax-deductible organization to help our programs there. A friend of mine, an American lawyer, did the entire job for free. Her expertise was the capital that she invested into the foundation. When all the papers were ready and I had spoken with everybody, it took only six weeks for the American government to approve the organization. Officers from well-known foundations—Rockefeller, Ford, plus others—advised me to create this institution, because having a partner institution in the States could be a great help given the situation with Cuba. That would provide us with a structure capable of developing programs together with different institutions in the United States. I don't say that they were our only partners because, since the very beginning, we had started to work with well-established institutions. We began a program with the Rhode Island School of Design, which was the first university to work with us. Later, we developed permanent relationships with other universities, mainly with New York University (NYU), as well as the Museum of Modern Art, the Whitney Museum, the Metropolitan Museum, and the Corcoran Gallery in Washington. We are working now with the Tisch School of the Arts, which is also at NYU. That is the way we are trying to create our own links with American society. And we are trying to do the same with the rest of the world, including Europe. We both had and have relations in Sweden, Denmark, Norway, Finland—especially in the dance world but also in design and other fields. We have accomplished this with the support and efforts of important partner institutions that have collaborated with us. Even in the worst political circumstances, when the European Union had no relations with Cuba, we received the help of the Swedish Institute. It currently seems important for the future of Cuban society for us to develop our programs for internships in renowned institutions in the US and other countries. That way, young professionals update their knowledge and experience international training.

RW How are you and your foundation involved in the process of selecting students from abroad or sending your people here? Are you part of the selection process?

HH Not at the very beginning, because our foreign partners sent whomever they wanted to Cuba. Sometimes now, me personally, or people from the foundation, go to teach and promote the courses we are going to have, like the one in the spring—photo and video workshops for a full semester. It is the only program in our country in which Cubans can study together with students from US universities. Of course, Cuban students don't have to pay tuition. That is part of the contribution we receive for organizing and hosting these courses. They bring faculty members. I also serve a teacher here in Cuba. Of course, this is just one example. In a similar way, we proceed with other partners in the US—for example with the Brooklyn Academy of Music, the Joyce Theater, the Lincoln Center Theater Lab, et cetera.

RW Can you tell us how many students you received here during the twenty years of your foundation? And from how many countries did they hail?

HH Believe me, it is listed in one of the charts which we are screening now to celebrate our twentieth anniversary. But I do not remember the numbers because I am getting older. We have received so many students in twenty years, mostly from the US but also from Germany, France, Denmark, and Sweden. We have also received others who are not students—professionals that come to Cuba receiving a grant, a very special kind of grant. We don't have money to bring people from Germany to Cuba. This is what we do instead: we write a letter to invite you to Cuba, and with that letter you raise the required funds for your trip. There is no question that you can receive the money from an institution if you say that I have this proposal from Cuba to do this and that. Once here, we do the paperwork to cover your migratory status as a student. Thus, you receive the same rights as a Cuban. We pay you a stipend equivalent to our salary. We are saying, "Would you like to live the experience of being a Cuban in the middle of our situation?" We offer them that experience, but mostly we offer the environment to develop their project—and always tutorial assistance.

In addition, we receive help from different institutions from all over the world. They send well-qualified people here to develop workshops and train artists and intellectuals in different fields. This is the way video art came to us, and its use subsequently expanded in the community of Cuban artists, owing to the help of some institutions and universities from Canada. Today, we are still receiving this kind of help from different Canadian partners as well as from those in Sweden, Denmark, and others. I don't want to finish without saying that ours were the first grants that Cuban artists received. Later, a lot of people started offering grants to Cuban artists. But at first, this was only offered by the Fundación Ludwig. Unfortunately, we cannot continue offering that in Aachen, because they were always living in apartments at the Ludwig Forum, and now these apartments are not available. I hope, and I tell you this as a member of the Board of Trustees of the

Peter and Irene Ludwig Foundation in Aachen, that we can find a new way to continue our programs there.

[Irene Ludwig] reorganized the German foundation; she did a good job with that.

RW That's clear, but let's come back shortly to the Ludwigs, Peter and his wife Irene, and the honorary medals that they received from the Cuban state. How did this respectively develop for Peter Ludwig and for his wife?

HH Since the very beginning, Thomas and Wolfgang told me, "Helmo, important, very important, is not only to be on time and to have everything perfect: you also have to offer a distinction or an order to Ludwig!" I didn't believe that, but we offered this to Ludwig, and he very early on received the Doctorate Honoris Causa at the arts university, which is the right place to receive that. Okay, all were very happy. Next year, we tried to do the same with Mrs. Ludwig. I talked with everybody in Cuba and she came that year together with Wolfgang Schreiner and his wife. The four of them stayed in a government house and she received the doctorate, but this time from the University of Havana.

After she received the honor, I brought them back to the house where they were staying. Surprise: Fidel was there, waiting for them, with all of his bodyguards and everything, to have lunch together. As I told you, I was not at this lunch, but I later learned that they started to discuss very diverse topics and even made some jokes. At some point Fidel asked Ludwig if he was related to Emil Ludwig. The answer was obviously negative, but Mr. Ludwig understood that Fidel had read much of Emil Ludwig's biographies, and especially the one on Napoleon. Immediately after that, Fidel teased Mrs. Ludwig: "Congratulations, now you are a doctor of the same university where I studied." And he added: "You know what, you are a real doctor. Peter is not, because he received the doctorate from a school that is not a real university." The minister of culture was there, and he didn't understand, perhaps he didn't notice that. We now have more than fifty universities in the country. Receiving a decoration in one university means you also received it from the rest of them. They are all the same system—a Socialist concept, you understand.

The following year Peter Ludwig arrived here with Schreiner again, and I think with Becker too. He arrived in Santiago de Cuba and on the way from Santiago de Cuba to Havana he told me, "Well, what about my doctorate?" And I said, "What?" Then began a big problem with the new doctorate and how it could be resolved. First, the Cuban government gave him a cultural decoration. Ludwig said to me, "Ok, thank you, but this is not enough." It was a big argument, as he was confronting me with a problem without a solution. Then, suddenly, he said to me: "Okay, I know what I am doing. I know it is against the regulations. I understand what you are saying. But this is the way I know I have to behave. I have to push to see how far I can go, because the president of your country offered the doctorate to me." That was the first lesson from him that I learned for life. The second one occurred when we were walking on a street, and I said, "I understand, but don't you think that is a little too much?" He answered: "Well, Helmo, what can I do? I am a megalomaniac, yes, what can I do?". We made jokes all the time about the second doctorate and everything. But he finally received it—don't ask me how—the second Doctorate Honoris Causa, this time from the University of Havana.

RW Do you have the impression that Irene Ludwig followed her husband in all of his expanding demands, in going to the limit?

HH After he died, her actions proved that she respected what he had been doing, and she preserved everything at the same level that he had left it. She reorganized the German foundation; she did a good job with that, also with preserving the principles that the two of them had developed during their lives. During his trips, Ludwig was telling her—always over the phone—what he was doing in Cuba. I don't think that they had the same goals in life. They were different people, but I believe he always discussed with her what to do regarding the most important decisions. And during this conversation with Fidel, she was there, and her presence was very important. She came only once to Cuba, and during that trip she received the doctorate. Later in 1998, at the Ludwig Forum in Aachen, we had a show called *Provisorische Utopien* (*Provisional Utopias*), the catalog is here. She organized a big party and a lunch at her house for the guests of honor of the foundation. For that occasion, several of our members travelled to Germany. Yes, she did everything in a good way, although the Cuban art collection didn't expand anymore, with the exception of one single piece. She did preserve what he had already done.

RW I have a last question, having spent now four days here with you visiting internationally successful artists and speaking with them. We saw the older generation, the middle generation, and the younger generation. What are your thoughts about the development of art here?

But the new customers of Cuban art were Americans. They started to come to Cuba after Ludwig, immediately after Ludwig.

HH First of all, concerning the international success of Cuban artists, some people love to talk about the Cuban "miracle." I think that, from the point of view of an art historian or an art critic, this phenomenon is overestimated. Nevertheless, it was not a miracle: it was the result of cultural policies and the fight for art schools. I remember how Wolfgang Becker told me many times during those years, "Helmo, if you run an art place, how many artists do you think you will work with?" I believe that a smaller group of good artists should be enough. The main problems happened when the concept of the market arrived in Cuba and a dollarization of the economy took place—new policies of the government allowing the artists to sell their works in dollars. First of all, the institutions were not at all prepared for that; nobody knew anything about the market. I was perhaps the only one because I learned how markets function from Thomas, Wolfgang, and mainly from Ludwig. And later I learned more in the States when I went to auction houses and galleries. But I wasn't interested in the market; I was interested in the philanthropic world and cultural management. At the very least, we don't sell art. But the new customers of Cuban art were Americans. They started to come to Cuba after Ludwig, immediately after Ludwig. And they came to buy Cuban art, mainly—in my opinion—because Ludwig, that great collector, showed to the rest of the world that Cuban art could be attractive. Perhaps it could have been a good investment to buy art for the price that Cuban art held at that moment: should the government fall down and the situation change, the value of the art would grow, which is what occurred in the former Socialist countries. Even though the government didn't fall and the situation didn't change in Cuba, the prices still grew higher and higher. I think that artists started to learn how to sell to their American customers. And then they stopped working for Cuban audiences, for whom they were working before. They started to paint for their new customers. Of course, what they made was what the customers wanted to find. Often, this so-called political art criticizing the government isn't that critical at all. They are not talking about the real problems of our society right now. They are talking about problems that are already well-known. That's one of the reasons why you don't see so much censorship now. You see how artists who want to sell have to construct stories that Americans can buy—you saw the nice way that they are living.

So, what is the situation of Cuban art? We are currently facing a big problem: they are learning how to deal with the market and with the contemporary art scene all over the world. Are they going to be successful at the end? Who knows? I don't think the schools were training new artists for that scenario, because the professors and the officials who organize this activity don't understand what is happening, they don't understand what is going on in the world in this new scenario. I don't think that the artists are really well prepared. But I believe—because I trust a lot in people—that they will learn by themselves step by step, perhaps it will take time. Their skills to make art are still good, more or less the same as they were in the eighties. I don't think that there was a miracle in the eighties, and I don't think that there is a miracle now, but I think it is important to continue working with Cuban artists and to promote creativity in Cuban society. We are increasingly living in an audiovisual world. Our foundation is currently placing a big emphasis on installing and developing the necessary equipment for media production at the foundation. The artists are able to work with cameras and they are increasingly creating audiovisual content and material. This will perhaps be the most important track to be developed in the future for Cuban artists. On the other hand, the world is not a homogeneous place, and Cuba is not a homogeneous country. It's mainly in Havana where people have contact with the museums, et cetera. We have many areas in our country, a lot of cities in the provinces, where young people need to see good art—

good visual art, good audiovisual materials, good literature. That's why we are also working with the schools I mentioned to you and with communities. Perhaps we have to place more emphasis on that in the future. But if you ask me, finally, what is the situation for Cuban artists in the contemporary world: only a few of them are in international art fairs, only a few of them are represented at the big events in the world. However, do we need that? Good question …

RW Thank you, thanks a lot, Helmo!

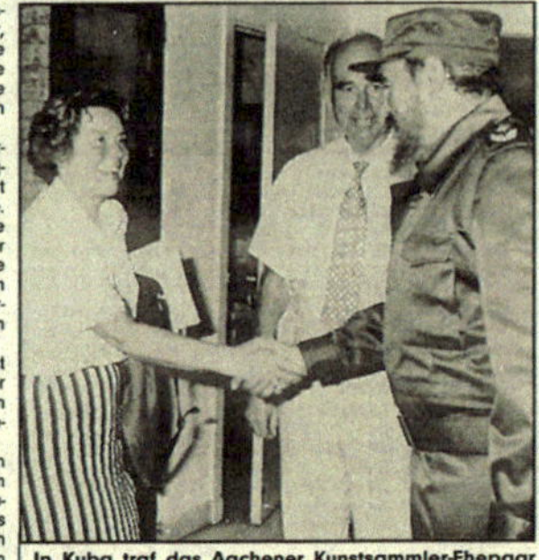

Peter Ludwig bei Fidel Castro:

„Der kennt sogar den Aachener Dom!"

Aachen/Havanna – Was fällt Ihnen zu Kuba ein? Klar: Zuckerrohr, Tabak und Fidel Castro. Doch die Sonneninsel hat auch jede Menge Kultur zu bieten. Und wer könnte das besser wissen als Kunstmäzen Peter Ludwig.

Der Aachener 'Herr der modernen Kunst' ist auf Kuba ein gefragter Mann. Jetzt war er wieder dort – zusammen mit seiner Frau Irene.

Knapp drei Stunden plauderte das Aachener Ehrenbürgerpaar mit Fidel. Wichtigstes Thema: Die Ausstellung 'Biennale der Dritten Welt', die in Havanna eröffnet wurde und bald in Aachen zu sehen sein wird.

Peter Ludwig: „Fidel Castro ist ein außerordentlich gebildeter Mann. Über die Stadt Aachen, den Dom und die Museen wußte er bestens Bescheid."

Während des Besuchs wurden Irene und Peter Ludwig mit dem Nationalorden für Kultur der Republik Kuba ausgezeichnet. Und was die wenigsten wissen: Seit einigen Jahren sind sie Ehrendoktoren in Havanna.

In Kuba traf das Aachener Kunstsammler-Ehepaar Irene und Peter Ludwig Präsident Fidel Castro.

Bild-Zeitung = Samstag 14.5.94

Newspaper article about Peter and Irene Ludwig's meeting with Fidel Castro.
"He Even Knows the Aachen Cathedral!," Bild-Zeitung, 14.5.1994

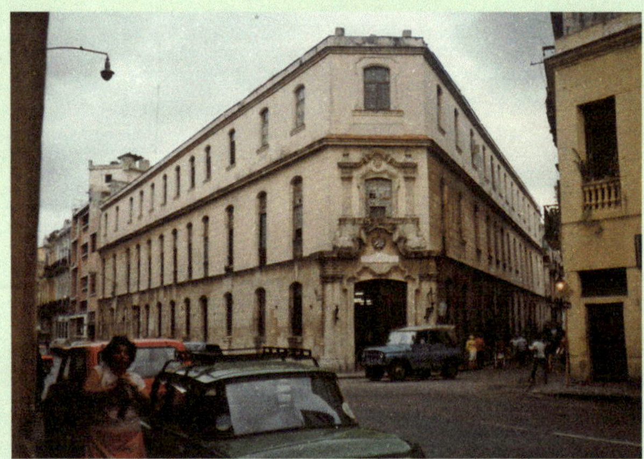

Former police headquarters building in Havana, which was considered as a possible location for a Ludwig museum, 1991.
Photo: private

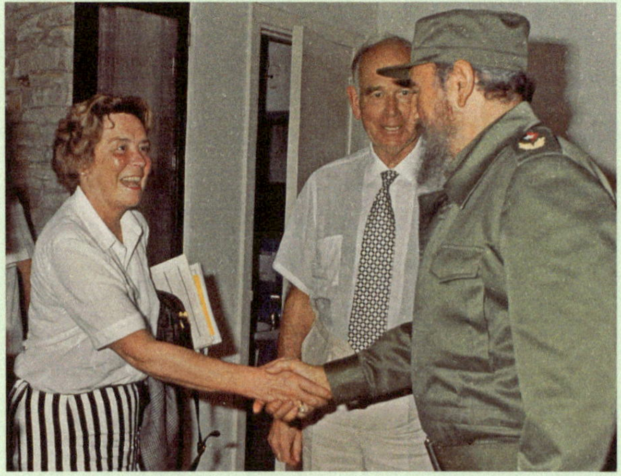

Meeting of Irene and Peter Ludwig with President Fidel Castro in Havana, 1993.
Photo: unknown

Accused/ blowtorch/ padlock – so lautet der Originaltitel dieser Collage aus Fotos und Schriften. Übersetzt heißt das 1986 entstandene Werk des US-Amerikaners Pat Ward Williams: „angeklagt/ Schweißgerät/Vorhängeschloß“

Aachens „Ludwig Forum“ zeigt die „Biennale der Dritten Welt“

Wie die Kunst Brücken schlägt

G.W. **Aachen**

Premiere im Ludwig Forum für Internationale Kunst in Aachen: Erstmals präsentiert sich die 5. Biennale der Dritten Welt jenseits des Atlantiks. In diesem Sommer zeigte die Biennale in Havanna 600 Werke von 200 Künstlern. In Aachen ist seit Donnerstag eine Auswahl zu sehen – 190 Werke von 84 Künstlern aus 25 verschiedenen Ländern. Sie wurde gemeinsam getroffen von Llilian Llanes, Leiterin des Wilfredo Lam-Zentrums in Havanna und Initiatorin der Biennale, und dem Leiter des Ludwig Forums Dr. Wolfgang Becker.

Die 1984 gegründete Biennale, damals noch Biennale von Havanna genannt, war als Forum für Künstler Lateinamerikas gedacht. Mittlerweile bietet sie Künstlern aus der gesamten Dritten Welt Gelegenheit, sich mit den gemeinsamen Problemen ihrer Länder auseinanderzusetzen. Schwerpunkte dieser einzigen themenbezogenen Biennale '94: Umwelt, Wanderungsbewegungen, Randgruppenbildungen, Diskriminierungen und kulturelle Einflüsse.

Der Aachener Sammler Peter Ludwig und Wolfgang Becker kamen 1990 nach Havanna und waren begeistert von der lateinamerikanischen Kunst. Als Becker den Mitarbeitern des Wilfredo Lam-Zentrums vorschlug, die Biennale nach Europa zu exportieren, begegneten sie ihm zuerst vorsichtig, mißtrauisch. „Die Vorgespräche waren geprägt von Berührungsängsten“, berichtet Becker, doch: „Gerade die bildende Kunst bietet die Chance zur Verständigung.“

Dem Einsatz Ludwigs und Beckers ist es zu verdanken, daß die Biennale jetzt in Europa zu sehen ist. Die beiden kubanischen Künstler Eduardo Ponjuán und René Rodriguez verewigten die zwei Aachener in ihrer aus Bildern und Skulpturen zusammengesetzten Installation „Traum, Kunst und Markt“ – nicht ohne ironisches Augenzwinkern.

Die Werke wirken oft provokativ. Der Umgang der Künstler mit sozialkritischen Themem mag Europäern zunächst befremdlich erscheinen, bietet aber vielleicht gerade dadurch die Chance, das Anliegen und Empfinden der Dritte-Welt-Länder besser zu verstehen. Auch Llilian Llanes, die ihre anfängliche Skepsis gegenüber den Europäern zugibt, meint: „Wir denken, daß wir uns näherkommen werden und uns besser verstehen, indem wir einen Teil unserer Ausstellung in Aachen zeigen.“

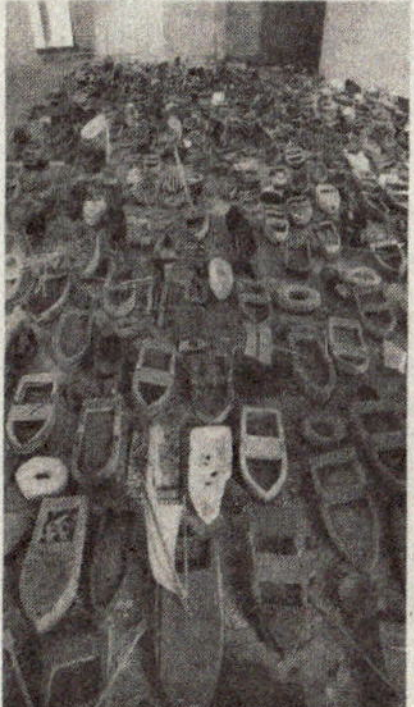

„Regatta“ nennt der Kubaner Alexis Leyva diese Installation aus vielen Booten

In den Mittelpunkt der Ausstellung rückt Llanes die Installation „Aus der Asche“ von Sue Williamson aus Südafrika, da sie ihrer Meinung nach Optimismus ausdrückt: Aschebahnen führen zu schwebenden Häuschen aus weißem Stoff, an denen Portraitfotos hängen, um an die Opfer der Apartheid zu erinnern.

Die Installation „Regatta“ des Kubaners Alexis Leyva, die aus vielen verschiedenen kleinen Booten besteht, erinnert in erschreckender Weise an die Pressebilder aus seiner Heimat, die uns fast täglich begegnen. Der Kolumbianer Arias Gaviria beschäftigt sich mit Aids: Der blauleuchtende Fußboden eines dunklen Raumes ist über und über mit den Glasplättchen von Blutproben bedeckt, darüber ist ein Mensch abgebildet. Die Skulpturen des Venezolaners Milton Becerra im Eingangsbereich des Ludwig Forums sollen an die Hängematten der Amazonas-Indianer erinnern.

Die Doppelmoral der Religion ist Thema mehrerer Installationen. So setzt sich zum Beispiel die Argentinierin Kuki Benski mit „Mea Culpa“ mit dem Bildnis einer Frau im Christentum – heilige Jungfrau und Hure – auseinander.

Begleitet wird die sehenswerte Ausstellung, die noch bis zum 11. Dezember zu sehen ist, von einem breiten Rahmenprogramm. Am heutigen Sonntag findet im Hof und Skulpturengarten des Ludwig Forums in Zusammenarbeit mit dem Dritte-Welt-Forum Aachen ein lateinamerikanischer Markt statt.

Newspaper article about the Fifth Havana Biennial at the Ludwig Forum, Aachen.
"How Art Builds Bridges," Welt am Sonntag, 18.9.1994

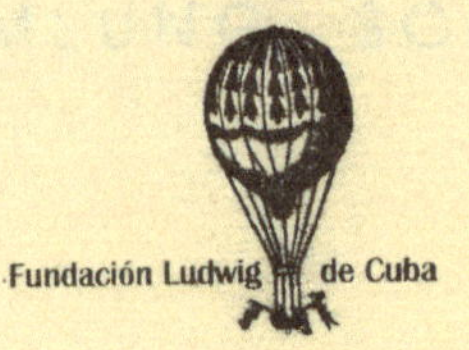

KUBA
KUNST
HEUTE

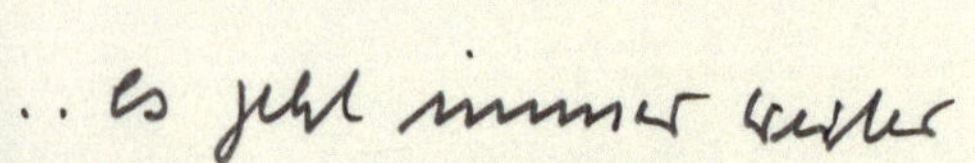

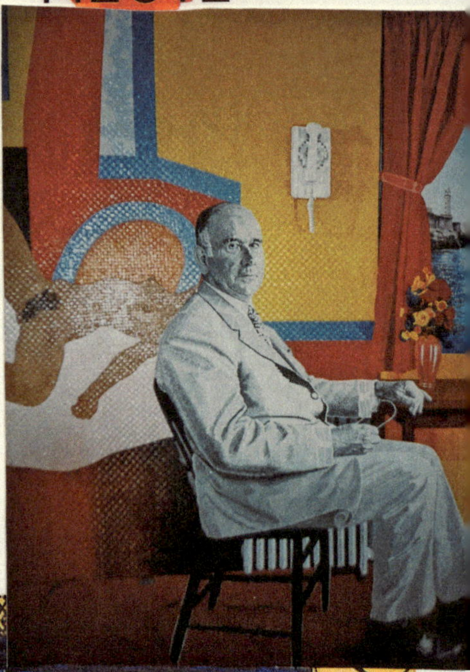

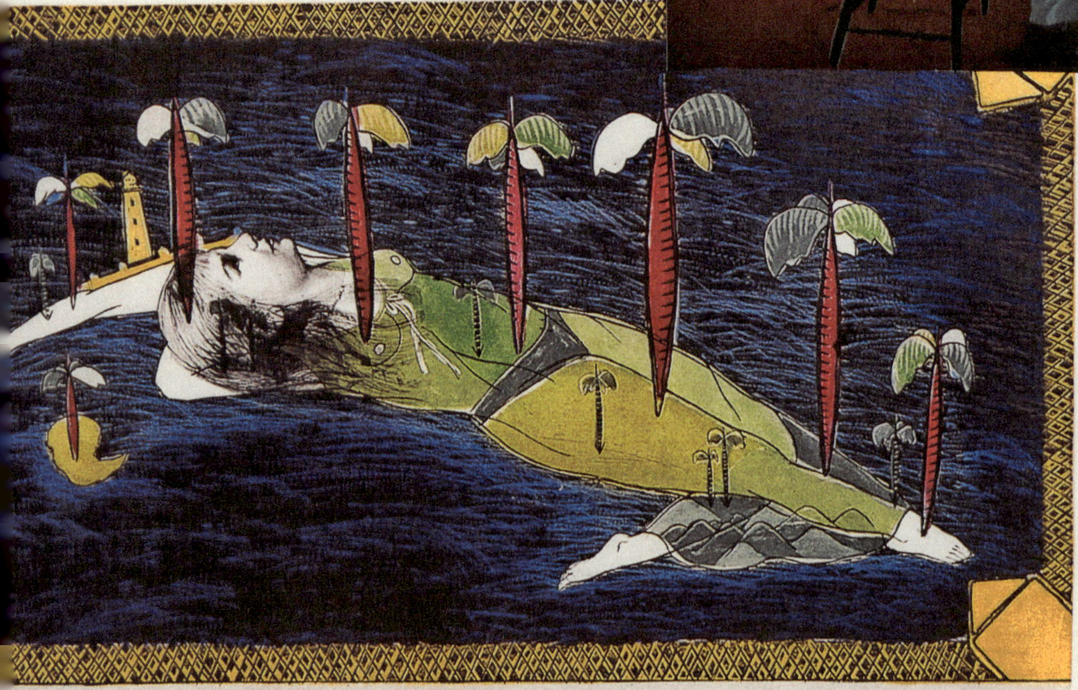

maldita circunstancia del agua por todas partes"

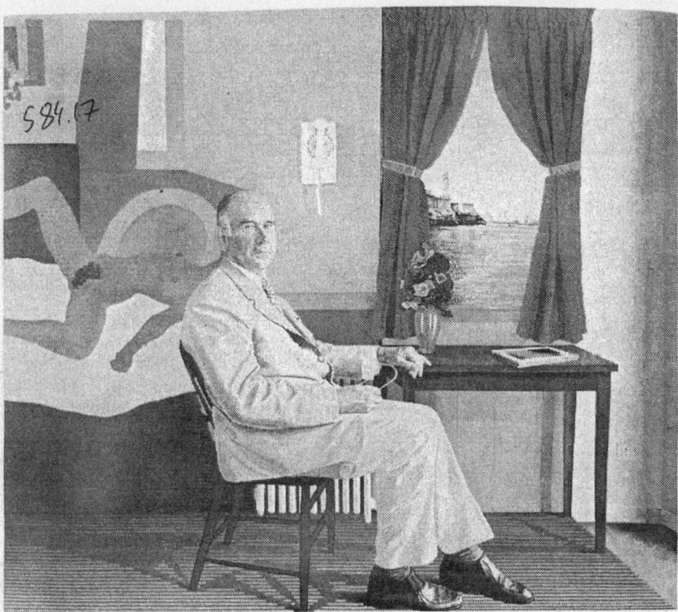

Newspaper article about the opening of the Fifth Havana Biennial at the Ludwig Forum, Aachen.
"A Vision Filled with Life," Stolberger Nachrichten, 17.9.1994

Teil des Ensembles „Traum, Kunst und Markt" von Ponjuan und Rodriguez: Ludwig vor Wesselmann-Akt. Durchs Fenster sieht man den Leuchtturm von Havanna. Foto: Krömer

Eine Vision mit Leben gefüllt

Biennale von Havanna: Starker Andrang im Ludwig-Forum

Von Gernot Geduldig

Aachen. Der Mäzen war bester Stimmung. Denn im Ludwig-Forum herrschte ein unbeschreiblicher Andrang. Nach dem großen Erfolg des Afrika-Projekts vor einem Jahr konnte der Sammler jetzt ein weiteres Kapitel seines ehrgeizigen, von Kritikern oft belächelten Zieles realisiert sehen: Die Vision eines Weltkunstzentrums wurde am Donnerstag erneut mit Leben ge-und erfüllt: Mehr als tausend Besucher waren zur Eröffnung der aus Havanna übernommenen Biennale gekommen. Etliche Ehrengäste waren dabei, so der kubanische Botschafter in Bonn, und auch rund dreißig Künstler aus der Dritten Welt. Als „Heldin des Abends" stellte Forumsleiter Wolfgang Becker die Biennale-Organisatorin Llilian Llanes vor. Ihr war es trotz der wirtschaftlichen Not Kubas gelungen, auch in diesem Jahr wieder die Biennale der Dritten Welt in Havanna zu veranstalten. Aachenwird der einzige Ort bleiben, wo diese Schau zu sehen ist.

Nach den Eröffnungsreden führte Peter Ludwig höchstpersönlich durch einen Teil der Schau. Während des kurzen Rundgangs rief er dazu auf, die Situation in Kuba differenzierter zu sehen und sich nicht nur auf die Fernsehberichte zu verlassen. Dem Lande Castros zollte er Hochachtung für „eine ernstzunehmende Utopie", die zu einer für Lateinamerika einzigartigen Förderung von Unterricht und Kunst geführt habe. Eingehend erläuterte Ludwig das Gemeinschaftswerk der beiden Kubaner Ponjuan und Rodriguez – ein Ensemble von Gemälden und Skulpturen, das auch ein Konterfei des Aachener Sammlers vor einem Wesselmann-Akt enthält, außerdem viele Dollarzeichen – als Chiffre dafür, daß erst mit dem Auftritt Ludwigs auf Castros Insel ein Kunstmarkt zu blühen begann.

Page from a private photo album belonging to the Ludwigs: collage containing the logo of the Fundación Ludwig de Cuba; a detail from the catalogue of the exhibition *KUBA KUNST HEUTE* (*Cuba Art Today*) in Bamberg and Bad Steben, 1995–1996; a portrait of Peter Ludwig with a detail from *Sueño, arte y mercado (Dream, Art, and Market)* by René Francisco Rodríguez & Eduardo Ponjuán, 1993; and *La isla en peso* by Sandra Ramos, 1994.

CHINA

In the years following 1976—that is, after the death of Mao Zedong—a political movement advocating for reforms and opening up took place in China. Tourists began to be allowed into the country. Irene Ludwig, travelling without her husband, joined one of the first tour groups in 1979.

Irene and Peter Ludwig had been fascinated by China's millennia-old culture since the beginnings of their art collecting, a fascination awoken by the many objects of ancient Chinese art that came to them as either gifts or heirlooms from Irene's parents. The Ludwigs continued to expand this collection until the mid-1990s, with the majority of it being given as permanent loans to the Museum für Ostasiatische Kunst (Museum for East Asian Art) in Cologne.

In contrast, the Ludwig's interest in contemporary Chinese art was first awakened by the exhibition *China Avantgarde!*, held in Berlin at the Haus der Kulturen der Welt (HKW, or House of the World's Cultures) in 1993. This was one of the first presentations of independent Chinese contemporary art in Europe. The Ludwigs didn't visit the exhibition themselves, but the gallerist Thomas Krings-Ernst asked **Andreas Schmid**, one of the exhibition's curators, to make a presentation to Peter Ludwig about the included artworks. The Ludwigs purchased a number of works from the Berlin exhibition, including two paintings by Fang Lijun and two by Wang Guangyi. Their initial acquisition consisted of around thirty works by more than a dozen artists, all made between 1985 and 1994. It also included works that Krings-Ernst had seen on a trip to China with Schmid in 1994, which he then offered to the Ludwigs. Among these were works by Ai Weiwei, Hu Zhiying, Huang Yong Ping, Ji Wenyu, Li Bangyao, and Xu Tan. Only a year later, in 1995, the Ludwigs acquired two further large groups of works. One consisted of 120 prints and works on paper by artists from the Central Academy of Fine Arts (CAFA) in Beijing, and the other was of photographs by Eva Siao, primarily taken in Beijing in the period between 1949 and 1966. This latter group included more than one thousand negatives and around one thousand signed and titled original prints.

End of April 1995, Peter and Irene Ludwig took their first trip together to China, escorted by the cultural envoy and interpreter **Chen Ping**. In October of the same year, Peter Ludwig travelled to China again, this time without Irene. Both trips had the aim of establishing cultural and business contacts. When it came to their cultural ambitions, the Ludwigs found a negotiating partner in Yang Lizhou, the deputy director of the National Art Museum of China (NAMOC). From early on, the Chinese Ministry of Culture also showed an interest in working with the Ludwigs. During his third trip to China, in March 1996, Peter Ludwig initialled a contract for a donation of eighty-nine works of international contemporary art, in connection to the founding of the Ludwig Museum for International Art as a division of NAMOC. However, Peter Ludwig passed away on July 22, 1996, and as such was unable to take part in the opening celebrations planned for September that year. One day before his death, he dictated a letter to Roman Herzog, in which he asked the then federal president to write a foreword for the catalogue for the opening exhibition in Beijing.

Irene Ludwig's ceremonial signing of the donation and founding contract finally took place on November 18, 1996. Two days later, the Ludwig Museum for International Art in the National Art Museum of China opened in Beijing, with the celebrations attended by the Chinese and German heads of state, Jiang Zemin and Roman Herzog.

A conversation with **Andreas Schmid** about the exhibition of contemporary Chinese art *China Avantgarde!* (1993) at the Haus der Kulturen der Welt in Berlin, which led to Peter and Irene Ludwig's first acquisitions of contemporary Chinese art

The interview was conducted at Andreas Schmid's studio in Berlin on September 23, 2021.

ANDREAS SCHMID (b. 1955, Stuttgart) has lived and worked in Berlin as an artist, curator, and expert on contemporary Chinese art since 1987. In 1983, he went to China on a scholarship from the Deutscher Akademischer Austauschdienst (German Academic Exchange Service), or DAAD. After a year of language studies in Beijing, he studied the practice and history of Chinese calligraphy and seal engraving at the Zhejiang Academy of Fine Arts, now known as the China Academy of Art, in Hangzhou from 1984 to 1986. He returned to Germany at the end of August 1986, settling in Berlin. Since then, Schmid has visited China regularly, as far as circumstances have allowed.

You can't study that art here, you can only learn about it in Asia. ... During my studies here in Germany, I had always focussed on lines; it's something that's interested me from the beginning.

REGINA WYRWOLL Mr. Schmid, we're very pleased that you're willing to talk to us, because you can provide additional context for Peter Ludwig's ambitious project in China. With everything you have done in your life, you must have many friends in China.

ANDREAS SCHMID Yes, I know many artists and mediators of art from various generations. There are also deeper friendships I've maintained since my studies, such as with the ink-wash artist Zheng Chongbin or the video artist Zhang Peili.

RW Are they in Hangzhou?

AS Zhang Peili lives in Hangzhou and Shanghai. Zheng Chongbin has lived in San Francisco for many years. My most important teacher, Wang Dongling, has again returned to Hangzhou after spending many years abroad. Back then, he was one of the youngest teachers and had just passed his calligraphy teaching exam, which is generally quite difficult. I have seen him many times, most recently at a performance in Hamburg in 2015. There was also the eighty-four-year-old calligraphist Sha Menghai, whose lessons I was lucky enough to attend for six months alongside a few other foreign students. He was a charismatic master of his art. His lessons were held in his small apartment. Very impressive.

RW What fascinated you so much about China? And why has the fascination continued?

AS It was actually an exhibition at the Museum für Ostasiatische Kunst (Museum for East Asian Art) in Cologne in 1982 that led me to apply for a DAAD scholarship. The director, Roger Goepper, put on an exhibition called *Worte des Buddha* (*Words of the Buddha*) with calligraphy by twentieth-century Japanese priests from the collection of Abbot Seiko Kono from the Daian-ji Temple in Nara, Japan. The exhibition was magnificent. It struck me like a bolt of lightning. You can't study that art here, you can only learn about it in Asia. I visited the eighty-year-old Seiko in Nara at the end of my studies in 1986. During my studies here in Germany, I had always focussed on lines; it's something that's interested me from the beginning. I have to confess that I also have a family connection to China, but that wasn't what inspired me to go there. My grandfather lived there for almost thirty years, from 1903 to 1931. He was a missionary and teacher for blind children in various places in the Guangdong province, along with my grandmother. They got married in Hong Kong, then moved to Guangdong where they periodically moved from place to place. At the time, my grandfather believed that Mao Zedong represented the only political option and chance for the country.

RW For it to develop?

AS Yes, to develop and to rid itself of a corrupt system. In 1929, my grandfather received a writ of protection from Zhu De, who would later be commander in chief of the People's Liberation Army, stating that the missions were not to be attacked.

RW And?

AS And they weren't. At the beginning of the 1930s, however, they were told they would either have to be part of the Long March or leave the country. My grandparents said, "With three children at home, we can't risk that." So they returned to Germany in 1931 and then, under National Socialism, practised inner emigration [a term that refers to Germans who remained in the country and kept a low profile while privately disagreeing with Nazi ideology].

RW When did you start curating? When did that become important to you?

At the opening of the exhibition of works from the Berliner Nationalgalerie, there was pandemonium owing to the size of the crowds and their desire to see original artworks.

AS At the end of the 1980s. I hadn't curated myself by then, but as an exhibition supervisor I oversaw the exhibition *Kritische Grafik der Weimarer-Zeit* (*Critical Graphic Art of the Weimar Period*) in Beijing and Hefei on behalf of the Institute for International Relations. In 1985, while I was still studying, the German embassy in Beijing hired me for the Berliner Nationalgalerie (Berlin National Gallery) under Dieter Honisch, who was installing an exhibition of nineteenth-century German art in Beijing, but was having problems with the interpreter. The embassy counsellor had called, and I was excused from my studies for two weeks in order to translate. I hung paintings, escorted people, and gave tours in Chinese. There were two exhibitions running at the same time, both with the theme of nineteenth-century paintings: one from Dresden in East Germany, and one from West Berlin, West Germany. It was unbelievably exciting. At the opening of the exhibition of works from the Berliner Nationalgalerie, there was pandemonium owing to the size of the crowds and their desire to see original artworks. The large numbers of Chinese people who took part in my tours were all extremely interested, not just in the art but also in its historical background. I was greatly impressed by that.

RW What was it like studying in Hangzhou?

It was powerful to see how these artists refused to allow repressive measures stop them from creating their art.

AS The calligraphy curriculum was extraordinarily intensive as there were only a handful of students—none of us from China. Chinese citizens were only allowed to start studying calligraphy again in 1986, as there were simply not enough teaching staff. Wang Dongling was a delightfully open and engaging teacher who was also interested in our artistic experiences. Liu Jiang, the old professor of seal engraving, was also a good communicator. In China, students had far more personal interactions with faculty than they do in universities here. We did a lot of things together. For instance, we travelled through China for three months with Wang, looking at calligraphy and art. We went as far as Xi'an in northwest China. During my studies in Hangzhou, I met young people, both students and teachers, who could not publicly exhibit their more experimental works outside the academy, sometimes only working on them at night. It was powerful to see how these artists refused to allow repressive measures stop them from creating their art. Such artists could be found in other academies besides Hangzhou. Editorial teams developed that increasingly highlighted discussion of contemporary issues in their publications. This movement later came to be known as the New Wave, Xin Chao, or the '85 Movement. The chief editor of the art journal of the academy in Hangzhou, Fan Jingzhong, was an unbelievably erudite individual who translated Ernst Gombrich's writings into Chinese during this time. He often slept at his desk so that he could start work again early the next morning. He also incorporated contemporary art—both from China and overseas—into the journal. The academy didn't initially want to accept this, as the director was very conservative. However, the director suddenly disappeared from the scene. It was rumoured that he had sold some of the academy's artworks to buyers in Hong Kong and committed suicide when news of this became public. His successor, Pan Gongkai, had a much more open attitude. At this time, information from the outside world was slowly but surely finding its way into China. A spirit of optimism prevailed. It was in this context that I was asked in 1985 which art journals were important in Germany. I answered, "*KUNSTFORUM international*, for instance, but it's in German." Those in charge replied: "That doesn't matter. There might be some people who can speak German." They began to order copies of *KUNSTFORUM international*, although at first only for the teacher's library. Later on, students were also allowed to read it. What some of the artists themselves experimented with and created, I found impressive. I was very moved by the absoluteness and power expressed in their art.

All the people in charge in Berlin told us: "That's unacceptable." ... We replied: "But you're attacking the wrong people."

RW What happened when you moved to Berlin?

AS I returned from China in autumn 1986. In January 1987, I moved to Berlin and was thinking about what I could do in relation to China. I had met Jochen Noth in China. He was living in Beijing at the time and was a generation older than me. Jochen really knew his stuff when it came to the literary scene in Beijing and was very good friends with some of the Beijing artists who were part of the "no-name" or Wuming group, which had been founded in 1973 during the Cultural Revolution.

Jochen and I worked together in 1990. Jochen had written a proposal for a potential exhibition about the Chinese avant-garde, to which I contributed my ideas. We visited a number of institutions with it, including the daadgalerie and the Künstlerhaus Bethanien. The Tiananmen Square massacre of protesting students in Beijing had just happened in June 1989, which meant it was the completely wrong time for this. All the people in charge in Berlin told us: "That's unacceptable. We can't hold an exhibition like that with China right now. It's completely absurd and politically incorrect." We replied: "But you're attacking the wrong people. We're on the side of the victims and those who need to be seen." Only the Haus der Kulturen der Welt (HKW, or House of the World's Cultures) in Berlin was open to hosting our project. We went to the head of the visual arts and film department, Wolfger Pöhlmann, first. "Very interesting, we were already thinking about China. Do you have more photographic material?" was his response. As I hadn't brought all of my material with me to this first meeting, we arranged for a second one, at which the general secretary of HKW, Günter Coenen, was also present. He was very taken with the idea: "We should discuss it in more concrete terms, and also in an international framework." And so I was contracted to curate the exhibition *China Avantgarde!* Jochen also received a contract that involved a lesser degree of responsibilities, as he was very busy at work.

[Hans van Dijk] spoke about wanting to write a new history of art that integrated Chinese art. His thought process completely reflected my thinking.

RW What was your approach?

AS It was clear from the start that we couldn't go through official channels to bring the artworks to Germany. Alternatively, we could have exhibited work by some professors who were officially recognised by China, but who were otherwise artistically unimportant—that would have been a laughable solution. We quickly realised that we had to do things differently. In May 1991, the recently-founded Heinrich-Böll-Stiftung (Heinrich Böll Foundation) in Bonn held its third conference, *Junge Malerei in China* (*Recent Art in China*), which included the curator Fei Dawei and the artist Huang Yong Ping, who I only knew of at that point from his works. Both of them travelled from Paris, where they were living in exile. During a coffee break I met Hans van Dijk from the Netherlands. He told me how frustrated he was, because he had recently presented a proposal for an exhibition of experimental contemporary art from China to no avail. Our conversation quickly became very intense. I had been in China from 1983 to 1986 and van Dijk had been there from 1986 to 1989. Along with the art itself, he was interested in Chinese independent art magazines: What subjects were the various magazines writing about? He collected them and spoke about wanting to write a new history of art that integrated Chinese art. His thought process completely reflected my thinking and seemed to me to be the perfect complement to my experiences, as I came more from the world of art and knew a lot of artists: "Hey, maybe I have something for both of us? I'll try to get two contracts from HKW." And, indeed, they got involved: shortly thereafter, Hans van Dijk and I were cocurators, forming a team together with Jochen Noth that nicely complemented each other. Sometime after the first open call, we received more than 150 packages containing pictures of artworks and applications. We spread them out in my studio, as we didn't receive office space for us in HKW until later. A number of research trips involving various people were planned to China, as well as the US and throughout Europe. In the process, new artists for potential inclusion arose again and again. Proposals were selected by the jury, composed of Wolfger Pöhlmann and the three of us, after intensive and sometimes vigorous discussion of the submitted material along with more recently provided documents. Unfortunately, there was far less exhibition space than there were good applications. As a result, some excellent works had to be left out, which pained us.

RW And how were the works smuggled out of China?

AS Jochen is an unbelievable organiser. He had good contacts in Beijing. Through them, the artworks could be transported to Europe via Hong Kong. It was completely crazy, because we had to smuggle the works back into China once the exhibition was over. That was problematic because prior to the HKW opening, the Berlin office of the Chinese embassy had protested that *China Avantgarde!* was not a representative exhibition: the art being shown was generally unknown in China and some of the invited artists didn't live in China. They argued that this gave a false impression of Chinese "cultural life."

RW How did Peter Ludwig come into the picture?

AS After the opening, I gave a large number of tours through the exhibition, as it became quickly apparent that the exhibition was not at all self-explanatory, especially the conceptual works. Context is very important. We had particularly considered developments in art in the 1980s, but had also included the most recent developments, up to 1991, that arose from our research trips. Contact with Peter Ludwig came through Thomas Krings-Ernst, the Cologne gallerist. He contacted me after the opening to arrange an exhibition tour. After seeing the exhibition, he said that he found it all very exciting and that I would hear from him. He eventually called me and asked: "Mr. Schmid, would you be prepared to give a talk to Mr. Ludwig about the exhibition and experimental contemporary art in China, perhaps with images? Mr. Ludwig would be very interested." Of course I said yes.

RW Was that in Cologne or Aachen?

AS It was in Cologne.

RW In the Museum Ludwig?

AS No, in Krings-Ernst's gallery. I gave a slide presentation that lasted around seventy-five minutes.

RW How did Ludwig react?

AS He was interested, very attentive, and asked a lot of questions. It was clear something had been awoken in him, even though he didn't say anything like "That's amazing!", or "That's really splendid!" He simply showed great interest and asked for background information. Finally, he said that he was interested in certain of the exhibition's works without specifying which ones. I had agreed with van Dijk that we would let the artists know if there was interest in buying their works, and that addresses would be exchanged if need be. But there were also artists who said, "No, please take care of it yourself as my representative," like the artist Yu Youhan from Shanghai. Van Dijk neither wanted nor was able to take part in that, as he was planning to open a consultancy for contemporary art in Beijing; he finally succeeded in doing so in 1994 after considerable obstacles. That was the NAAC, the New Amsterdam Art Consultancy, which existed for a number of years and advised foreign curators and collectors like Uli Sigg from Switzerland.

In any event, it was through me that Krings-Ernst gained access to many of the studios where he saw art and made purchases.

RW Did you sell art to Krings-Ernst or directly to Ludwig?

AS It was done through Krings-Ernst.

RW Did he organise an exhibition in his gallery?

AS No, not in his gallery. He acquired the works of particular artists in the exhibition for the Ludwig Collection. I then went to China with Krings-Ernst in autumn 1994 and travelled throughout the country. We visited a lot of studios and spoke to the artists, including Ai Weiwei, who had just returned from studying in the US. At the time he was living with his mother and brother in an old courtyard house in Beijing. I could see that Krings-Ernst was deeply interested in him. There was a spark between the two of them. Ai Weiwei later told me, "I sold some things to the Ludwig Collection through Mr. Krings-Ernst." They were the works *Double Mao* (1985), *Hide 1* (1991), and *Hide 5* (1991). That happened without my involvement, directly between the two of them—as was occasionally the case. In any event, it was through me that

Krings-Ernst gained access to many of the studios where he saw art and made purchases. We—that is van Dijk, Noth, and myself—had a good reputation among the artists. On the basis of that trust, we had first access to their studios.

RW So Peter Ludwig travelled to China with Krings-Ernst afterwards?

AS I didn't know anything about it at first. Krings Ernst travelled with Ludwig independently of me. In any case, on our trip he got the idea that he wanted to, at all costs, acquire an older work by Huang Yong Ping. However, Huang Yong Ping was in exile in Paris and not in China. His brother was in Xiamen and I was supposed to pick up the painting, commonly known as *Haymakers* (1983), which is now in the Ludwig Forum in Aachen. It's splendid, one of the key works in his oeuvre. Unfortunately, the handover didn't work out as his brother returned too late and I had to leave China. Krings-Ernst then organised it himself. He was always good at such things, just as he was with negotiating prices. In general though, it must be said, our views and goals often differed.

RW How many works did Ludwig acquire from the *China Avant-garde!* exhibition?

AS I think it was around eight or nine.

RW Did he buy them directly?

AS Through Krings-Ernst. With the agreement of the artists, those works didn't return to China. But the process was quite chaotic. I had to write a lot of letters and, when possible, make phone calls, as that was before email; this included communicating with people like Michaela Raab, a German who worked in Beijing and who was then married to Fang Lijun. She made sure that everything was above board and that Fang was not taken advantage of. That was important and I was pleased about it, but it meant a lot of back and forth. I visited Fang with Krings-Ernst. He had just moved into a new apartment and his fellow artist Yue Minjun lived next door. One could see that some artists, particularly those involved in the cynical realism movement, were doing extremely well for themselves at that time. Fang, for example, had bought himself a new car. Krings-Ernst then directly contacted Wolfger Pöhlmann, in other words HKW, to arrange the transport of the works acquired from the exhibition.

RW The artists were compensated for their participation in the exhibition. HKW paid them a kind of loan fee through you. Can you remember how much that was?

The government didn't really keep a close eye on that, nor on the works that went in and out.

AS Three hundred or four hundred deutsche marks.

RW And that was paid in deutsche marks, as foreign currency?

AS Yes, deutsche marks, foreign currency. That was very useful, as the artists could then exchange it for US dollars or renminbi, the Chinese currency. The choice was up to them.

RW Could the artists decide that, or was it overseen by the Chinese government?

AS No, the state knew nothing about it. That was between HKW and the artists; I was the "money postman" for the loan fees. The government didn't really keep a close eye on that, nor on the works that went in and out. That's why the earliest gallerists in China could, for example, tell customs that a painting was worth 1,000 marks, even though the work would command a much higher price in the West. That changed drastically over the years. It had a beneficial side, however, as artists could take their own small works that were going to be exhibited overseas with them, with few major formalities to worry about.

RW How long was your trip with Krings-Ernst?

AS We were travelling for roughly two weeks.

RW You didn't work together again after that?

AS No, I was neither kept in the loop about further developments nor did I actively take part in any talks. That's another way of saying that I wasn't involved, for instance, in the preparations and negotiations for the Ludwig Museum for International Art in the National Art Museum of China.

RW Mr. Schmid, thank you very much for taking the time to talk to us.

A conversation with **Chen Ping** about his work as an adviser and interpreter for Irene and Peter Ludwig during the negotiations for the Ludwig Museum for International Art in the National Art Museum of China (NAMOC) in Beijing

The interview was conducted at the Embassy of the People's Republic of China in Berlin on July 13, 2017.

CHEN PING (b. 1964, Jiangsu), envoy and counsellor for culture for the People's Republic of China, worked at the Chinese embassy in Bern from 1986 to 1989, the embassy in Bonn from 1989 to 1992, and in Bonn and Berlin from 1998 to 2003. He was head of the Western Europe Unit at the Ministry of Culture in Beijing for four years. When he met Peter and Irene Ludwig for the first time in 1995, he was working for the Chinese Ministry of Culture to facilitate cultural exchange between China and German-speaking countries. At the time of this interview, Chen Ping was an envoy and counsellor for culture at the Embassy of the People's Republic of China in Berlin. Since 2019, he has been a counsellor for culture at the embassy in Vienna.

Peter Ludwig was a huge figure in the world of art and culture. … He was described as a passionate individual, a man with vision and many ideas. This was clearly evident through my direct interactions with him.

REGINA WYRWOLL Envoy-Counsellor Chen, in preparation for our conversation, I looked through the archives of the Peter and Irene Ludwig Foundation and discovered that Peter Ludwig began negotiations with the People's Republic of China in 1981. These concerned a proposed business partnership for instant hot chocolate and cold desserts, in return for which he would provide his expertise to the Chinese chocolate industry. Ultimately, nothing came of it. When did you first become personally acquainted with Peter Ludwig? That is to say: When did it become about art?

CHEN PING I met Peter Ludwig in 1995, just over a year before his death, in preparation for his and his wife's first visit to China, which took place between April 24 and May 4, 1995. We had received a letter from our embassy, which was then in Bonn, informing us that the well-known German collector Peter Ludwig planned to visit China. The ambassador at the time, Mei Zhaorong, had already met with him a few times in Germany and had begun negotiations. The Chinese embassy asked the Ministry of Culture in Beijing, where I worked at the time, to put together an itinerary for the Ludwigs' visit and to arrange for meetings with individuals at a variety of cultural institutions in several Chinese cities.

At the end of April, Peter Ludwig, his wife, Irene, and Thomas Krings-Ernst came to Beijing. His stated intention was to get to know the country better. This initially had nothing to do with his business. However, before he departed China, he expressed a wish to conduct a joint venture arrangement with a Chinese firm. A colleague from Bonn had already informed us of this, and we had taken it into account when preparing the tour. To this end, we had contacted the Inner Mongolia Yili Industrial Group, which produced sweets and hard candy, as well as bread. Ludwig had a productive discussion with the firm's executive management, but I don't know if it led to anything.

RW Where did you meet Mr. Ludwig for the first time, and what was your personal impression of him?

At every meeting ... he spoke of his great interest and admiration for China and for Chinese art and culture.

CP I picked the Ludwigs up at Beijing Airport in April 1995. That was our first meeting. Peter Ludwig was a huge figure in the world of art and culture, and I had already read about him. He was described as a passionate individual, a man with vision and many ideas. This was clearly evident through my direct interactions with him; he had goals and was determined to achieve them. Ludwig displayed great interest in Chinese art and culture. In the nine days he stayed in China, we visited many museums and cultural institutions and inspected numerous pieces of Chinese cultural heritage. It was an amazing experience for me, too!

RW Can you remember what the Ludwigs were interested in? Were they focussed on different subjects or did they share common interests?

CP Mrs. Ludwig told me that she had already been to China in 1979. That was shortly before China opened its doors to the world. She came as a tourist and was part of a tour group that visited a number of cities. When the opportunity arose in 1995 to intensively engage with Chinese culture together with her husband, it was a new experience for her. She was very interested in everything we did, although she had already visited some of the sites during her first trip.

RW The couple collected ancient Chinese art, such as the nine fabulous bronze bells from the eighth century BCE and the wonderful painted porcelain plates and vases from the sixteenth and seventeenth centuries, among other similar pieces. Did the Ludwigs already have all that, or did they acquire it over the course of this trip?

CP That collection predated their trip. During their stay in China, Peter Ludwig told me a number of times that he collected ancient Chinese art. His parents-in-law were also interested in ancient Chinese art and had a collection in their house. At every meeting, whether it was with functionaries from the Ministry of Culture, the mayor of Beijing, the governor of Xi'an, or any number of museum directors, he spoke of his great interest and admiration for China and for Chinese art and culture. I only saw his collection later, in Cologne. In August 1995, the Ludwigs personally invited me to visit the Museum für Ostasiatische Kunst (Museum for East Asian Art) in Cologne, where the majority of their collection of ancient Chinese artworks are on permanent loan.

In 1995, contemporary Chinese art was still unrecognised, even by official authorities and cultural institutions.

RW Did you show him any contemporary Chinese art then?

CP No, we could show him almost no contemporary pieces at the time, but together we visited the Central Academy of Fine Arts (CAFA) in Beijing, the most important art academy in China. Ludwig spoke with the then president of the academy, Jin Shangyi, and during the tour expressed his interest in acquiring some of the graphic works by professors at the academy. We immediately organised that. The CAFA staff sent photos and relevant information to Aachen; there were about one hundred works in total. In 1995, contemporary Chinese art was still unrecognised, even by official authorities and cultural institutions. It was referred to as "underground art" and could not yet be seen in museums, which was why we were unable to present any to Ludwig. However, Krings-Ernst had previously informed Ludwig about developments in Chinese contemporary art; in 1993, the first important exhibition of contemporary Chinese art had been presented at the Haus der Kulturen der Welt (House of the World's Cultures) in Berlin—*China Avantgarde!*

RW Didn't Krings-Ernst, who owned a gallery, also buy works from that exhibition? He then offered many of those works to Ludwig.

CP Yes, that could be.

RW The big names in Chinese contemporary art since the middle of the 1980s are almost all represented in the Ludwig Collection: Huang Yong Ping, Ai Weiwei, Fang Lijun … It's amazing, the prescience with which he would purchase works.

CP Yes, works like those can no longer be found on the market. If they are, the prices are astronomically high. The National Art Museum of China (NAMOC) in Beijing is currently being expanded. A new building with around 130,000 square metres was put to tender in 2005. The permanent exhibition that will be housed in it will include Chinese art from the twentieth century. NAMOC essentially has sufficient works from this period, but there are gaps for the years after 1980, as there are no collections that include works from those years in China's public museums.

RW Was there any talk at the time that Ludwig wanted to present his collection in Beijing?

CP No, he didn't mention that. But Yang Lizhou, the then deputy director of NAMOC, wanted to show Ludwig's Picasso collection in Beijing—despite the obvious difficulty of such an undertaking.

As a starting point, Ludwig had prepared a list of chosen works from his collection for donation. Initially, there were around sixty works by European and American artists.

RW Negotiations with NAMOC for a donation of works from the Ludwig Collection developed astonishingly quickly: on November 20, 1996, the Ludwig Museum for International Art opened as an independent division of NAMOC.

CP They did indeed. Negotiations only began in earnest in summer 1995, after a visit by Ludwig in May, during which he discussed a cooperative arrangement with Yang Lizhou. As a starting point, Ludwig had prepared a list of chosen works from his collection for donation. Initially, there were around sixty works by European and American artists. Yang discussed the selection with him in writing and also clearly expressed his own wishes. He was very keen to have works by Pablo Picasso for the museum. At the time, there wasn't a single museum in China, or even in Asia as a whole, with a Picasso painting in its collection! Yang travelled to Aachen at Ludwig's invitation to personally discuss the list and the general conditions of the donation with Ludwig, to set down the fundamental conditions of the agreement and as such lay a solid foundation for further negotiations. It's worth mentioning that Yang asked Ludwig to include Roy Lichtenstein's *Cubist Still Life with Lemons* (1975) on the list after he had seen it in Ludwig's office—it was love at first sight. Ludwig hesitated for a few seconds and then decided to donate it to China as well. The number of donated works grew from sixty to eighty-nine. They consisted of works of contemporary art from 1965 onwards, representing a cross section of the international pieces in the Ludwigs' collection: works from the US, Europe, the Soviet Union, and Cuba, which included pieces by, among others, Gerhard Richter, Anselm Kiefer, Jean Tinguely, Natalya Nesterova, Renato Guttuso, Hervé di Rosa, Roy Lichtenstein, Andy Warhol, and Jasper Johns. The former GDR was also well represented through works by Bernhard Heisig and Willi Sitte. As it so happens, four of Picasso's late works were also included: three paintings and a work on paper.

RW Did Beijing know about Ludwig's collaboration with the Russian Museum in St. Petersburg and his subsequent donation?

CP Yes, Yang knew about that. The Chinese embassy had already reported that Ludwig had founded a number of museums in a number of countries with his donations. The most recent was in St. Petersburg, the Ludwig Museum at the Russian Museum. At dinner one evening, Yang spoke openly of wanting to convince Ludwig to also make a donation to NAMOC in Beijing. Ludwig didn't want to commit immediately. He worded his answer carefully, saying that he could imagine doing such a thing but would need more time to consider. Although he had read and heard a great deal about China and Chinese culture and had collected Chinese art, he didn't know the country well enough yet to make such a decision. He wanted to gather further impressions and experiences in order to determine what form such a collaboration might take. And then, at our last stop in Shanghai, something happened that none of us was expecting.

RW And that was?

CP The official itinerary was over and we were staying at Jin Jiang Tower, a modern hotel in the city centre. It was the afternoon and we had some time off when I received a call from Peter Ludwig. He asked me to come to the hotel's café. I did as he asked, and

Ludwig said to me, "Siegfried, I would like you to take down the following sentences and pass them on to Beijing." It was his wish to make a donation to China. I wrote this down on some of the hotel's stationery and sent it that day by fax to my supervisor at the ministry. Before he flew back to Germany, Peter Ludwig wanted to meet with the deputy minister of culture, Liu Deyou, who had received him in Beijing, to tell him in person. Naturally, I made the arrangements.

RW He called you Siegfried?

CP We talked a lot on the trip. I had told him, among other things, that during my German language and literature studies at the university in Beijing, I had been given a German name, Siegfried. From then on, Ludwig, his wife, Irene, and Krings-Ernst always called me Siegfried. You know, in the 1980s we already had teachers from Germany at our university. It wasn't easy for them to memorise our Chinese names, so the students were all given German names. That was normal at the time. And so I became Siegfried.

RW Were you able to get the deputy minister to come to Shanghai?

CP No, we flew back to Beijing the next day, as the Ludwigs were to return to Germany from there. Peter Ludwig was able to meet with Deputy Minister Liu Deyou before his departure for Germany on May 4, 1995.

RW You attended and interpreted?

CP Yes. Ludwig personally expressed his wish, which he had already put down in writing, to the deputy minister of culture. The deputy minister was delighted, acknowledged Ludwig's generosity, and expressed his heartfelt thanks. The two of them agreed that the details of the donation would be discussed through the channels of the Ministry of Culture and the Chinese embassy in Bonn. It was a short meeting because it had been arranged spontaneously. Afterwards we drove to the airport.

The idea was that the two sides—that is, the Chinese government and the Ludwig Foundation—should each establish an endowment fund.

RW In the foundation's archive, I read that these negotiations also discussed an endowment fund that both Ludwig and the People's Republic of China were to pay into. The same model had been used for the Österreichische Ludwig-Stiftung für Kunst und Wissenschaft (Austrian Ludwig Foundation for Art and Science). Why didn't it work in China?

CP Yes, that's right, we also discussed this subject on Ludwig's initiative. He was already thinking about the possibility of expanding the donation and of future exhibition projects. The idea was that the two sides—that is, the Chinese government and the Ludwig Foundation—should each establish an endowment fund. That meant that the Chinese state would provide one part of the financial support, and the foundation would provide the other part. Eventually, the two funds would be merged. The aim was to support young artists, to provide scholarships, and to hold exhibitions in order to increase artistic and cultural exchange between Germany and China. The foundation would have been independent, meaning the money would not have gone exclusively to NAMOC. This was a completely new approach for us. Such a model didn't exist in China at the time. Even the establishment of a fund was by itself a completely new idea to us. From today's perspective this wouldn't be a problem, but it wasn't possible in 1995. We had made enquiries, but there was no authority that could tell us which procedure we needed to follow. We received no answers to our questions. In the mid-1990s, this bordered on being a cumbersome demand for us, as there were no regulations for combining state and private money.

Translation alone was insufficient for this ambitious project. I often had to first clarify issues for both negotiating parties, because the cultural background, political structures, and, above all, the ways of thinking are so different.

RW Mr. Chen, I could see from the archival records that you personally played an important role in setting up the Ludwig Museum for International Art in the National Art Museum of China. You were extremely supportive of this project. I have the impression that you did a great deal behind the scenes in order to ensure smooth communication and to prevent misunderstandings. Did Ludwig personally take part in the negotiations, or did he leave it up to Krings-Ernst?

CP Both. He himself negotiated and he asked Krings-Ernst to do so as well. Personally, I tried go beyond my role as an interpreter to build bridges and foster long-term understanding on both sides. Translation alone was insufficient for this ambitious project. I often had to first clarify issues for both negotiating parties, because the cultural background, political structures, and, above all, the ways of thinking were so different. I had to teach the people from NAMOC how "the Germans" think and what their intentions were. For instance, Krings-Ernst complained that some processes that seemed simple from a German perspective proved to be difficult and protracted. On the other hand, I sometimes had to explain to the German side the structures and procedures that existed in China—and what needed to be taken into consideration. It was all about mutual understanding.

For example, Ludwig wanted to sign the contract stipulating the terms of the donation at the beginning of March 1996, during a planned visit to China. To this end, he commissioned Krings-Ernst to travel to China in February of that year and negotiate the final details with the Chinese side. However, the suggested dates coincided with the spring festival of Chinese New Year. As you know, Chinese New Year, or Chun Jie as we call it, is the most important event of the year for us, comparable to Christmas in Europe. Everybody travels home to celebrate with their whole family—myself included. Accordingly, we couldn't receive Krings-Ernst during this period. So we put forward an alternative suggestion: the unresolved points should be discussed during the next visit by Peter Ludwig in March. Ludwig didn't agree to this and was worried that there wouldn't be enough time in March, because he wanted to visit other cities as well. He insisted on a guarantee that the contract could be signed in March. After consulting with Yang, we came to a compromise, and Krings-Ernst came to Beijing directly after the Chinese New Year celebrations. I had to cut my holidays short as a result.

RW Did Peter Ludwig visit Beijing again?

CP He came as planned in March 1996. Krings-Ernst came by himself in February for the contract negotiations, despite the fact that very important discussions were involved. I can remember it very clearly, it was a very cold winter that year. Yang and his team talked through all the details with Krings-Ernst at NAMOC. I was there for all of it. The two sides discussed questions of transport, the organisation of exhibitions, catalogues, text contributions from political figures, and so on in great detail, ultimately finalising the content of the contract. Peter Ludwig came to China the following month. Shortly before the end of his trip, on March 27, 1996, he and Yang initialled the contract together at NAMOC. It was a special moment for Peter Ludwig.

RW How many times did Peter Ludwig visit China altogether? Twice?

CP No, three times. He first visited in April 1995, and then he came again in October of the same year. Unfortunately, I wasn't there for that as I was overseeing the exhibition *Das Alte China – Menschen und Götter im Reich der Mitte* (*Ancient China: Men and Gods in the Middle Kingdom*) at the Villa Hügel in Essen. I was there for more than three months. During that time Ludwig travelled to China again with Franz-Josef Zimmermann, the CEO of Ludwig Schokolade GmbH, and Wolfgang Schreiner, his former general representative for all his businesses in Eastern Europe, who had also set up a private graphic arts museum in Bad Steben. Together they travelled throughout the country and visited many cities.

RW Did they also buy art?

CP Yes, the graphic works by the CAFA professors, which Ludwig had wanted to acquire on his first visit. These included works by Zhou Ji Rong, Yan Han, and Wang Weixin, among others. He then had a catalogue called *Meisterwerke chinesischer Grafik* (*Masterpieces of Chinese Graphic Art*) produced, covering the one hundred graphic works from the CAFA group. I assisted from Essen, translating his introduction into Chinese.

It was clear to me from the beginning that this was an important project for both sides in terms of the exchange of culture and art between Germany and China.

RW You played an extremely important role as an intermediary, as can be seen in the file notes in the archive of the Peter and Irene Ludwig Foundation in Aachen, which describes your role along these lines: there was Mr. Chen Ping in Beijing, who could be relied upon; if there were problems, then you asked Mr. Chen Ping. That brings me to a fundamental question: Why did you put so much effort into this initiative?

CP It was clear to me from the beginning that this was an important project for both sides in terms of the exchange of culture and art between Germany and China. And there was another reason: my travels in the company of Peter and Irene Ludwig had a huge influence on me. You could say that Peter Ludwig opened the door to contemporary art for me. I had gained some experience in Europe before meeting the Ludwigs. I had worked for three years at the Chinese embassy in Bern and then another three years in Bonn. During that time I had the opportunity to familiarise myself with contemporary art in Europe, but couldn't really study it in depth. From then on, I increasingly paid attention to contemporary Chinese art. In 1995, I was also working on another project. Together with the Hahn Produktion – Gesellschaft für Theater, Management und Kulturaustausch (Hahn Production Company for Theatre, Management, and Cultural Exchange), we were organising the Chinese festival *China Heute* (*China Today*), which was to have taken place in Munich in 1996. It was supposed to present contemporary Chinese culture—music, dance, theatre, and recent Chinese art too. During preparation for the festival, I had direct contact with young Chinese artists, many of whom were still unknown at the time. In this context I also got to know the Dutch curator, Hans van Dijk, who had done a great deal for the development and dissemination of contemporary Chinese art. I saw many works from a variety of artistic directions and styles with him, some of which shocked me a bit, if I'm being honest. There were some really interesting works with new ideas, as well as things I didn't understand.

As I've already mentioned, in the mid-1990s there wasn't a single public museum in China which possessed a collection of contemporary Chinese art. When I was chatting with Yang, I told him that NAMOC, the most important museum in China, would have a gap in its collection fifty years from now if it didn't start to buy this kind of art soon. Whether we officially recognised this art is besides the point—it is a part of our art history. Peter Ludwig had told me all about the Russian avant-garde. The Soviet Union had also missed the opportunity to collect its own avant-garde art because they dismissed it at the time as bad quality art; later, it would turn out to be the most important movement in Soviet art history.

Peter Ludwig donated art to a number of countries and founded museums in order to promote international understanding. ... There are a great many people in the world who collect art, but what Peter Ludwig did is exemplary.

RW Were you surprised that Ludwig was an effective cultural politician? Were you surprised that an art collector acted with such foresight and political understanding? He was, after all, concerned with nothing less than global art history.

CP I would go a step further and say I marvelled at it. The fact that a collector collected art not for himself but for museums made an enormous impression on me. Peter Ludwig donated art to a number of countries and founded museums in order to promote international understanding. After all, art can build bridges and foster understanding between peoples. That's important. There are a great many people in the world who collect art, but what Peter Ludwig did is exemplary.

RW Peter Ludwig passed away suddenly on July 22, 1996. It moved me greatly to see how emotionally you reacted to it in China. This can even be seen in the archive.

CP I was tending to a German travel group at the time. On that day I was in Chongqing, a city in southwestern China, where I received the terrible news and was overcome by a deep sadness. I just couldn't believe it. In March 1996, when Peter Ludwig was in Beijing, I was unable to join him as I was busy with a project in Munich. A younger colleague, who had just returned from Bonn, tended to him. But as soon as I returned to Beijing I visited him in his hotel. The next morning we went to Beijing University together and met with Lao Zhu, a young professor who had studied art history at Heidelberg University and received his doctorate there. He was head of the newly-formed art history department. In the afternoon we went to NAMOC once more, where Ludwig signed the contract.

For those who had been heavily involved with the donation, his death was a bolt from the blue, as the saying goes. However, there was something that really puzzled me. During his visit to China in March, I had the feeling that Ludwig was quite agitated and impatient rather than his usual calm and composed demeanour. He wanted to get everything done quickly and couldn't wait. He said to me, "I really want to sign the contract on this occasion," and that's exactly what happened. And with that his wish came true. After his sudden passing I recalled this scene, and I asked myself several times whether he had already suspected or sensed that he didn't have much time left, similar to an old Chinese superstition. It was all very mysterious!

RW Was there a chance that the entire project might fall apart after his passing?

You can imagine the emotions we experienced as we waited for the foundation's decision.

CP Yes. At the time I occasionally worried that the project wouldn't come to fruition. I could also understand quite well that Irene Ludwig had other things to worry about after the death of her husband. At the Ministry of Culture, a big question mark hung over the whole endeavour. At that time, the two governments were in talks regarding the state visit of the German president Roman Herzog to China in November 1996. We had informed the Ministry of Foreign Affairs about the donation and expressed our wish for Herzog and President Jiang Zemin to visit the exhibition together. The idea had the support of the Chinese embassy in Bonn and the German embassy in Beijing, as well as the personal support of the German ambassador Konrad Seitz. After coordinating through diplomatic channels, the Chinese Ministry of Foreign Affairs arranged for the two heads of state to visit NAMOC. That was our main goal. You can imagine the emotions we experienced as we waited for the foundation's decision. I imagine that the matter was discussed at length by the foundation in Aachen. I was overjoyed that Irene Ludwig chose to fulfil the wishes of her husband. It was wonderful!

RW How did the visit of the two heads of state go?

CP Prior to the opening celebrations, the protocol department of the Ministry of Foreign Affairs told us that the opening ceremony would have to last less than thirty minutes, as President Jiang and President Herzog had subsequent political meetings that they had to attend. This meant that, along with the speeches—and the translations from both sides—there was only around twenty minutes left to view the exhibition. The allotted time was anything but sufficient for such a large exhibition. Following the concept developed by Barbara Thiemann, the curator of the Museum Ludwig in Cologne, the donated works were spread across three rooms on the ground floor of NAMOC. In the western room, works from Western Europe were presented; in the middle room were those from America; and in the eastern room was art from the former GDR, the Soviet Union, and other Eastern European countries. Clearly, there wasn't enough time to see all three rooms, so the Ministry of Culture suggested to only visit the western and middle rooms, which we agreed to. After the opening celebrations, the then director of the Museum Ludwig in Cologne, Marc Scheps, gave President Jiang and President Herzog a guided tour and I interpreted. We stopped in front of Gerhard Richter's painting *Eifellandschaft (Morgenstimmung) bei Hubbelrath* (*Eifel Landscape (Morning Atmosphere), near Hubbelrath*) (1969), and Scheps told them about the artist. It was a peaceful German landscape in which the sky took up almost the entire canvas, with only a small part of the horizon below visible. The painting reminded Jiang of a verse from the Tang poems: *ping sha wu yin* (平沙无垠). I translated it for Herzog and Scheps as "sweeping and flat land." It was astounding that the president could experience the same atmosphere in a European landscape painting as that described in a thousand-year-old Tang poem. As the two heads of state left the exhibition, President Jiang looked toward the eastern gallery and asked Ambassador Mei what was in there. Mei answered that there were further works from the Ludwig Collection on display. Jiang asked why they were not also going to look at those, and the head of protocol reminded him that they had run out of time. To this Jiang responded, "That's OK, it won't take long." In the end, the two presidents saw the entire exhibition. That made everyone very proud. President Jiang was a man who appreciated art, and his interest was genuine.

I was greatly moved that she visited China only a few months after her husband had passed away in order to fulfil his final wish. She was a strong woman!

RW When Irene Ludwig came to Beijing with Marc Scheps, what was your impression of her?

CP I went to the airport, as always, to meet the delegation. That was November 16, 1996. Mrs. Ludwig stepped out of the plane carrying a bouquet of flowers. I went up to her and greeted her. She was in a good mood and was happy to be in Beijing and to see me again. I asked her if she wasn't tired after the nine-hour flight, and she replied that she had slept on the plane. I was greatly moved that she visited China only a few months after her husband had passed away in order to fulfil his final wish. She was a strong woman! I'm very grateful to her. In the evening, all the members of the delegation sat together in the Grand Hotel. Along with Scheps, Thiemann, and Krings-Ernst, there was Elke Beyer, Ludwig's secretary; Walter Queins, chair of the Ludwig Stiftung für Kunst und Internationale Verständigung (Ludwig Foundation for Art and International Understanding); Rainer Jacobs, the foundation's lawyer; Ilka Husmann, an employee of the foundation who spoke Chinese; and Hans Ewald Schneider, general manager of the art transport and logistics company hasenkamp. I was there too. Irene Ludwig gave a short speech before dinner.

RW What did she say?

CP Just a few words. With tears in her eyes, she said that we were all gathered in Beijing because that was what Peter Ludwig had wanted. She wanted to make his wish come true. It was a very moving moment. Two days later, on November 18, the contract was signed in a special ceremony in the Great Hall of the People. The state counsellor Li Tieying was there, as was Li Yuancho, the new deputy minister of culture. Yang Lizhou, Irene Ludwig, and Walter Queins formally signed the contract. It was a dignified ceremony. Peter Ludwig would have been very pleased.

RW Did you see Irene Ludwig after that visit? Did you have regular contact with her?

CP Yes. In autumn 1998, I returned to Bonn to again work in the Chinese embassy. In 1999, during my time there, Yang Lizhou and I attended a directors' meeting at Irene Ludwig's house in Aachen. In 2001, I was transferred to Berlin, where the Chinese embassy had its new headquarters. In summer 2002, I travelled to Cologne at the foundation's invitation to celebrate Irene Ludwig's seventy-fifth birthday on June 17. We saw each other again there at the Museum Ludwig. She still called me Siegfried and introduced me to her guests: "This is Siegfried, who Peter and I got to know in China. He's currently working at the Chinese embassy."

RW Can you describe Irene Ludwig in a bit more detail?

CP She was a very emotional person. There's a particular moment I remember very clearly: It was the day after the opening of the exhibition of donated works, in November 1996. Yang Lizhou had already said goodbye to her, as she was flying back to Germany with the other members of the foundation the next day. To relax, we went on a day trip to the Summer Palace, which is just outside the city. That autumn in Beijing was very beautiful and so we went for a walk along the shore of Kunming Lake. Suddenly, she said to me: "Siegfried, I need to go back to the city, I want to go to the museum again. Please let Mr. Yang know that I would like to meet with him again." Then we drove back to NAMOC together. Yang was waiting for us when we arrived and accompanied us through the museum. Irene Ludwig toured the three exhibition galleries where the donation was on display, and looked closely at all eighty-nine works of art. Then Irene Ludwig said to Yang: "Now our donation has found a home with you. You know, for me it feels as if my heart is being ripped out a hundred times over. You must take good care of all this art!"

RW I found a letter from Peter Ludwig in the archive that he wrote when he was assembling the works for China. Some very valuable pieces were going to Beijing, and they came from a number of museums where they were then being exhibited on loan. He wrote at the time, "We must choose very carefully, so that the other collections are not disadvantaged." The selection was very important to him. It's easy to understand why Irene Ludwig again emphasised this. Are there any other memories you'd like to share with us?

CP In October 1995, I was in Essen, while Peter Ludwig was visiting China for the second time. One morning the telephone rang and woke me from a deep sleep. It was Krings-Ernst, who was calling because Ludwig had just called him from Beijing. Ludwig had told him that Beijing's deputy mayor, Zhang Bei-Fa, had invited him for a meal. During the meal he had let Ludwig know that the City of Beijing was also interested in receiving a donation. He had told Ludwig that a new museum for contemporary art was being planned, offering him a large gallery in the future building for a permanent exhibition of donated works. Presumably, Ludwig allowed himself to be talked into this a little, as NAMOC's limited exhibition space for the permanent display of his donation had been a sticking point in the negotiations. However, he was unsure and wanted to hear my opinion.

I made two points to Krings-Ernst on the phone: First, a new museum was being planned. That's good! But the deputy mayor hadn't revealed any details about the location, the architecture, the budget, or the construction timetable. In my experience, it could be a long road until its completion. If everything was still up in the air, why should Ludwig collaborate with the City of Beijing? Second, even if we accept that a new museum for contemporary art would be built in Beijing and that a gallery would be offered to Ludwig for his collection, it was still only a city museum and its status and importance couldn't be compared to that of a national museum. Such differences are still of great significance in a country like China.

Krings-Ernst passed my comments on to Ludwig. When he returned from China, he invited me to his house in Aachen. At lunch he spoke with me about this subject. I explained the structures and the decision process within the Chinese administration to him very clearly. I believe that my telephone conversation with Krings-Ernst was instrumental for his deciding on the location of the donation. It's worth noting that there is still no city museum for contemporary art in Beijing.

RW Envoy-Counsellor Chen, thank you for taking the time to talk to us!

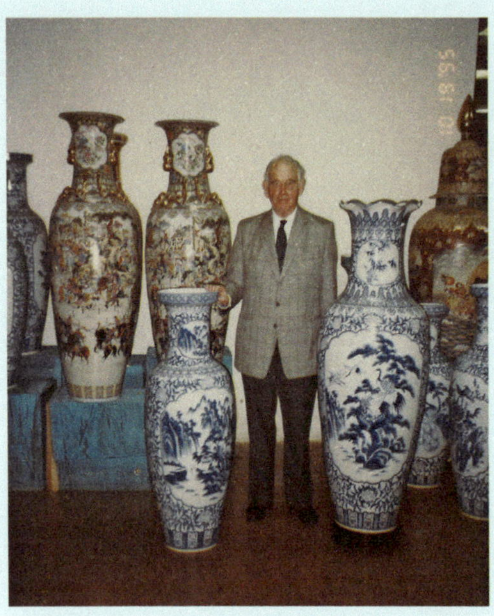

Peter Ludwig among Chinese porcelain vases, Beijing, March 1996.
Photo: private

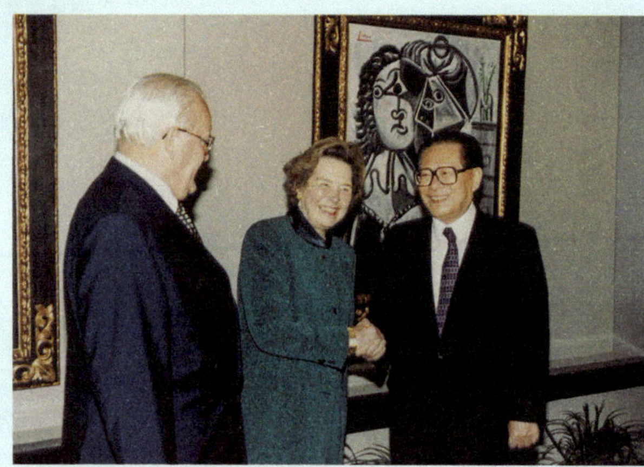

After the signing of the donation contract in Beijing, November 1996. From left to right: Roman Herzog (president of Germany), Irene Ludwig, Jiang Zemin (president of China).
Photo: private

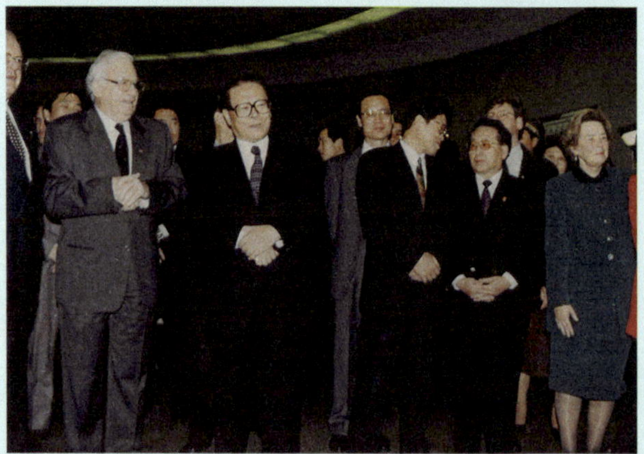

Tour of the exhibition of the Ludwig Collection in Beijing on the occasion of the signing of the donation contract, November 1996. Front row, from left to right: Roman Herzog (president of Germany), Marc Scheps (director, Museum Ludwig, Cologne), Jiang Zemin (president of China), Li Tieying (minister of economic affairs, China), Mei Zhaorong (Chinese ambassador), Irene Ludwig.
Photo: private

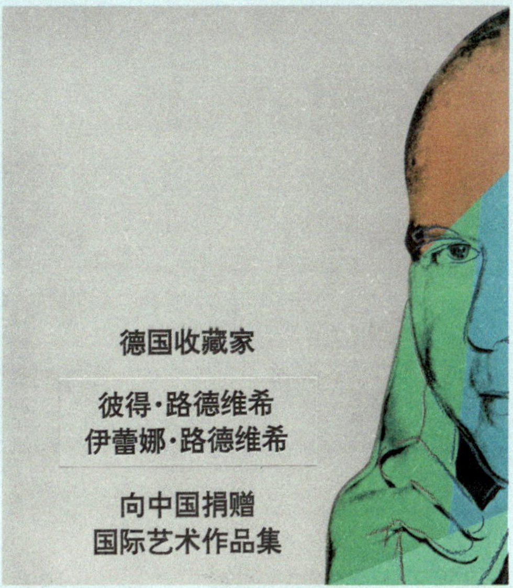

Collection catalogue from the opening of the Ludwig Museum for International Art in the National Art Museum of China: ***The Well-known German Art Collectors, Peter and Irene Ludwig, Donate Artworks From Throughout the World to China*****. Beijing, 1996.**

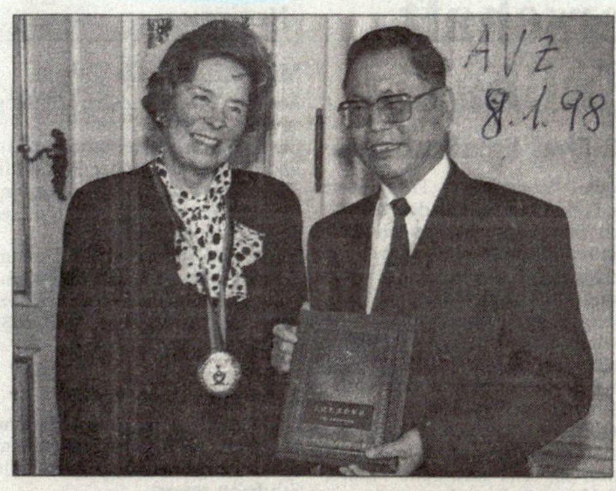

Chinesischer Preis für Irene Ludwig

Hohe Auszeichnung für Professor Irene Ludwig: Im Weißen Saal des Aachener Rathauses ist der Aachener Kunstmäzenin gestern die Auszeichnung für Verdienste um den Kulturaustausch der Volksrepublik China verliehen worden. Die Ehefrau des verstorbenen Peter Ludwig nahm den Preis aus den Händen des chinesischen Botschafters Lu Quitia entgegen. Zu den Gratulanten gehörten neben Aachens Oberbürgermeister Dr. Jürgen Linden auch NRW-Kulturministerin Ilse Brusis. Foto: Michael Jaspers

Newspaper article about Irene Ludwig being honoured for her work in cultural exchange with China.
"Chinese Award for Irene Ludwig," Aachener Volkszeitung, 8.1.1996

Ludwigs Name auch in Peking verewigt

Im November wird das neue Museum eröffnet

Aachen. Was der Direktor des Aachener Ludwig Forums, Prof. Dr. Wolfgang Becker, vor einigen Tagen andeutete, wurde nun offiziell bestätigt: Bereits im November soll in Peking ein „Ludwig Museum für Internationale Kunst" eröffnet werden. Ein entsprechender Vertrag wurde jetzt in der chinesischen Hauptstadt unterzeichnet, teilte die Ludwig Stiftung für Kunst und Internationale Verständigung am Dienstag in Aachen mit.

Die Sammlung vor allem westlicher Kunst als Schenkung des Aachener Sammlerpaares Irene und Peter Ludwig sowie der Ludwig-Stiftung wird als eine eigenständige Abteilung unter dem Dach des Nationalen Museums für chinesische Kunst in Peking eingerichtet.

Mit diesem Schritt werde „die Politik der Öffnung und der internationalen Zusammenarbeit" Chinas auch auf dem Gebiet der bildenden Kunst vorangebracht, hieß es. Damit trägt nun auch im fernen China ein Museum den Namen des Aachener Kunstmäzens. Den Schwerpunkt der Schenkung bilden über 100 Kunstwerke aus Deutschland, Westeuropa, den USA und Rußland. Damit soll der Beitrag Chinas zur Kultur der Menschheit sowie „die heutigen Leistungen des chinesischen Volkes" gewürdigt werden, heißt es in der Erklärung der Stiftung.

Das Pekinger Ludwig-Museum will aktiv den Kunstaustausch mit dem Ausland fördern und darüber hinaus eine ständige Sammlung außerchinesischer Kunst aufbauen. Die jetzige Schenkung ermögliche als „einen ersten Schritt den Aufbau einer Sammlung im weltweiten Maßstab".

Das Ludwig Forum in Aachen widmet in diesem Jahr eine ganze Ausstellungsserie der Kunst Chinas.

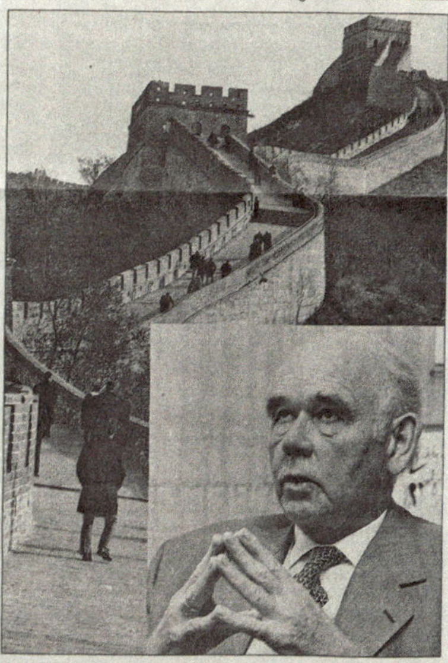

Auch die chinesische Mauer hält Kunstsammler Peter Ludwig nicht auf: Im fernen Peking wird im November ein Museum Ludwig eröffnet.

Newspaper article about plans for the Ludwig Museum in Beijing.
"Ludwig's Name Also Immortalised in Beijing," Jülicher Volkszeitung, 3.4.1996

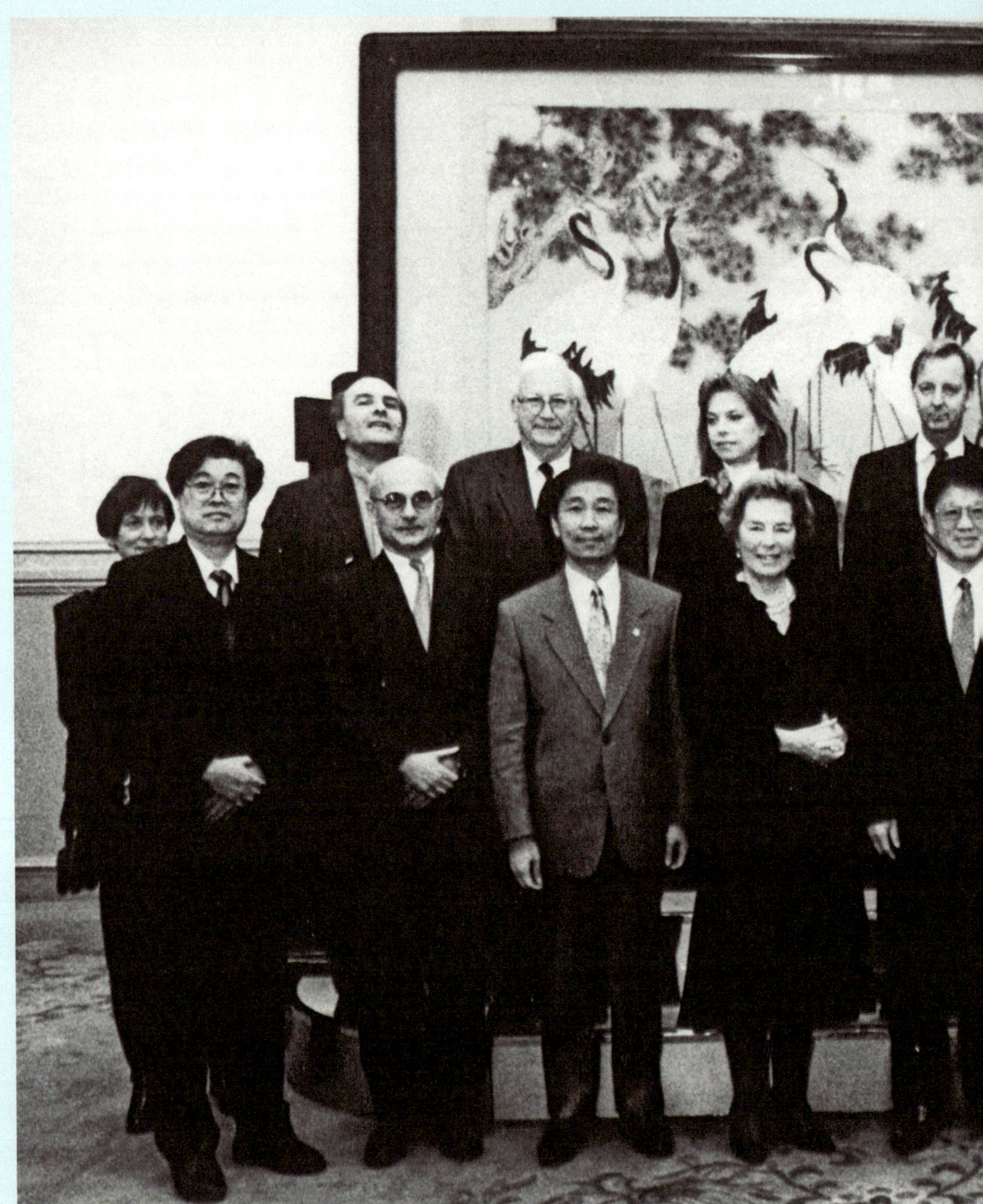

On the occasion of the signing of the donation contract in the Great Hall of the People, Beijing, November 1996. Front row, from left to right: Yang Lizhou (deputy director, National Art Museum of China), Rainer Jacobs (lawyer), Li Yuanchao (deputy minister of culture, China), Irene Ludwig, Li Tieying (minister of economic affairs, China), Walter Nocker (chargé d'affaires, German embassy, Beijing), Yuan Xue (deputy general director, Department of International Cultural Exchange, Ministry of Culture, China), Walter Queins (CEO, Ludwig Foundation), Bai Yang (head of Western Europe Division, Department of Cultural Exchange, Ministry of

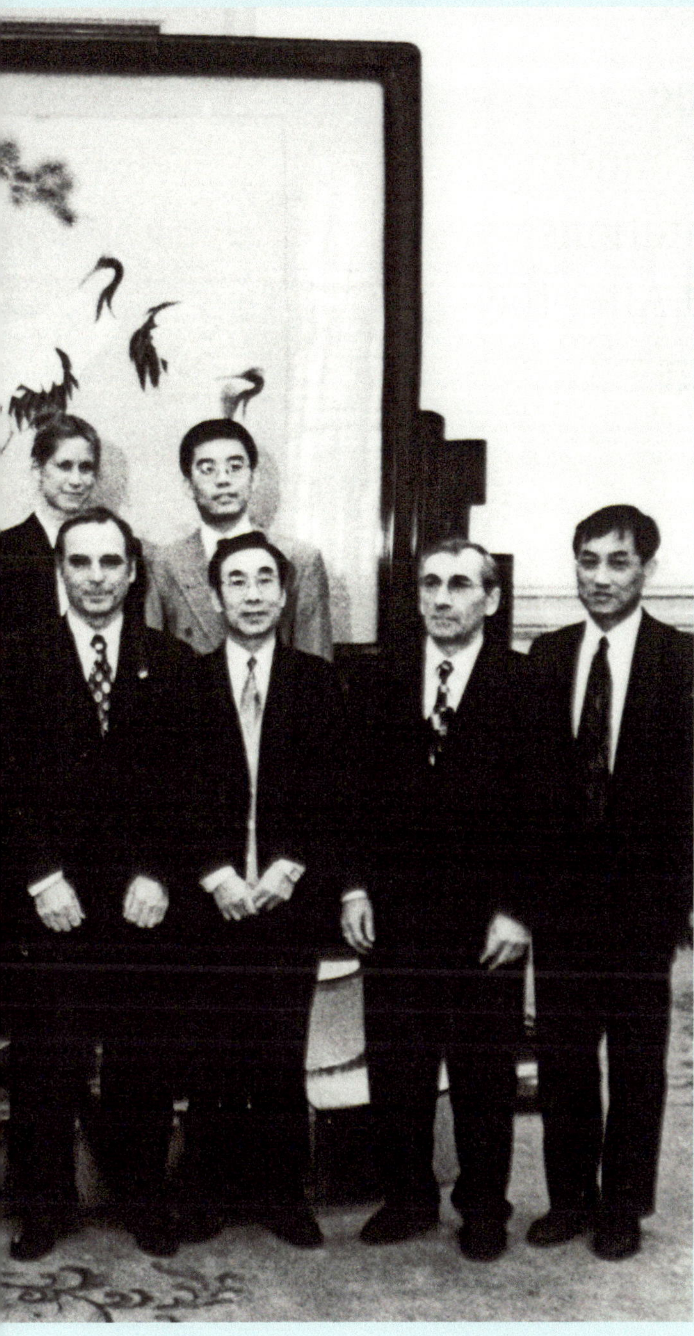

of Culture, China). Back row, from left to right: Elke Beyer (secretary, Ludwig Foundation), Thomas Krings-Ernst (gallerist),Marc Scheps (director, Museum Ludwig, Cologne), Barbara Thiemann (art historian at the Museum Ludwig, Cologne, and guest curator for the collection exhibition in Beijing), Hans Ewald Schneider (hasenkamp Fine Art), Ilka Husmann (former assistant to Peter Ludwig, project supervision, China), Chen Ping (envoy and culture counsellor, China).
Photo: unknown

Timeline of the Founding of Institutions Named After the Ludwigs

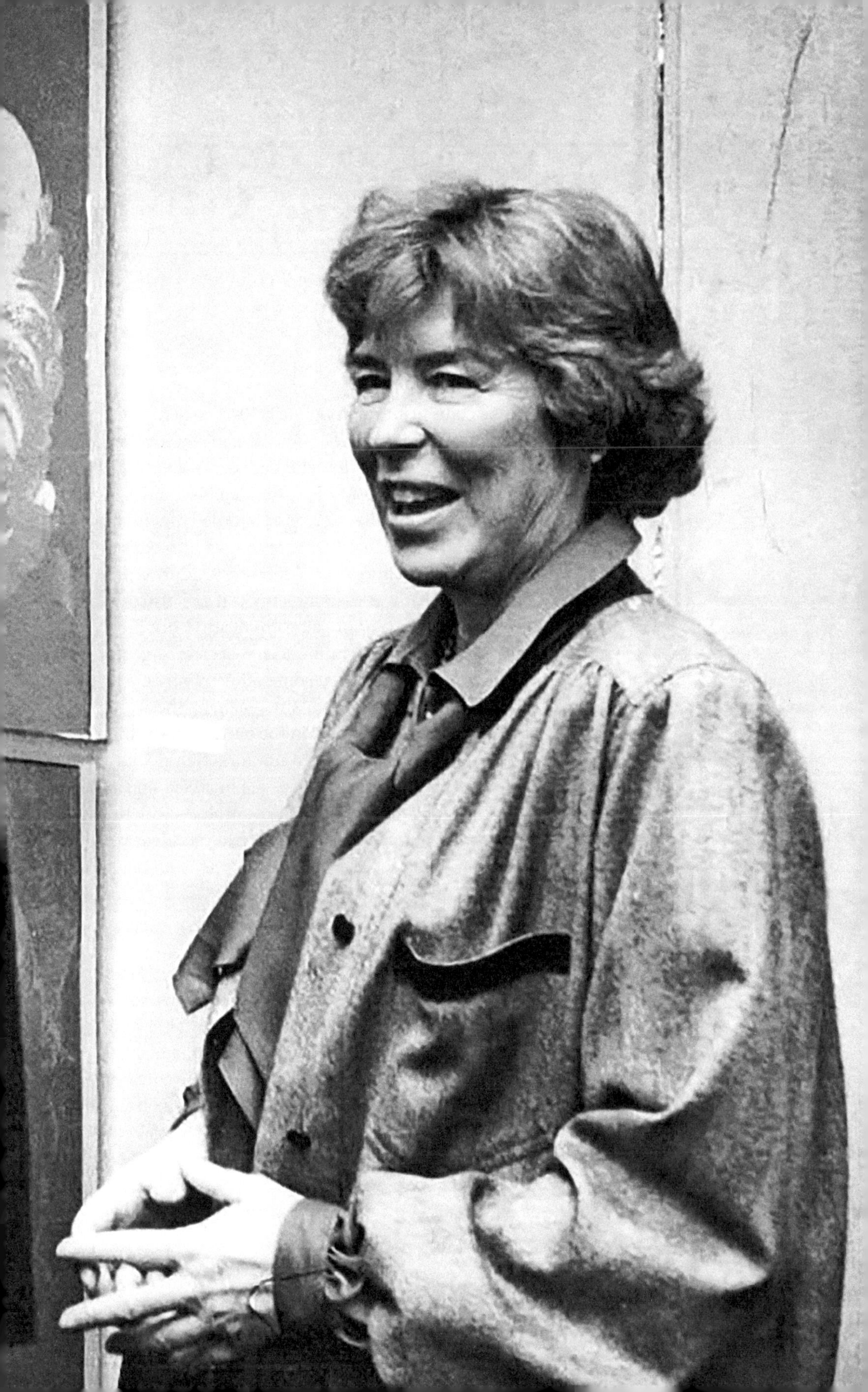

A Personal Afterword

"Yes, what is memory?
We ourselves are memory."
Esther Kinsky, *Rombo*

During my time as a cultural journalist in the 1980s, I once received a letter from Peter Ludwig. Like many of my colleagues at the time, I had criticised both him and his forceful collection policy. He responded with inimitable politeness: He extended his thanks, as well as those of his wife, for the attention I had afforded him in my article. However, he requested that I be sure to take into consideration certain other pieces of information if I were to address this topic again. And at first, that was that. It seems as if any criticism just rolled off Peter Ludwig. Later on, after his death, I occasionally worked with his widow, Irene, in my role as secretary-general of the Kunststiftung NRW (NRW Art Foundation). Twice a year, she would invite me to lunch at her villa in Aachen. She was a highly educated lady. She had remained in the background while her husband was alive. Naturally, she had not forgotten my past journalistic attacks, but with grace and care she focussed on the possibilities created by collaborating on funding projects with the Peter and Irene Ludwig Foundation, which she had founded.

And now? Why these interviews?

In 2012, I was invited to join the Board of Trustees of the Peter and Irene Ludwig Foundation, a great honour that, nonetheless, immediately reactivated the gene that had driven my past journalistic curiosity. Who were these two great collectors, and what influence did they actually have on cultural politics? Which of their projects had been realised and which had not gotten off the ground? Had Peter Ludwig really been the most influential cultural figure in the former Federal Republic, as some had believed him to be (and fought against him for that reason)? What impression did Peter and Irene Ludwig leave on their contemporaries and partners? Who among them was still alive and could provide information and insights? I began my research.

In 2015, Brigitte Franzen became CEO of the Peter and Irene Ludwig Foundation (a position she held until 2021). She had previously spent seven years as the director of the Ludwig Forum für Internationale Kunst (Ludwig Forum for International Art) in Aachen and knew the Ludwig Collection well. When we discussed the extensive archive stored in the Haus Ludwig, the founders' former private residence in Aachen and now the foundation's home, we both had the same idea: to begin an intellectually rigorous reappraisal as soon as possible, in order to establish future ways forward for the Peter and Irene Ludwig Foundation. Let's face it: the chocolate entrepreneur and holder of a doctorate in art history Peter Ludwig was (and is) one of the most controversial figures of the German cultural landscape since the 1960s, when he exhibited his sensational Pop Art collection in Aachen and Cologne and, among other things, derived from it a claim to power that many found unbearable. To this day his actions—unlike those of his wife, Irene, who tended to be active in the background—are still perceived in the same light as the critical publications of those years, as there has been no subsequent reassessment of the Ludwigs.

In 2015, the "Voices" project—a series of interviews of contemporaries of Peter and Irene Ludwig who had personally collaborated with them—took shape. The Board of Trustees of the Peter and Irene Ludwig Foundation gave its approval and tasked me with finding and interviewing these individuals. Initially beginning with ten people, the project grew over the years into sixty authorised interviews. The first fourteen of these interviews, focusing on the Ludwigs' founding of international museums and foundations, are gathered in this volume.

However, how "objective" are these individuals' testimonies?

In fact, it is precisely because of their subjectivity that these personal recollections contribute to a more objective picture of Peter and Irene Ludwig's impact on the public sphere of their times, as well as on the opinions and behaviour of particular stakeholders in the art world. In terms of further scholarly appraisal, the subjective can contribute to a greater objectivity in scholarly analysis—for example, through the comparison of various accounts, including those of the Ludwigs themselves.

Before I move on to giving thanks for the support I received during my work, I would like to say one more thing. For many years, I was a freelance investigative cultural journalist, including two years as the editor in chief of the publication *KUNST INTERN*, which, among other things, questioned Peter Ludwig's actions and sought to investigate and uncover hard information behind the scenes. I was unsuccessful at the time. Peter Ludwig frequently enjoyed using a provocative style of communication. His public relations work, which he directed alone and without the assistance of agencies, was legendary. Other journalists with more money and larger archives, such as those from *Der Spiegel* or the *FAZ*, also fought their way through the tangle of rumours and conjecture about his political influence and lobbying. Particularly prominent were Peter Ludwig's efforts to establish a national Ludwig Foundation, which stretched across several years (1979–1982) but ultimately proved fruitless.

The shimmering kaleidoscope of background information that has been provided by the many interviews has fundamentally altered my image of the Ludwigs. We owe a debt of gratitude to this astoundingly active couple from Aachen for their enormous collection that covers all genres and all periods and has been loaned or donated throughout the world: twelve public museums carry the Ludwig name, and a further sixteen public museums manage loaned or donated works. We also owe them gratitude for the Peter and Irene Ludwig Foundation in Aachen, which has been designed to continue in perpetuity and, together with the associated museums and foundations, keeps their legacy alive. It is time to get to the bottom of things: What were the social and political conditions that allowed the Ludwigs to proceed as they did, what made their actions unique, and what lessons can we learn from them for the future in light of the current dramatically changing challenges facing museums?

I would like to thank the many contemporaries of the Ludwigs who have so generously shared their knowledge. I would like to thank the Board of Trustees of the Peter and Irene Ludwig Foundation—particularly its chairperson, Isabel Pfeiffer-Poensgen—for its willingness, in the form of the “Voices” project, to begin a rigorous investigation of the collection. My thanks to Brigitte Franzen for her sage advice in the many situations in which I needed it.

And I would like to thank the current team at the foundation, its CEO Carla Cugini, as well as research coordinator Benjamin Dodenhoff and trainee Larissa Grotebrune, who worked together with me in the preparation of this volume. A first step in examining the national and international activities of the Ludwigs has been taken.

REGINA WYRWOLL
Member of the Board of Trustees
Peter and Irene Ludwig Foundation

List of Works and Copyright

The permanent loans and donations listed here all come from the Ludwig Collection.

List of acronyms:
mumok: Museum moderner Kunst Stiftung Ludwig
NAMOC: National Art Museum of China

Front Cover:

Pablo Picasso, *Couple au Vase de Fleurs* (*Couple with Flower Vase*), 1970, Donation, NAMOC Peking © Succession Picasso / VG Bild-Kunst, Bonn 2023

Back Cover / P. 284/285:

Peter and Irene Ludwig in Berlin, 1990. Photo: unknown © Peter and Irene Ludwig Foundation Aachen

Andy Warhol, *Marilyn*, 1967, Donation, Museum Ludwig, Cologne © 2023 The Andy Warhol Foundation for the Visual Arts, Inc. / Licensed by Artists Rights Society (ARS), New York

P. 60

Tatjana Nazarenko, *The Circus Artist*, 1969, Permanent Loan, Ludwig Forum für Internationale Kunst, Aachen © VG Bild-Kunst, Bonn 2023
Galina Neledva, *Workshop*, 1975, Donation, NAMOC

N.N., "Soviet Art Exhibition, a Cultural-Political Event," Aachener Nachrichten, 5.7.1982
© Medienhaus Aachen

N.N., "The King of Art's Cosmonauts Landed Hard in the West," Express, 2.7.1982
© Express Cologne/Bonn

P. 61

Olev Subbi, *The Girl and the City*, 1979, Permanent Loan, Ludwig Forum für Internationale Kunst, Aachen

Vitalij Ivanovic Tjulenev, *Town for Two*, 1979, Permanent Loan, Ludwig Forum für Internationale Kunst, Aachen

Vitalij Ivanovic Tjulenev, *Boy and Dove*, 1972, Permanent Loan, Ludwig Forum für Internationale Kunst, Aachen

Igor Alexandrovic Popov, *Before Work*, 1966, Permanent Loan, Ludwig Forum für Internationale Kunst, Aachen

Anatolij Jurgevic Nikic, *The Red Shelf*, 1987, Permanent Loan, Ludwig Forum für Internationale Kunst, Aachen

Michail Vladimirovitsj Ivanov, *The Lenin Library*, 1965, Permanent Loan, Ludwig Forum für Internationale Kunst, Aachen © VG Bild-Kunst, Bonn 2023

Kaisa Puustak, *Passersby*, 1976, Permanent Loan, Ludwig Forum für Internationale Kunst, Aachen

Velo Vinn, *Dwelling*, 1973, Permanent Loan, Ludwig Forum für Internationale Kunst, Aachen

Georgij Georgievic Poplavskij, *Contact with the Faraway Cosmos*, 1977, Permanent Loan, Ludwig Forum für Internationale Kunst, Aachen

P. 62

Kcho (Leyva Machado Alexis), *La regata* (*The Regatta*), 1994, Permanent Loan, Museum Ludwig, Cologne, Photograph: Anne Gold © Leyva Machado Alexis (KCHO), Cuba 2022

Sebastian Preuss, "Cheeky Pathos: Young Cuban Art at the Ludwig Forum in Aachen," FAZ, 7.5.1992
© Sebastian Preuss/FAZ

Raúl Martínez, *Siempre Che* (*Always Che*), 1970, Museo Nacional de Bellas Artes de La Habana © Estate of Raúl Martínez / Corina Matamoros, Cuba 2022

Ines Anselmi, "Havana Biennial in Europe for the First Time," Der Bund, 20.10.1994 © Der Bund

Silke Nievenhuis, "Sparks Flew at Opening," Aachener Nachrichten, 17.9.1994 © Medienhaus Aachen

P. 63

Svetlin Rusev, *The Ballad of Nosat Peak*, 1983, Donation, Ludwig Forum für Internationale Kunst, Aachen

Gernot Geduldig, "Double Mao and a Naked Venus," Aachener Nachrichten, 29.3.1996 © Medienhaus Aachen

Fang Lijun, *Group One, No. 2*, 1990, Permanent Loan, Ludwig Forum für Internationale Kunst, Aachen © Fang Lijun Studio

Wang Jingson, *The Big Bright Day*, 1991, Permanent Loan, Ludwig Forum für Internationale Kunst, Aachen © Wang Jingson

P. 112

Klaus Gruber, "Ludwig Works Stir Vienna Up," Aachener Volkszeitung, 5.1.1979 © Medienhaus Aachen

Duane Hanson, *Football Vignette*, 1969, Donation, mumok © VG Bild-Kunst, Bonn 2023

Robert Indiana, *Der Mond – Die Braunschaft*, 1969, Donation, mumok © Morgan Art Foundation ARS, New York / VG Bild-Kunst, Bonn 2023

P. 113

John De Andrea, *Woman on Bed*, 1974, Donation, mumok © John De Andrea

P. 114

N.N., "Ludwig is Coming," Profil, 1.3.1977 © Profil Redaktion GmbH

John De Andrea, *Woman on Bed*, 1974, Donation, mumok ©John De Andrea

Jean-Olivier Hucleux, *Portrait of the Ludwigs*, 1975/1976, Donation, mumok © VG Bild-Kunst, Bonn 2023

Ralph Goings, *Airstream*, 1970, Permanent Loan, mumok ©1970 Ralph Goings

N.N., "Visiting Vienna: The Ludwig Collection," Die Presse, 7.10.1978 © Die Presse

Anne and Patrick Poirier, *Ostia Antica*, 1972, Donation, mumok © VG Bild-Kunst, Bonn 2023

P. 164

Jan Tabor, "Crash Course in Western Art," Kurier, 18.6.1983 © KURIER

David Hockney, *Self-Portrait with Blue Guitar*, 1977, Permanent Loan, mumok © David Hockney

Cover of the exhibition catalogue International Art Since 1960: Exhibition of the Museum Moderner Kunst Stiftung Ludwig, Budapest, 1983, from: Tibor Helényi, "Ludwig in the Art Gallery," URL: https://tiborhelenyi.com/wp-content/uploads/2021/03/Ludwig-in-the-Art-Gallery-1024x476.jpg © Tibor Helényi / www.tiborhelenyi.com

P. 166

Pablo Picasso, *Femme se coiffant* (*Woman Doing Hair*), 1906, Donation, Museum Ludwig, Cologne © Succession Picasso / VG Bild-Kunst, Bonn 2023

Pablo Picasso, Eight Plates with Bullfighting Motifs, 1959, Permanent Loan, Ludwig Múzeum, Budapest © Succession Picasso / VG Bild-Kunst, Bonn 2023

Konrad Klapheck, *Angst* (*Fear*), 1971, Donation, NAMOC © VG Bild-Kunst, Bonn 2023

Horst Antes, *Der Maler* (*The Painter*), 1968, Permanent Loan, Ludwig Forum für Internationale Kunst, Aachen © VG Bild-Kunst, Bonn 2023

Hans Erni, *Sibylle beim Würfelspiel, Fassung 1* (*Sibylle Playing Dice, Version 1*), 1966, Permanent Loan, Ludwig Forum für Internationale Kunst, Aachen

Hans Erni, *Der Tod und das Mädchen* (*The Death and The Girl*), 1963, Permanent Loan, Ludwig Forum für Internationale Kunst, Aachen

Andy Warhol, *Dr. Peter Ludwig*, 1980, Donation, NAMOC © 2023 The Andy Warhol Foundation for the Visual Arts, Inc. / Licensed by Artists Rights Society (ARS), New York

Roy Lichtenstein, Exhibition View, 1987 (*Vicki*, 1964, Permanent Loan, Ludwig Múzeum, Budapest / *Ruins*, 1965, Donation, Ludwig Museum at the Russian Museum, St. Petersburg) © Estate of Roy Lichtenstein / VG Bild-Kunst, Bonn 2023

Nancy Graves, *Bathymet-Topograph*, 1978/1979, Permanent Loan, Ludwig Forum für Internationale Kunst, Aachen © Nancy Graves Foundation, Inc./VG Bild-Kunst, Bonn 2023

P. 198

N.N., Cover of art, April 1982, titled "Collector Ludwig: New Art from Moscow," Photograph: Dirk Reinartz

P. 199

Eckhard Hoog, "The Most Beautiful Museum Ludwig Opened," Stolberger Volkszeitung, 14.3.1995 © Medienhaus Aachen

Pablo Picasso, *Arlequin, les mains croisées* (*Harlequin, Hands Folded*), 1923, Donation, Museum Ludwig, Cologne © Succession Picasso / VG Bild-Kunst, Bonn 2023

P. 242
N.N., "He Even Knows the Aachen Cathedral!," Bild-Zeitung, 14.5.1994 © Axel Springer SE

P. 243

N.N., "How Art Builds Bridges," Welt am Sonntag, 18.9.1994 © Axel Springer SE

Pat Ward Williams, *Accused/Blowtorch/Padlock*, 1968, Whitney Museum of American Art, New York © Digital Image, Whitney Museum of American Art / Licensed by Scala

Kcho (Leyva Machado Alexis), *La regata* (*The Regatta*), 1994, Permanent Loan, Museum Ludwig, Cologne, Photograph: Anne Gold © Leyva Machado Alexis (KCHO), Cuba 2022

P. 244

René Francisco Rodríguez & Eduardo Ponjuán, *Sueno, arte y mercado* (*Sound, Art and Market*), 1993, Havana © René Francisco Rodríguez & Eduardo Ponjuán, Cuba 2022 / Peter and Irene Ludwig Foundation

Sandra Ramos, *La Isla en peso* (*The Island by Weight*), 1994, Fundación Ludwig de Cuba © Sandra Ramos, Cuba 2022 / Peter and Irene Ludwig Foundation

P. 245

Gernot Geduldig, "A Vision Filled with Life," Stolberger Nachrichten, 17.9.1994 © Medienhaus Aachen

René Francisco Rodríguez & Eduardo Ponjuán, *Sueno, arte y mercado* (*Sound, Art and Market*), 1993, Havana © René Francisco Rodríguez & Eduardo Ponjuán, Cuba 2022 / Peter and Irene Ludwig Foundation

P. 279

Andy Warhol, *Dr. Peter Ludwig*, 1980, Donation, NAMOC © 2023 The Andy Warhol Foundation for the Visual Arts, Inc. / Licensed by Artists Rights Society (ARS), New York

N.N., "Ludwig's Name Also Immortalised in Beijing," Jülicher Volkszeitung, 3.4.1996 © Medienhaus Aachen

N.N., "Chinese Award for Irene Ludwig," Aachener Volkszeitung, 8.1.1996 © Medienhaus Aachen

Acknowledgements

We would like to express our sincere gratitude to the individuals previously mentioned by name in the foreword and afterword. In particular, we would like to thank Regina Wyrwoll, the contemporary witnesses, and all those who contributed to this project.

We would additionally like to thank the Board of Trustees and the entire team of the Peter and Irene Ludwig Foundation, as well as Wilfredo Benitez, Sonja Benzner, Beatrix Biesemann, Renate Buhren, Katharina Eloshvili, Thomas Fillitz, Drew Goings, Victoria Haas, Tibor Helényi, Ellen Jordans, Tatjana Kalugina, Franz König, Walther König, Louis K. Meisel, Eva Möller, Sebastian Preuss, Christian Rein, Nora Riediger, Barbara Roosen, Christoph Siekmann, Vanessa Taeter, and Klaudia Wojtczak.

Imprint

Irene and Peter Ludwig: Insights into
the Collectors' International Activities
Regina Wyrwoll in Conversation
with Contemporary Witnesses

A publication of the
Peter and Irene Ludwig Foundation, 2023
Edited by Carla Cugini and Benjamin Dodenhoff
Interviews and Transcription: Regina Wyrwoll
Editorial Assistance: Larissa Grotebrune,
Corinna Schröder
Image Editor: Larissa Grotebrune
Copyeditors: Luise Pilz (DE), Renate Voget (DE),
Andrew Wagner (EN)
Proofreading: Stefan Ripplinger (DE)
Translation: Darren G. Mann (EN),
Stefan Ripplinger (DE)

Graphic Design: Michael Pichler
Production: Maren Katrin Poppe
Lithography, Printing, and Binding:
DZA Druckerei zu Altenburg GmbH,
Gutenbergstraße 1, 04600 Altenburg

The interview with Helmo Hernández was originally conducted in English and has been written in American English. The other interviews have been translated from German into British English by Darren Mann.

Printed in Germany

Paper: FLY white 100 gsm (contents)
and 115 gsm (jacket), Colorplan bright red
270 gsm (cover)

Copies: 1,200 (DE), 700 (EN)

English Edition: ISBN 978-3-7533-0435-9

Published May 2023 by: Verlag der Buchhandlung
Walther und Franz König, Ehrenstraße 4,
50672 Köln, Tel.: +49 (0) 221 / 20 59 6 53
verlag@buchhandlung-walther-koenig.de

Bibliographic information of the Deutsche Nationalbibliothek (German National Library). The Deutsche Nationalbibliothek lists this publication in the Deutsche Nationalbibliografie (German National Bibliography); detailed bibliographic data is available at http://dnb.d-nb.de

Peter und Irene
Ludwig Stiftung